SOCIOLOGISTS BACKSTAGE

From the Foreword by Howard S. Becker:

> "The stories in *Sociologists Backstage* tell how the contributors, who differ in so many ways, dealt with the situations they found themselves in as they did their research, and how who they were and what they had become in their lives intersected with those situations. The stories will fascinate you, and give you a lot to think about as you go ahead with your own research adventure."

Sarah Fenstermaker is Professor of Sociology and an affiliate of the Feminist Studies Department at the University of California, Santa Barbara. She is the Director of UC Santa Barbara's Institute for Social, Behavioral and Economic Research. She received her Ph.D. from Northwestern University. Her research on women and work, domestic labor, family violence, and the workings of gender, race, and class have resulted in a long list of publications. She is the author of *The Gender Factory: The Apportionment of Work in American Households*, an edited volume (with A. Goetting), *Individual Voices, Collective Visions: Fifty Years of Women in Sociology*, published by Temple University Press, and *Doing Gender, Doing Difference: Inequality, Power, and Institutional Change* (with C. West), published by Routledge. Sarah is presently co-PI (with J. Mohr and J. Castro) of a Ford Foundation funded project, "Individuals and Institutional Cultures: Faculty as Change Agents," a national survey of the professoriate.

Nikki Jones is an Associate Professor of Sociology at the University of California, Santa Barbara. She earned her Ph.D. in Sociology and Criminology from the University of Pennsylvania in 2004. Her areas of expertise include urban ethnography, urban sociology, race and ethnic relations and criminology and criminal justice, with a special emphasis on the intersection of race, gender, and justice. She is the author of *Between Good and Ghetto: African American Girls and Inner-City Violence*, which is published in the Rutgers University Press Series in Childhood Studies. She is also a William T. Grant Scholar (2007–2012).

CONTEMPORARY SOCIOLOGICAL PERSPECTIVES

*Edited by Valerie Jenness, University of California, Irvine
and Jodi O'Brien, Seattle University*

This innovative series is for all readers interested in books that provide frameworks for making sense of the complexities of contemporary social life. Each of the books in this series uses a sociological lens to provide current critical and analytical perspectives on significant social issues, patterns and trends. The series consists of books that integrate the best ideas in sociological thought with an aim toward public education and engagement. These books are designed for use in the classroom as well as for scholars and socially curious general readers.

Published:

Political Justice and Religious Values by Charles F. Andrain

GIS and Spatial Analysis for the Social Sciences by Robert Nash Parker and Emily K. Asencio

Hoop Dreams on Wheels: Disability and the Competitive Wheelchair Athlete by Ronald J. Berger

The Internet and Social Inequalities by James C. Witte and Susan E. Mannon

Media and Middle Class Moms by Lara Descartes and Conrad Kottak

Watching T.V. Is Not Required by Bernard McGrane and John Gunderson

Violence Against Women by Douglas Brownridge

Gender Circuits: The Evolution of Bodies and Identities in the Technological Age by Eve Shapiro

Social Statistics: The Basics and Beyond by Thomas J. Linneman

The State of Sex by Barbara Brents, Crystal Jackson, and Kathryn Hausbeck

Gender Circuits: The Evolution of Bodies and Identities in the Technological Age by Eve Shapiro

Surviving the Holocaust by Ronald Berger

Forthcoming:

Transform Yourself, Transform the World by Michelle Berger and Cheryl Radeloff

Issues, Implications and Practices in Mixed Method Design by Jodi O'Brien

Stargazing: Celebrity, Fame and Social Interaction by Kerry O. Ferris and Scott Harris

SOCIOLOGISTS
BACKSTAGE
ANSWERS TO
10 QUESTIONS
ABOUT WHAT THEY DO

SARAH FENSTERMAKER
NIKKI JONES
University of California, Santa Barbara

Routledge
Taylor & Francis Group

NEW YORK AND LONDON

First published 2011
by Routledge
270 Madison Ave, New York, NY 10016

Simultaneously published in the UK
by Routledge
2 Park Square, Milton Park, Abingdon, Oxon OX14 4RN

Routledge is an imprint of the Taylor & Francis Group, an informa business

© 2011 Taylor & Francis

Typeset in Minion by EvS Communication Networx, Inc.
Printed and bound in the United States of America on acid-free paper by Walsworth Publishing
Company, Marceline, MO.

Library of Congress Cataloging in Publication Data
Fenstermaker, Sarah, 1949–
Sociologists backstage : answers to 10 questions about what they do / Sarah Fenstermaker and
Nikki Jones.
p. cm.— (Contemporary sociological perspectives)
1. Sociology—Research. I. Jones, Nikki, 1975– II. Title.
HM571.F46 2011
301.072—dc22
2010033735

ISBN13: 978-0-415-80658-9 (hbk)
ISBN13: 978-0-415-87093-1 (hbk)
ISBN13: 978-0-203-84036-8 (ebk)

To our teachers, who first answered the questions about what they do

Elijah Anderson

Howard S. Becker

John Kitsuse

Robin Leidner

Allan Schnaiberg

CONTENTS

Foreword   xi
HOWARD S. BECKER

Series Foreword   xiv

Preface and Acknowledgments   xv

Introduction.   1

SECTION I
URBAN SOCIOLOGY IN THE POST-CIVIL RIGHTS ERA   13

1   Mary Pattillo   15

    *Pattillo explores her research on Black middle-class communities and
    considers how it reconfigured the boundaries of studying urban Black
    populations. She describes how moving into the neighborhoods she studies
    presented rich opportunities for data collection, as well as considerable
    challenges.*

2   Scott Brooks   28

    *Brooks shares insights from his years spent coaching young Black men in
    South Philadelphia. He describes how studying young men's transition
    from playing streetball to more formally organized basketball reveals
    structural patterns of inequality. Drawing from his field observations and life
    experiences, Brooks stresses the importance of good mentoring practices,
    particularly for people of color and women.*

3   Alford A. Young, Jr.   41

    *Young highlights the importance of reframing more traditional sociological
    approaches to the study of Black men. Rather than focusing on behavior,
    Young strives to understand the varied ways in which Black men construct
    social meanings, and how those constructs impact their social conditions.
    He discusses how his own experience of growing up in East Harlem informs*

his complex approach to analyzing the intersections of race and class that
define fatherhood and manhood in low-income urban communities.

4   Mitchell Duneier   ↳↲   49

Duneier discusses the idea of moral worth and unpacks the centrality of
this theme in his studies of disadvantaged urban Black men. He explains
the difficulty of conducting ethnography, and weighs in on the longstanding
debate over theory's rightful place in the practice of fieldwork.

SECTION II
GLOBAL ETHNOGRAPHY AND THE STUDY OF TRANSNATIONAL
LABOR MIGRATIONS   61

5   Miliann Kang   ↳◐   63

Kang reflects on her theoretical transformations as a researcher. She
describes how her earlier study of Korean nail salons privileged gender
as the main focus of analysis, and explores how her recent work captures
the shifting dynamics of gender, race, and class. Kang discusses how
her examination of Asian "model minority" discourses takes up this new
theoretical demand. She also explores the notion of respondents as
co-collaborators in research.

6   Hung Cam Thai   𝟪   73

Thai discusses how his interest in researching transnational marriage and
migration was ignited during a return to Vietnam after many years. He
describes how his multiple identities as a refugee, an immigrant, and a
transmigrant offer a unique advantage in making connections between
macro processes and individual relationships. His discussion of his present
research on Viet Kieu—those Vietnamese workers who have returned to
Vietnam—exemplifies these connections.

7   Nazli Kibria   81

Kibria locates the struggles of studying Islamic identity in the Bangali
Diaspora in a post-September 11 world. She addresses the economic and
cultural strains that transnational forces have in shaping social relations
within Bangladesh. She stresses her desire to produce scholarship that can
inspire her students and inform policy agendas.

8   Rhacel Parrenas   88

Parrenas draws upon her three major studies of transnational Filipina
workers to stress the need for complicating analyses of migration and class
mobility. She contextualizes her working concepts of "serial migration" and
"destination hierarchies" through a discussion of the research processes that
led to their development.

Contents

SECTION III
STUDYING GENDER, CRIME, AND VIOLENCE IN THE ERA
OF MASS INCARCERATION   **99**

9   Meda Chesney-Lind   101

Known as the "mother of feminist criminology," Chesney-Lind shares her passion and motivation for researching women and crime for over 30 years. She traces the dramatic shifts and changes in the acceptance of women in criminology, but insists that there is still much to be done if we are to improve the lives of girls and women.

10   Victor Rios   9   111

Rios reflects on how his own youth involvement with gang culture in Oakland informed his study of Black and Latino youth experiences. He explains how discovering patterns of punitive social control within these two youth groups called into question his own reflexivity. He provides some startling accounts of field experiences, and speaks candidly about the consequences that resulted from certain decision-making during the research process.

11   Mercer Sullivan   120

Sullivan explains how growing up in the "still segregated South," coupled with his coming of age in the 1960s, shaped his early interests in social justice. He describes how cutting his teeth in New York during his grad school years helped him to shed his idealistic expectations, and grow as a researcher. In tracing his unconventional career path, Sullivan recounts how he managed to successfully straddle the boundaries between academia and think-tank research, while keeping intact his studies of disadvantaged inner-city youth.

12   Valerie Jenness   22   139

Jenness opens a portal into her experience conducting transgender inmate and sexual assault research in California men's prisons. She frankly discusses the complexities involved in interviewing respondents behind prison walls, and reflects on managing the collision between a researcher's curiosity and the contraints of systematic data collection. Jenness explains how traversing the basic/applied divide is achievable and offers insight into obtaining self-respect, and respect from others in the field.

SECTION IV
THE RESEARCHER AS...   **163**

13   Karyn Lacy *II*   165

Lacy details the process of conducting and completing her first research project which focuses on the housing decisions of middle-class Black suburbanites. She brings to light how an inductive approach to data collection and analysis creates spaces for innovative thinking. Lacy describes how the concept of "strategic assimilation" emerged from this process, and is currently being deployed by graduate students studying racial and ethnic communities.

14   France Winddance Twine) S   176

Twine discusses the impact that growing up in segregated Chicago has had on her sociological imagination, and how this experience continues to shape her scholarly journeys. Trained as an anthropologist and sociologist, Twine discusses why she embraces an interdisciplinary perspective in her work. She weaves theory, narrative, and empirical rigor to provide intricate understandings of racial formations in places such as Brazil and Great Britain.

15   Denise Segura   191

Segura reflects on the trials of advancing as one of the few University of California Chicana scholars, beginning in the late 1980s. She explores the choices and consequences of valuing public sociology, and balancing her life as a mother, feminist scholar and community organizer. Segura describes the importance of a feminist borderlands consciousness, and discusses how the projects she works on are informed by personal experiences, as well as by larger social realities.

16   Christine Williams   206

Williams stresses the importance of applying an intersectional lens to sociological inquiry. In rethinking her earlier work, in which she developed the concept of the "glass escalator," Williams describes how she has learned to incorporate an intersectional approach to her research that includes race, class, and sexuality, in addition to gender. She discusses how theoretical shifts within the discipline ultimately work to improve the sociological stories we tell. She offers insight into the consequential differences between the interview study and participant research.

17   Verta Taylor and Leila J. Rupp   217

Taylor and Rupp discuss their experiences studying drag queens, and explain how they moved beyond theory to understand embodied accounts of their research. They speak to the political nature of drag shows, and share vivid details of how drag queens push the boundaries of respectability for themselves and their audiences. Taylor and Rupp credit their dynamic research process, which spans 30 years, to the commitment that they bring to their studies and to each other.

Editors' Afterword   231
References   237
Contributors   242
Index   248

FOREWORD

Howard S. Becker

Sociologists have forever had a thing about methods, beguiled by the idea that if they just use the right method they will eventually produce "real science," that real thing which has somehow eluded us all these years. But we have been fooled over and over again. One methodological fad replaces another, only to be exposed as also lacking that certain something. And yet sociologists continue to work, to collect data and analyze it, to write articles and books and give papers at scholarly meetings. And some of what they do seems to tell the world things it hadn't known before, even if it doesn't have all the marks of conventional science.

If it isn't science we are doing, we've still been doing something all these years. What is it? The contributors to this book have done their share of discovering things that we and others find interesting and useful. But the methods debates ("wars" is far too drastic a term for our little disagreements) continue, always chasing after the elusive title of "science."

When I used to teach I followed, as best I could (being only human, and then some, I didn't always succeed), a simple rule: never lie to students. Which is harder than it sounds. Because students ask questions to which the honest answer, the one that isn't a lie, is often "I don't know" or, more hopefully, "Why don't you try X? It might work but, then again, maybe not." My efforts at this kind of truth telling had some positive consequences, mainly that when I did say something less wishy-washy students often took me seriously.

But why couldn't I truthfully give surer answers, ones guaranteed to give kosher results? I think I know the answer to that. People in the physical and biological sciences do their work in a sanitized world in which they insulate their materials from interference by other phenomena which would affect what happens, so making it possible to pin down more or less exactly the kind of causal relationships we social scientists would like to similarly establish. But we do our scientific work in the world we live in, in which we have no such control over anything, and thus never know for sure that what we think caused something really did.

And that's what we find it hard to confess to our students. We'd rather not say that we can't do it the way it's supposed to be done. We can't assign people or communities or organizations randomly to differing experimental treatments, and all of that. Much of the methodological apparatus that obsesses us tries to get around that problem, although it never really does. The sizeable literature built on Donald Campbell's recommendations for quasi-experimental design testifies to the difficulties standing in the way of such getting-around tactics. But we hate to confess that truth to students, so we cheer them on with promises that it all really does work, maybe not now, but soon. Those assurances are the lies I stopped telling, just admitting that all our knowledge was even more provisional than what the "hard" scientists came up with, as I learned from the work of sociologists and historians of science.

Most of us do our best, keeping the faith and soldiering on. We write "methods" sections for our articles and books, giving a cleaned-up version of what we actually did. We tell how we followed the procedures laid out in the manuals on method. We leave out all the things we did that those manuals, and the experts who write them, warn against. Why admit to doing something that might introduce errors into our work?

And that's why everyone so welcomes the behind-the-scenes story of "how I really did it," how I dealt with the many contingencies the world put in the way of my best efforts to do real science. Such stories let everyone in on the truth that we can't do that kind of real science and that we have to live with the unforeseen and the uncontrollable and figure out how to move knowledge forward even so. They tell what the problems really were and what kinds of solutions we cobbled up to deal with them.

We can never get enough of these stories, because cases differ. Even cases that look similar differ in details which shape how we can gather our data and what we can make out of them. The situation we study unexpectedly reveals a feature whose existence we had no reason to suspect but which grossly affects what we're trying to understand. The world keeps producing variations, the same variations natural scientists get rid of by controlling their work conditions, but we can't exert that kind of control and have to find ways to get the work done even so. Variations continue to appear, and that means we can't find The Method, because there isn't any sure thing solution to any of our problems. A generation of questionnaire constructors knew how to ask a foolproof question about marital status: "Are you single, married, widowed or divorced?" What else was there? Well, suddenly there were people who lived together and slept together just like married people, except they weren't married, and weren't necessarily one woman and one man. Now we know that we have to ask about "living together" too. But we don't know what further changes in mating and living arrangements lie ahead of us, that will one of these days require some more revisions in our instruments and thinking. We always have to improvise and adapt what we do to what the people we study so unexpectedly do.

The need for improvisation means that sociologists have to rely on their personal resources, dig into what they have learned in their lives outside of school, in order to find ways around and through the thickets of doing science in the midst of real life, which is somehow not behaving the way it ought to so that we can follow the rules of method we've learned.

The stories in *Sociologists Backstage* tell how the contributors, who differ in so many ways, dealt with the situations they found themselves in as they did their research, and how who they were and what they had become in their lives intersected with those situations. The stories will fascinate you, and give you a lot to think about as you go ahead with your own research adventure.

SERIES FOREWORD

This innovative series is for all readers interested in books that provide frameworks for making sense of the complexities of contemporary social life. Each of the books in this series uses a sociological lens to provide current critical and analytical perspectives on significant social issues, patterns and trends.The series consists of books that integrate the best ideas in sociological thought with an aim toward public education and engagement. These books are designed for use in the classroom as well as for scholars and socially curious general readers.

What are some of the "hidden realities" of sociology as a worksite? In *Sociologists Backstage* seventeen sociologists take us behind the scenes for a glimpse into the decisions and activities that shape their field research. They address questions such as the motivation behind their research projects, most embarrassing moments while conducting research, and most difficult issues and ethical considerations. The interviews in this book turn the lens of inquiry back onto the sociologist to reveal the process of doing sociology. Readers of these experiences and insights will learn and how sociological work transforms both the researcher and ultimately, the practice of sociology.

Valerie Jenness
Jodi O'Brien
Series Editors

PREFACE AND ACKNOWLEDGMENTS

The idea for a book that asked sociologists to talk about what they do and why originated with Sarah Fenstermaker. Indeed, it sat in her "book ideas" file for about 10 years. Sarah has always been fascinated with what lies just beyond what one can see (or is allowed to see). "I was bequeathed a fascination with and some talent for discerning the 'hidden' realities, the variety of 'real' truths, and the ambiguous message," she wrote in her chapter for a book entitled *Feminist Sociology* (1997: 212). "This fascination has fueled my interests in sociology and specifically the powerful sociological vantage of social construction, the nature of stigma, and the backstage qualities of anything—especially work organizations. In all of that, it is always the *process* of it that is so compelling to me. The outcomes are visible, but the hidden realities lie elsewhere."

When Sarah approached her new colleague at UC Santa Barbara to join her in this endeavor, Nikki Jones enthusiastically accepted the opportunity to engage in dialogue with some of the most interesting social scientists in the field. Like Sarah, Nikki has an insatiable curiosity about why and how we do what we do, especially when it comes to ethnography and field research. Her first book was nearly complete and Nikki was eager to take on the role of co-editor and looked forward to learning how other researchers managed the various challenges and choices that come along with representing the social world, from the methodological to the political.

The format was simple. We sent each contributor nine questions, in large measure custom-crafted from what we knew about her or his research, with the tenth question asked of everyone. The 10th question was asked in three parts: What was the worst (or most difficult or most embarrassing) interview/field encounter you've had? What did you really want to do for a living and what were you afraid you would end up doing? What is the study you never pursued, but always wanted to? In our letter of invitation to prospective contributors we said, "We have long believed that there is far too little discussion in published works about the actual *doing* of Sociology, making it look like magic, or at least relatively easy. This book is intended to right the balance a bit by illuminating the craft and the choices made as the research process unfolds." The dialogic process of crafting responses typically took two rounds—back and forth—between us and the contributors, and we are happy to report that nearly all of our contributors spontaneously declared that they had a good time in the process.

Who should we invite? And how many? We had been advised initially to invite a lot of people, on the presumption that no matter what they promised, many ultimately would bail out of the project. So we invited around twenty, thinking ten would deliver. That turned out to be a huge miscalculation, to which our seventeen contributed chapters attest. While there are clear substantive themes that ultimately emerged from the interviews and which helped us group the chapters, we were led in our invitation list largely by our own curiosity, with each of us suggesting contributors whose work represented a backstage worth exploring. Additionally, we wanted to maximize the diversity of research locale, and we tried to reflect the range of contributors' professional networks. Finally, because of our own differences in age, race, and sociological interests we ended up assembling a diverse group in those conventional ways as well.

Ultimately, however, we assert no claim that we were systematic in who we invited; indeed there is only one contributor whom neither of us had met before. This non-systematic selection process also resulted (only in part by accident) in the preponderance of contributors who are qualitative sociologists, and all the projects discussed being either qualitative, ethnographic, or both.

We worried about this, but only for a few minutes. What we realized when we saw the array of invitees is that the "backstage" of field research is far richer and more mysterious than those projects that proceed with a tool-kit that is applied to relatively static and thus more predictable data sets. We are not suggesting that there is no craft or creativity demanded in the design and implementation of quantitative study. We are suggesting that those who embark on field research are called upon to invent (and re-invent) ways of making sense of their social worlds as they *unfold*, and this results in ways of working that typically aren't articulated or apprehended in published form. Thus, while the challenges addressed by our contributors are many of the same ones confronted by all researchers (e.g., issues of internal and external validity, sample selection, reliability, etc.) *how* they address them in the various contexts presented by their research sites renders each "backstage" unique—and uniquely fascinating. As a result we hope that the book will be especially useful to those whose research questions lend themselves to a mix of methods.

We also had little inkling that the responses to questions about methods would be so uniformly engaging and often downright inspirational. However much we thought we knew some of our contributors, and however much we had previously gleaned from their publications, their responses took us by surprise again and again. For us, this quality transformed a good little idea for a book into a much more substantial product, and one that we hope has real value for readers.

While we aspired to create a collection that was interesting to professional researchers of all persuasions, we were especially mindful of the uses to which graduate students could put this volume. We collaborate in our department's field research methods sequence: Nikki takes the first 10 weeks, and Sarah the second. The sequence is designed to escort each student from the first moments in the field to the crafting of a sociological story. Of course, 20 weeks is a ridiculously short time in which to imagine such a process, but it proves to be good practice nonetheless, and is roughly modeled from Howie Becker's field methods course at Northwestern in which Sarah was a student—albeit centuries ago.

One goal with our graduate students is for them to appreciate—through their own field research and reading the results of others' efforts—the myriad choices that go into crafting a research project. We don't mislead our students into believing that *every* choice is consequential, or that there is always something important at stake. However, we do emphasize that whatever the choices made, they are still *choices*: that research does not unfold *itself*, and that the researcher ultimately is the one creating the story that results. In short, it *isn't* magic. It's craft. It is the result of a set of decisions, deliberate or otherwise. Thus, one aspect of each and every contribution to this volume is the unveiling of craft, the pulling back of the curtains to reveal what choices lie behind. The cover photo of the volume is intended to convey that when the reader parts the curtains, a sociologist will reveal the backstage of the craft, and while the mystery may be fascinating, it is in fact, no mystery at all.

In any book the furthest backstage one usually goes is the acknowledgments, where authors reveal who has made the actual creation of the work possible. Developing our book has likewise left us with debts of gratitude. We want to thank our home departments at UC Santa Barbara—Sociology, and the Institute for Social Behavioral and Economic Research—for their continuing support of our work. Such support often came in the form of ISBER's IT director, Randall Ehren, who provided frequent consultation and aid. We are especially grateful to Sarah's Research Assistant, UCSB graduate student Joan Budesa, who was so helpful in the preparation of the volume. What she *wanted* to do was think about social change in Croatia; instead Joan attended to the small but weighty matters of our volume. We thank her. Our gratitude also goes to Stavros Markopoulos, far away on the Island of Crete, who graciously allowed us to use his photograph "Through the Curtains" for our cover. Thanks to Ali Hendley for clerical assistance, Heather Tirado Gilligan and Lori Sexton for their editorial assistance, and to Anita Anthony-Huebert, Bryan Farley, and Dasa Francikova for advice on the cover art. Thanks go to series editors Jodi O'Brien and Valerie Jenness. Val's helpful intercession early on in the process made the book possible. Thanks to Routledge's Leah Babb-Rosenfeld for her editorial help, and our gratitude to Routledge publisher, Steve Rutter, for just the right advice at just the right time. And thanks to Howie Becker for a thoughtful start.

Finally, and foremost, to our contributors: the stories you tell are memorable, insightful, and inspirational. Thank you for making our project a success.

INTRODUCTION

The contributors to this volume fit a rather flexible definition of sociology. The authors of the following chapters are affiliated with a range of departments, programs, and institutional centers, including Sociology, Women's Studies, Criminal Justice, Feminist Studies, African American Studies, and Chicano/a Studies, among others. It is not their departmental affiliations that make their works sociological. Instead, it is that each of the contributors reveals in her or his work and in the responses provided in the following pages a vibrant sociological imagination. They are adept at linking biography—their own and that of their respondents—with history and the larger social forces that compel both. For some, it is experiencing large-scale historical shifts first hand that sparked their sociological imagination. The contributors to this volume are also experts at illuminating the often invisible links between private troubles and public issues (Mills 1959). They think critically about how institutions shape lives and the difficulties associated with undertaking research that makes a difference. These scholars have taken these common concerns to field research sites in far-flung locales—from Philadelphia to Saigon—and in a variety of settings—from neighborhoods to nail salons. The set of responses included in the following pages provides an invaluable and often intimate, survey of what sociologists do, how and why.

As a discipline, sociology is one of the most diverse subfields in the social sciences (STEM Trends, 2009), and is reflected in the range of contributors to this volume. Many of us recognize this diversity as a manifestation of the victories won by various social movements over the last sixty years. In the following pages, contributors reflect on how their own identities, and how they imagine others may perceive them, inform how they collect, analyze, and eventually represent their field research to others. Other demographic trends have shaped sociology as well. The baby boom generation is now nearing retirement and the wisdom shared by our contributors regarding how the profession has changed over the course of their careers is illuminating. For example, several senior contributors to the volume describe a more acci-dental path to the academy than is often imagined by a younger generation of scholars. The professionalization of sociology has implications for how new knowledge is produced, and several of the contributors reflect on these implications and dilemmas in their responses. The value of a social science perspective does not translate easily into careerism. Its benefit often lies in the skills required to gather and analyze evidence about the social world, and an analytical point of view on all things social to motivate the questions: what is happening, how is it happening, and what are the implications for things happening in this way? The contributors bring this way of thinking to various settings and events: rural Georgia, the basketball court, Bangladesh, a drag show, and so on.

In addition to capturing large-scale demographic and historic changes, many of the contributors' responses also reflect key theoretical questions that have shaped sociology over the last few decades. For example, how do intersections of race, gender, class, and sexuality influence our research and analysis? How can feminist questions and analyses enhance and complicate how we approach a question? What does it mean to do community-based research? What does it mean to do work in the so-called post eras: the post-feminist era, the post-Civil Rights era, the post-Chicano/a Movement era or post-racial era? A number of scholars challenge the notion that we are, in fact, living in a post-moment, and their research testifies to those convictions.

These responses to the interviews in this volume are obviously relevant for contemporary sociology, yet there is also a timeless quality to them. The volume includes responses to questions that both Sarah and Nikki—decades apart—encountered as graduate students. These are questions that we now hear from our own students, and we are confident that the research undertaken by students of field research at all levels will resonate with the responses: How to find respondents; how to get into a setting; how to share oneself with respondents without losing a grip on one's research; how to make respondent lives visible and voices heard while still being systematic in one's approach; how to tell the story that is true. The answers vary, of course, but the questions will be asked over and over by each researcher in each new field setting.

How This Book Is Organized

The volume is organized around four themes that include some of the areas most current in contemporary sociological research. The first section of the book, "Sociology in the Post-Civil Rights Era," includes interviews from sociologists Mary Pattillo, Scott Brooks, Alford A. Young, Jr. and Mitch Duneier that consider the benefits, privileges and challenges of conducting field research among African Americans in urban settings. Despite commonly held beliefs that the academy is somehow removed from the real world, these responses make clear that academia is a contested site too: race, gender, class and sexuality inflect individual and political battles in both the field and the discipline.

We begin our interviews in chapter 1 with Mary Pattillo, author of *Black Picket Fences* (1999) and *Black on the Block* (2007), who reflects on how her biography was shaped by shifts in residential patterns of segregation, a process later described by her mentor, William Julius Wilson, as African American out-migration or Black flight (e.g., Wilson 1993). Pattillo's work has helped to expand the focus of urban sociology from urban poverty to the experiences of the Black middle class, and she describes how she came to carve out this niche for herself. Mary has focused her research on a group that was hailed as symbolic of the triumph of the Civil Rights Movement a decade ago, yet remained relatively understudied in sociology. Ten years later, Mary notes, the amount of scholarship in this area is significant. Pattillo speaks of methodological challenges too, including those she faced as an ethnographer who moved to a neighborhood primarily for research purposes: "the biggest challenge of being a fully embedded ethnographer: data collection exhaustion." She also considers, as do others, the benefits of stretching beyond one's disciplinary boundaries in trying to make sense of what one finds in the field. Pattillo's chapter ends with a personal story about a downtown Chicago encounter with now President Obama and the implications of the Obama presidency for future research agendas in sociology.

In chapter 2, the questions directed to Scott Brooks draw on fieldwork conducted for his book, *Black Men Can't Shoot* (2009), an ethnography based on four years of field research in Philadelphia. In this interview, Scott explains how he came to the discovery revealed in his book about how young Black men with hoop dreams move from being seen by others as good, to being "known" as great, and the significance of these designations for their life course trajectories. In response to our questions, Brooks extends this discussion from the court to the academy. In doing so, and like Mary Pattillo, Brooks also complicates our understanding of how race, class, and gender operate there. Brooks's interview also reveals how intersecting identities—in his case, male, African American, Christian, and heterosexual—influence how he is seen in the field and shape the story he tells about his respondents. His interview includes a reminder that although there are more people from underrepresented backgrounds in the discipline than ever before, the types of mentoring resources that ensure success for scholars of color are often in short supply.

Alford A. Young, Jr. responds to our questions with a discussion of the motivations for his research on poor and working-class African American men in chapter 3. He explains the power of field research to re-frame conversations, a task he takes on successfully in his book, *The Minds of Marginalized Black Men* (2006). Young advances a cultural framework for studying the lives of African American men. He encourages researchers to shift their focus from the *behavior* of Black men to *how men construct meaning* about various aspects of their social worlds. He encourages field researchers to imagine their respondents as "practical theorists" of their social worlds as a way to better capture and understand the complexity of people's lives. In his account of a "surprising finding," we see how the sustained engagement with a community of scholars is essential to the production of new knowledge. His interview reminds us that sociological discoveries do not simply spring from the data, but they are pulled, finessed, and refined over time and in participation with others. Young knew he wanted to be a professor by age 20, and his account of growing up in East Harlem reveals an early interest in stratification, inequality, and social difference. His life experiences, including his roles as father and son, continue to influence his work. Like Pattillo, Young also reflects on the utility of drawing on interdisciplinary approaches to understanding the lives of African American men.

Mitch Duneier, author of *Slim's Table* (1994) and *Sidewalk* (2000), concludes this section with a set of provocative responses to questions about the central concerns that motivate his research on the moral worlds of poor and working-class Black men. In his books Duneier critically considers how men construct meaningful lives in the face of burdens and barriers. His chapter provides a compelling and informative account of the various methodological and disciplinary challenges that face ethnographers and ethnography. His chapter includes instructive lessons on the little discussed problem of transparency in field research methods, the unique position occupied by ethnographers, and the difference between ethnographers and novelists. Like the other contributors in this section, Duneier considers how lines of difference inform the field research process, including how the classics, Stack's *All Our Kin* (1975) and Liebow's *Tally's Corner* (1968), offer instruction in navigating white privilege in the field. Duneier reminds us that ethnographers play an important role in the study of social life: "Ethnographers are on the front lines of a zone of confrontation where theories developed through survey methodologies, experiments and armchair reflection meet the actual people whose behavior has sometimes already been explained with these other methods."

In the second section of the volume, "Global Ethnography: The Study of Transnational Labor Migrations," Miliann Kang, Hung Cam Thai, Nazli Kibria, and Rhaceal Parrenas provide an engaging set of responses based on their research on labor migrations. The topics we asked them to consider cut across what is now wide-ranging scholarship on the movement of work and workers. The study of work, labor, and occupations in sociology began (as did virtually all American sociology) firmly fixed in the domestic case. Not so today. The interviews in Section II serve as exemplars of ethnographies done about people and their labors as they seek opportunity around the globe. Miliann Kang reflects on the discoveries made from her study of nail salons (Kang 2010). She explains how she came to select this setting as a site to focus on interracial engagement among women, specifically the set of relationships that emerge when working-class Black women are served by Korean women. Looking back, she comments on how theoretical concepts used in her earlier work have changed or evolved over time. She writes that she no longer sees gender as "*the* central axis in all social settings or exchanges." (Others in this volume likewise describe the increasing complexity they perceive retrospectively in their past analyses.) If she were to do the same study today she would likely view the enactment of body labor through the shifting lens of gender, race, and class, as she has done in her recent research. Kang draws important parallels between her work and the work of scholars such as Mary Pattillo and Karyn Lacy, who study middle-class Blacks, along with those who study Black families more generally. Like others in this section, Kang also reflects on the importance of feminist research to sociological analysis. In ways that parallel some of Young's discussion, Kang encourages us to consider respondents less as "subjects" and more as "agents in the co-construction of knowledge."

Hung Cam Thai offers a compelling account of how his personal biography informed his eventual analysis of Vietnamese transnational marriage (Thai 2008). In no interview are we reminded as forcefully of how one's occupational fate can hang on so many random and seemingly arbitrary turns of events. The type of diasporic movements that he now studies shaped Thai's professional trajectory. He speaks, as France Winddance Twine does in a later interview, about the challenges of conducting field research over a period of years in settings that are far away from his home institution. Thai's chapter also reveals, as do a number of others in the volume, the challenges of crossing lines of difference; in Thai's case it was the experience of interviewing women. Like Brooks's interview, Thai's interview reminds us that the perceptions of the researcher are consequential for the conduct of research. While lines of difference exist, and can be challenging to navigate, there are still ways that respondents can develop genuine rapport and trust with their respondents.

Nazli Kibria and Rhaceal Parrenas round out this section with interviews that reflect on field research examining the Bangladesh Diaspora and Filipina migrant workers, respectively. In ways similar to Thai's, Kibria's interview encourages us to ponder "how social and economic capital obtained abroad is 'converted' to social status" in home countries. The returning worker is subject to both new and old perceptions of their status and value as they negotiate a new existence in once familiar territory. Kibria draws on her study of migration and social displacement and is explicit about making connections in both her personal and professional work between "private troubles" and larger social and political realities (Kibria 1995). She provides an account of what it is like to conduct research on Islam and identity formation in the Bangali Diaspora after the 9/11 attacks. She also considers the challenges that come along with teaching social change and what she hopes her students draw from her research. Along with several other contributors to the volume, Kibria also disputes the notion that we live in a post-racial world.

Section II ends with Rhaceal Parrenas's interview, drawing from her three major studies of globalized workers (Parrenas 2001, 2005, 2008). She explains how she came to the concept of "serial migration" and "destination hierarchies" in her research on Filipina workers in Rome and Los Angeles. Parrenas also describes how she came to study the children of migrant workers and what it is like to interview them (a challenge that Pattillo also notes). Parrenas's research and analysis complicates our understanding of the experience of migration and contradicts common expectations of class mobility. Parrenas also speaks of the important contribution of the work of feminist sociologists to the study of global migration and some thoughts on the "gender revolution" against women's emancipation in the settings she has visited. Finally, she offers an account of how to get to the right question—the answer, she has discovered, does not always already exist in the literature.

The third section of the volume, "Gender, Crime, and Violence in the Era of Mass Incarceration," contains interviews from scholars who have produced and are producing key studies bearing on mass incarceration (for discussion see Western 2006). Meda Chesney-Lind, Victor Rios, Mercer Sullivan, and Valerie Jenness consider topics that reflect the nation's shift to incarceration as the first response to criminal behavior and of a generally punitive approach to criminal violations in schools and neighborhood settings. Along with the increasing number of Americans incarcerated since the late 1960s, schools have embraced zero tolerance policies toward violations on school grounds, and officers in many jurisdictions have focused their energies on the broken windows-style policing, exemplified by Mayor of New York City Rudolph Giuliani in the 1990s. These policy shifts have had serious consequences for those who are most likely to come into contact with the criminal justice system. The scholars interviewed in this section speak to how such changes influence what they study, with whom, and how. Several address directly the issues related to engaging in progressive work in a period where the criminal and juvenile justice system has expanded so dramatically. How can social science influence policy? Is social science any match for "tough on crime" legislatures? The interviews consider these questions, among others.

Meda Chesney-Lind opens this section with an interview that includes a candid disclosure about what has motivated her work over the span of her 30-plus year career: to make the world a better place for women and girls. Chesney-Lind is now widely regarded as the mother of contemporary feminist criminology, yet she also admits that she took a somewhat accidental path to her current career. She began her career with "energy, youth, and the 60s" at her back. The optimism of youth couldn't soften the realities that she and other feminist scholars confronted early on—colleagues who focused on the study of women and crime were frequently denied tenure. Chesney-Lind now looks back with amazement at the dramatic changes that have taken place since she began her career. Today, gender and crime is a major part of many criminology and criminal justice programs, and the study of gender is a centerpiece of the annual meetings of the American Society of Criminology. This success is not without its challenges, as Chesney-Lind explains. Chesney-Lind ends her interview with a powerful comment on what it has meant to do critical scholarship during the era of mass incarceration: "The fact that during my 'watch' the U.S. has become the world's largest incarcerator horrifies me. As many have noted, the criminal justice system has functioned really for the past 30 years or so as the 'new Jim Crow.'"

Victor Rios describes his comparative analysis of the punitive social control of Black and Latino youth in Oakland, California (Rios forthcoming). He describes his own movement from being the target of punitive social control to studying its penetration into the daily lives of Oakland youth. Rios reflects on how his identity influenced his interactions, especially his ability to build trust equally among Black and Latino young men. His chapter also echoes responses from other contributors about the importance of understanding how lines of difference influence field research. Like Thai, Rios encourages field researchers to remain respectful of the barriers between researchers and respondents while also appreciating the fact that they are rarely insurmountable.

Mercer Sullivan, author of the widely respected *Getting Paid: Youth, Crime and Work in the Inner City* (1989), provides an account of how his early interest in social justice developed during the course of a childhood spent in the "still segregated South." Much like Meda Chesney-Lind, Sullivan began his academic career with the energy of the 1960s at his back. He eventually became hooked on efforts to "save" the inner cities. Experience gained while working in an inner-city neighborhood in Harlem as an undergraduate helped Sullivan to develop a more realistic sense of the challenges associated with such an ambition. Trained as an anthropologist at Columbia University, Sullivan worked to develop a "set of tools to study the ways of life in poor urban neighborhoods." He had a particular concern for youth coming of age in poverty, especially in the adaptive responses young people develop to structural disadvantage. We see again a somewhat accidental route to an eventual faculty position for Sullivan at the Rutgers School of Criminal Justice. He explains that he took advantage of research opportunities as they emerged (as if following the guidance of Christine Williams in a later chapter). Mercer speaks of his intellectual and methodological mentors near and far, who helped him to make sense of what he was seeing in the field. The interview ends with some provocative statements on how a "sociological imagination" might be more effective in solving contemporary problems than are popular criminological theories.

Valerie Jenness's interview—one of two interviews in the volume that focus on transgender life and identity—begins with an explanation of what led her to this understudied population in prisons. Jenness provides a lively and engaging account of the lessons she has learned in this unique study— lessons methodological, theoretical, and, at times, personal (Jenness, forthcoming). Her interview, like others here, raises important questions for field research: what impact can research effect beyond its contribution to an academic literature? How and when can qualitative research best inform policy? Jenness also describes the challenges facing researchers who study vulnerable populations. For this study, Val had to navigate three separate Institutional Review Boards, train a research team to conduct face-to-face interviews with transgender inmates, and enter the field herself to collect data and conduct interviews. She speaks quite candidly about venturing into this "foreign social terrain," including how her first round of interviews can be likened to a first kiss. Val's honest account reveals both the stresses and surprises of studying transgender in a prison context. She explains how Gloria Anzaldua's (1987) concept of "open-hearted listening" helped her when she heard story after story of serious victimization, and how her study made her think critically about herself, her humanity and what constitutes "a real woman."

The final section of the book, "The Researcher As...," features interviews with researchers who each offer examples of how to break new ground in qualitative sociology. In their reflections—from Karyn Lacy, France Wind-dance Twine, Denise Segura, Christine Williams, and co-authors Leila Rupp and Verta Taylor—each reveal how the adaptive method of field research offers startling reflections on everyday life. Karyn Lacy begins the section with a set of responses that include invaluable information on the process of conducting and completing a first research project (Lacy 2007). In her interview, we see the researcher as novice. She offers an account of the benefit of the "novice's authenticity" that can be found in many classic "first books" and she speaks of what is at stake for researchers during difficult or embarrassing encounters in the field. Lacy explains how her project evolved from a study of how middle-class Black suburbanites make housing decisions to a book on how middle-class Blacks understand their own identities and distinguish themselves from others in the Black community. In doing so, her account provides an example of how grounded theory and inductive approaches to data collection and analysis can help to generate new knowledge. Eventually, this approach led Lacy to the concept of "strategic assimilation," a concept that is now being tested by graduate students who are exploring other racial and ethnic communities.

In the next chapter, France Winddance Twine speaks of the researcher as boundary-crosser. Twine describes how her childhood in Chicago shaped her sociological imagination and a career with a distinct multidisciplinary character. Like Pattillo, Sullivan, and Chesney-Lind, Twine observed the world changing around her: over the course of her childhood she lived in a white neighborhood, an integrated neighborhood, and the infamous Ida B. Wells housing project. Twine continues to cross boundaries as a "disciplinary hybrid"—trained as both sociologist and anthropologist at UC Berkeley. She provides an account of how her anthropological training informed the writing of her first book, *Racism in a Racial Democracy: The Maintenance of White Supremacy in Brazil* (1997), and continues to influence her journey toward becoming "a certain sort of sociologist who integrate[s] theory, narrative, and empirical rigor." Twine's interview touches on a variety of seemingly disparate topics but all have some quality of breaking through or maintaining "borders": she speaks of the difficulties of conducting a longitudinal ethnography in a country not her own; she describes the place of visual sociology in her ethnographic toolkit and the utility of drawing on other forms of evidence to tell a story; and she explains how to position oneself as "researcher" in the field when respondents want and need more.

In the interview following, Denise Segura—the researcher as pioneer— offers a compelling account of her path into the academy. Throughout her career, Segura thought critically about what it means to do work for her community and we believe she serves as an exemplar of a public sociologist. Segura describes the crafting of a union of research, teaching, and social change, all the while accumulating the common markers of success in the discipline. Segura provides an informative account of how the choices she made in developing pedagogical, activist, and academic aspects of her life as a researcher shaped her career. Segura explains how she draws on her own experience as a scholar of color to shape her strategy as a mentor. Her interview ends with a description of her current "Old Timers" research—a study of the retrospective accounts of men from the Los Angeles Watts neighborhood.

Christine Williams speaks to the researcher as "observant participant" (to use her phrase). She describes her first book, *Still a Man's World* (1995) and the concept of the "glass escalator" that she introduced to the field. Revisiting her important contribution to the field with a critical eye, Williams observes how an appreciation of intersectionality might have productively complicated her original analysis. Her discussion reveals how theoretical shifts in the discipline over time can improve how we make sense of what we encounter in the field and the sociological stories we tell. She embarked on the research for her recent book, *Inside Toyland* (2006), with a better appreciation of intersections of race, gender, class, and sexuality and was better able to understand what she was seeing—or not seeing—in her field research. Her experiences lend credence to the notion that it is more difficult to enter the field as "blank slates" as one becomes a more seasoned sociologist and the work that one must do to not evaluate or judge. In her set of responses, we see the researcher as observer-participant. Her responses reveal the importance of being with people in the field as they are in order to get the story. In this interview, Williams also provides a rare but instructive description of the "physical and emotional intensity" involved in field research, for example, in contacting gatekeepers and locating respondents, and the pressure of completing the first project when so much is at stake. She addresses timeless questions for field researchers: What do you do if a respondent declines your interview request? What if you can't "get in"? She instructs field researchers to cultivate a balance of "confidence and humility." Finally, she offers a useful comparison between the results of interview studies and what Mitch Duneier refers to as "context-driven" research.

The final chapter in the volume is co-authored by Verta Taylor and Leila Rupp. Taylor and Rupp—nicknamed the "professors of lesbian love" by Sushi, a drag queen featured in their book *Drag Queens at the 801 Cabaret* (2003)— answer our questions about their interdisciplinary collaboration, which has spanned a 30-year period. Here, we see the researchers as "performers." By this we mean not only their research into (and some participation in) the transgressive performances in the Key West cabaret they studied, but also the ways in which these two scholars have had to be mindful of being "out" to all their audiences: colleagues, administrators, students, and the public more generally. Taylor and Rupp reflect on the assumptions they brought to their study of the drag queens and their performances (on and off the stage). They speak of their own epiphany that the drag queens knew relatively little about the variations in and realities of, transgender. In this interview, we raise the question of the role of politics in field research: do we make the work our respondents do political or do they make it that way? Taylor and Rupp comment on the challenges of "high risk activism" and how being out as lesbians, and being a lesbian couple, have made them vulnerable to subtle and not so subtle forms of discrimination. Both Taylor and Rupp are now in administrative positions at the university and they consider the difficulties of moving into administrative roles, while noting the commonalities between drag queens and academics. Finally, they provide some valuable descriptions about what can be at stake as the researcher commits to telling the "truth" about one's respondents to a variety of audiences.

A postscript to the volume—in the spirit of turnabout is fair play—is Sarah and Nikki's answers to the 10th question, one common to all the contributors.

Other Ways to Read This Book

The order provided by the Table of Contents is just one way to read this book. Over the course of the preparation of the volume, as we lived with the interviews we saw many ways in which contributor responses overlapped, effectively commented on each other, and when read in concert, offered new insights. Three examples must suffice here, but there are countless others which we hope readers discover for themselves.

Those who are particularly interested in the intersection of biography and the sociological imagination might benefit from the childhood memories offered by Pattillo, and how white flight and then black flight shaped her experience as an adolescent girl, or Sullivan's reflection on how growing up in a small, segregated Southern town shaped his understanding of race and racism, or Alford Young's understanding of how growing up in East Harlem shaped his first appreciation of the workings of social stratification. Read together, Thai's and Rios's interviews reveal how dramatic international and domestic policy shifts influenced the trajectory of their adolescent lives and ultimately, their research: moving Hung from a small village in Viet Nam to a federally subsidized housing project in Mississippi, and moving Victor from being the target of the police to being a collaborator in research endeavors with police officials. Each of these accounts—among many others—reveal how history shapes biography and, as the work of scholars inform new research and policy agendas, biography shapes history.

Readers interested in feminist and gender studies will gain a deeper appreciation of the costs and consequences of a feminist lens by reading the interviews with Chesney-Lind, King, Williams, Twine, and Taylor and Rupp, side-by-side. What does it mean to be a feminist scholar? How do feminist scholars think about the intersections of gender, race, class and sexuality? How can one have a career as a feminist scholar? And, as Chesney-Lind asks in her chapter, are "academic articles enough" to ameliorate many of the real world problems we research?

Finally, in many of the interviews, contributors reveal that much more inspires social scientists or sustains them that others never see: family, friendships, and relationships. Perhaps the most important relationship to the successful development of a career over time is that with one's mentor. Those interested in mentoring relationships might read Chesney-Lind's responses alongside those of Brooks, since both illuminate the importance of mentoring those on the margins. Segura's interview illustrates how such mentoring can reverberate to the next generation, where those previously guided spend their lives reciprocating such gifts in relationship with their own students.

Ultimately we hope that each of the interviews will make an engaging supplement for anyone reading or teaching the books authored by the contributors, and we hope that the volume becomes a new way to appreciate the complexities of the research process, including those hidden backstage.

SECTION I

URBAN SOCIOLOGY IN THE POST-CIVIL RIGHTS ERA

1.
MARY PATTILLO

1. *With your study of the Black middle class (*Black Picket Fences *[1999] and* Black on the Block *[2007]) you join a group of scholars who have opened new (or long neglected) areas of sociological interest. In the case of the Black middle class, you make the observation that we are at once declaring the Black middle class symbolic of the triumph of the Civil Rights Movement, but yet we know very little about them. What difference has this odd dynamic made to your choices as a researcher?*

As I read that question now, I immediately think—"now we know a lot about the Black middle class." You are so right that my work is among that of many other youngish scholars in exploring the lives of middle-class Blacks. And as a result, I don't think now—as much as I did when I began—that we know very little about this topic. This is amazing since I finished graduate school in 1997, and in just over 10 years there has been significant scholarship in this area. I think Bart Landry's *The New Black Middle Class* (1988) was really at the vanguard of this line of research, and since then the number of studies—both quantitative and qualitative—has swelled. Honestly, I think it became pretty obvious after the volumes of "urban poverty" research (read, "Black urban poverty," for the most part) that something was missing; that this focus among sociologists on poor African Americans was misleading. I think it became especially frustrating for teachers to not have any books or articles to assign to students on any other facet of Black life aside from poverty. As a result, I am happy to say that we know a lot more about the Black middle class now than we did when I was first starting the research for *Black Picket Fences*. There is still a lot more to know, but there is no longer a vacuum.

Still, the question asks me about my choice to study the Black middle class. In many ways it was very personal. I knew that my life was symbolic of the supposed "triumphs" of the Civil Rights Movement. My parents grew up in segregated Louisiana. My mother remembers not being able to go to the public library in New Orleans, and Louisiana State University *paid* my father to go to medical school outside the state so that they did not have to admit a Black student. My own high school education was the direct result of civil rights activism in Milwaukee. I participated in a desegregation busing program that opened up suburban high schools to inner city students. In some ways, my schooling epitomized the kind of "Black middle-class out-migration" that William Julius Wilson wrote about extensively in *The Truly Disadvantaged* (1993), and argued was the result of civil rights triumphs.

Both the words *triumph* and *out-migration* connote finality. Yet I knew the civil rights agenda was not fulfilled because there were still protests in my city against racially motivated police brutality, and because in the 1990s my mother was the unwitting victim of racial discrimination by an apartment management agency in Milwaukee, and became a party to a lawsuit. Similarly, it was not clear to me what the "out" meant in Black middle-class "out-migration." Out of what? When I was an infant, my neighborhood babysitter was white, but by the time I started school that family had left, and nearly all my neighbors were Black. Maybe my family had initially moved "out" of the Black community, but the Black community quickly moved back "in" with us. All of this motivated me to want to know more about middle-class African Americans, and how, as the subtitle of *Black Picket Fences* states—they (we) were both privileged as a result of civil rights struggles and imperiled by the continuing realities of discrimination and segregation.

2. *In* Black on the Block *you document the role of the Black middle class in a changing Chicago neighborhood—one in which you lived. You have written of a worry that you would take all your "insider" knowledge (that served you so well in many respects) for granted. What challenges did you confront as an ethnographer—someone who lived and worked in the neighborhood under study? What advice would you give to ethnographers facing similar challenges?*

For the research in both *Black Picket Fences* and *Black on the Block,* I lived in the neighborhoods I studied. This is different from studying the neighborhood you live in. I think the latter method is even more likely to lead to overlooking one's insider knowledge because studying where you live means that you've already skipped the crucial step of documenting your early experiences in the neighborhood. In my case, I had a topic of interest and chose neighborhoods that might help me explore that topic. Every experience—from house/apartment hunting to getting settled to meeting new neighbors to learning where to shop to learning where and where not to walk—was data. And this was indeed the biggest challenge of being a fully embedded ethnographer: data collection exhaustion.

I have to admit that I wrote far fewer field notes for *Black on the Block* than I did for *Black Picket Fences.* I was a graduate student for the first project, and doing fieldwork and writing field notes was my full-time job. For the second project, I was expected to teach (and grade), advise students, serve on committees, and I had to actually leave my study neighborhood and commute 45 minutes to Northwestern to do all of that. On top of that I was a newlywed and a new homeowner with new domestic responsibilities. As a result, the data from North Kenwood—Oakland (study no. 2) come much more from meetings (of which there were many) and much less from hanging out, which I did a lot of in Groveland (study no. 1).

I also had challenges with insider knowledge, but less so about the neighborhood and more so about the lives of Black professionals like myself. At this point, I have several colleagues who have moved to North Kenwood—Oakland. It is the kind of place that attracts Black doctors, bankers, consultants, IT workers, and, yes, professors. In interviews, I had to avoid the temptation to skip an interview question because I assumed I'd know how the person would answer just because we shared a lot in common. But this is a lesson quickly learned, because all Black professionals clearly do not think alike. Sticking with your interview guide—even when you feel like it's a dumb question—will quickly reveal this diversity of perspectives.

One more thing: getting to be an insider *is* incredibly helpful when there is information being shared on the *inside* that is not presented in public.

Joining the group of community residents charged with overseeing all new development in North Kenwood—Oakland proved invaluable for seeing the back stage of community negotiations and the front stage at public meetings when, often, decisions had pretty much already been made.

3. *You recently co-edited a book,* Imprisoning America: The Social Effects of Mass Incarceration. *What led you to this topic? Is there some continuity of sociological interest between the prior and the present research reflected in your editing of this volume?*

This is an easy one. Early in my time at Northwestern I got corralled into putting together the annual signature conference for the Institute for Policy Research (IPR). I was honored that they made me a Faculty Fellow, which reduced my teaching by one course, and so I felt kind of obligated when they asked me to chair a conference. I honestly don't even remember if I chose the topic—the collateral consequences of mass incarceration—or if it was delegated to me. Of course it was relevant to my larger interests in urban and racial inequality, and in my focus on youth, gangs, and crime in *Black Picket Fences*. But I had not done any original research on the topic. Still, being dutiful and interested, I ran with it.

As I invited presenters and created session topics, Fay Cook, the director of IPR, gently suggested that the conference papers could be turned into an edited volume. *Beware*: When people make this suggestion they will always understate the amount of work required in putting together an edited volume. Granted, it is not like writing your own solo-authored book, and you still end up with a book with your name on the front. But, it's also not as easy as getting a three-ringed binder to hold the submitted papers together for review by a publisher. Fay was utterly convincing and I took on the book project as well. She also gave me the great advice of inviting co-editors (David Weiman and Bruce Western) to share the load. Overall the volume does not really constitute clear continuity with my own original research, but surveying this field, meeting the authors, working with my co-editors, and reading (and re-reading and re-reading) the chapters has definitely enhanced my teaching, and, I think, broadened my profile professionally.

4. *In your recent work, you focus on the role that the Black middle class plays in changing "bad" neighborhoods. What role do you think you and other Black middle-class scholars play in changing Sociology?*

There is no doubt that the range of topics that Black (and Black middle-class) scholars are exploring has broadened the scope of the discipline. This is not to say that non-Black scholars have been narrow in their questions or research, but I think the firsthand experience of DuBois's *twoness* is highly motivating for understanding the complexities, and indeed the intersectionalities, of race, class, gender, and sexual identities. I also think that our *bodies* add legitimacy. While this somewhat smacks of tokenism, I think it is becoming increasingly untenable to have a conference on racial segregation in cities, for example, and not have any Black people on the program. This is also now true of making sure that Latinos are also on the program. This is somewhat unfortunate because, as the adage goes, "all skinfolk ain't kinfolk," which is to say that skin color alone is not assurance that one is getting a perspective any different from that of someone who is white. And, of course, one of the points I make most forcefully in my research is that the Black community is not a monolith, and so no one should expect a Black scholar to represent *the* Black position (which does not exist anyway). Nonetheless, if speaking bluntly, I still think that we have changed sociology by first demanding to be at the table (thanks to the pioneers) and now convincing others that we *must* be at the table, especially when *we* are the topic of conversation.

To extend this question a bit, how do you think your work—and the presence of your own body—influences the field of urban ethnography, which has focused so much on the social worlds of men?

There is no question that the "title characters" of so many classic urban ethnographies are men: Tally in *Tally's Corner* (1968), Doc in *Streetcorner Society* (1965), Herman in *A Place on the Corner* (1978), Slim in *Slim's Table* (1994). Still, I did not think of urban ethnography as all about the social worlds of men. Of course there are the classics: *All Our Kin* by Carol Stack (1975) and *Tomorrow's Tomorrow* by Joyce Ladner (1971) about women's worlds. But, also, there are women all throughout all of the books that are purportedly about men's worlds. Black women have also been the topic of much discussion as a result of the infamous *Moynihan Report* (1965). Of course this often garnered negative attention to Black women and Black families, but there was also a loud response in the work of sociologists like Robert Staples (e.g., 1971) and Andrew Billingsley (e.g., 1972), that gave a more balanced portrayal. Finally, more recent ethnographies by Kathy Edin (e.g., 2005) and Sharon Hays (2004), for example, have very much represented the worlds of women. So I do not see my work as making any particular impact on the representation of women in urban ethnography because I study Black men and women relatively equally. And while I think there is a certain *authority* attributed to those of us who are Black and study Black people, there is also the kernel of skepticism that we are *too close* to our subjects (i.e., indigenous ethnographers) and thus not fully objective.

> 5. *Another of our contributors to this volume, Mitchell Duneier—like you, an urban ethnographer—has written about how his privileged status position as a white, highly educated, secular Jewish, heterosexual man influences his ability to tell the stories of marginalized Black men. Are there moments when you feel you occupy a privileged status position? How does your status position(s) shape your engagement with your respondents, the stories they tell, and, ultimately, the stories you tell about them?*

There is no question that I occupy a privileged position in my research because, at the end of the day, I write the book. Because I study the Black middle and professional class (as well as many white professionals who circulate in this world), I do not necessarily make more money, have a bigger house, drive a better car, or have a bigger vocabulary than the people I write about. But I do go home and work *their* words into *my story*. Of course being a light-skinned, heterosexual woman professor at an elite school with an elite education all matter, and I try to stay conscious of these things in my research and writing. But, as Duneier's work has itself shown, people in the world open up to folks who are quite different from themselves. It is what we do with what they tell us that constitutes our true moment of privilege and power.

> *How have your respondents responded to the way you've worked their words into the stories you've told? Or, is it the case that your respondents care less about what you write (especially since the academic writing process is so drawn out) than you (and other scholars) do about how you write it? If the latter is true, to what or to whom do you hold yourself most accountable when writing and telling these ethnographic tales?*

In general, I think it is much more the case that I stress over how I represent my respondents and the social processes within the Black community than it is that they care a lot about how I write up my research. When I gave people a draft of the section where they would be quoted in *Black on the Block* few of them responded with any objections or changes. Those few who did respond wanted to clarify themselves (and I made changes for the final book), but they were in the minority.

Overall, I have found that no matter how much I try to write a book with graceful prose, most people outside the academic world find my (our) books too technical and not thrilling enough. I had a book club in Oakland, California choose my book as their reading one month, and they contacted me to join them for their discussion via speaker phone. I was, of course, honored, and agreed to do so. They began their meeting by going around the room and giving first impressions of the book. I spent the first 10 minutes listening to most of them say some version of: "I didn't completely finish reading the book because I didn't know it was going to be a textbook." Ouch! This is particularly funny because so many academics and graduate students say how "well-written" the book is. The point of this story is that we have to realize that our concerns as sociologists—connecting our work to other literatures, developing theoretical generalizations from micro-level interactions, finding patterns of similarities across social worlds—are not often what our respondents (or our readers) will find interesting. So, my primary concern when writing is to try to be true to my data and to be respectful of the people who gave me a piece of their lives by letting me interview or observe them. And "respectful," here, means taking care to avoid words and descriptions that *evaluate* people's behaviors and words, or judge social situations. Instead of evaluation, I aim for description and interpretation.

6. *African American scholars typically encounter the pressures of accountability. In* Black on the Block, *you write about members of the Black middle class who are sometimes perceived as "sellouts" by others: Is that a pressure you've encountered or observed in your own career? Is it a pressure that your students encounter? If so, how do you/they respond to these pressures?*

I don't actually use the term *sellout* in either of my books. While my books deal with diversity and schisms within the Black community, I still study *Black communities*. It's kind of hard to call someone a sellout who purposefully moves into a Black neighborhood, and a relatively poor one at that. I also think that the term is not particularly helpful as an analytic concept, even if it can be used powerfully as a sanctioning label among Black folks.

Personally, I've never been called a sellout (that I know of). Honestly, that would hurt. And maybe I craft my writing to avoid that, which probably is not the most rigorously scholarly thing to do. Still, I think my central argument from *Black on the Block* is relevant here.

These debates—over how to be Black and what Black people need to do to prosper—are what bind the Black community into one nation, rather than two. When those debates subside, then the Black community is no more. (p. 100) … Overall, "the Black community," and Blackness itself, are not fixed realities. They are projects. The words exchanged between Black professionals and Black public housing tenants in North Kenwood—Oakland were painfully harsh. To parents of teenagers whose test scores were below average, the conversion of King High School to a magnet school was misguided. Home owners with gas grills in their fenced back yards find serious fault with renters (with no back yards) who pull their old charcoal grills onto Drexel Boulevard for a barbecue. North Kenwood—Oakland is fraught with debates over what makes a community a community. And in this case, what makes a Black community a Black community. But instead of listing the top 10 things that constitute racial identity and membership in this community, I conclude that the engagement itself is the definition. (p. 302)

However exclusionary the new schools in the neighborhood might be, the Black leaders and professionals who brokered them intended for them to better educate Black students. And when Black newcomers made comments like the following—"What I wanna know is for the 25 percent that's gonna be low income are there going to be some guidelines for these people that when I go to work I don't need to worry about anything going on in my house. That people won't be up partying all night when some of us need to go to work?"—the sting for poor residents was particularly bad because they clung to a notion of racial solidarity that such statements seemed to violate. But in just these moments, when the Black community threatened to be torn apart, other voices spoke up: "These people? Wait a minute, wait a minute, what is 'these people'?" The points and the counterpoints, the suggestions and the counter-suggestions, the values and the other values all make up the ongoing project of Blackness, the constant pulling apart and pushing together that characterizes the Black community. There is no unitary Black political agenda and there is no "Black" way of doing things. There are only the manifestations of a Blackness project in the discussions and debates like those taking place in North Kenwood—Oakland.

So, I remain engaged in the Blackness project. And any student who would seek me out (as a Black professor) to talk about accusations of having "sold out" is obviously also still engaged in this project. If he weren't so engaged, he would not have even been networked enough to know that he was being so labeled. If she weren't so engaged, she would not come to talk to a Black professor. If she weren't so engaged, she wouldn't care.

In what ways do you see these dynamics play out in the academy? Not all Black professors share similar class backgrounds. Are there Black middlemen there/here too? If so, in what ways are they or others sanctioned or rewarded?

The dynamics of policing the "boundaries of Blackness" (as political scientist Cathy Cohen discusses it [1999]) definitely play out in the academy, as they do in any organization, firm, neighborhood, city, or even family. Universities often have Black faculty organizations, and almost always have Black student organizations that rely on faculty for guidance, advising, and support. Black faculty often play a middleman/woman role between university administrators and Black students—speaking for Black students who are less powerful to deans and provosts and other officials who are making decisions about the curriculum, student life, and campus climate issues. Such middlemen also enact and translate university policies and plans that affect Black students. Black faculty (and staff) also, of course, speak on behalf of their own interests regarding such topics as minority faculty or student representation, or campus/community relations. In all of these matters, there are debates among the group of Black spokespeople about what is in the best interest of the Black campus community.

I would say that faculty members who are Black in their appearance but never participate in such brokering, advocacy, representational, or protest roles are more the topic of conversation among Black *students* than among other faculty members. At this stage, most professionals assume that each of us is a complex adult with many communities of membership (including off-campus and family commitments), and there is no need to spend energy on pressuring or sanctioning anyone based on their involvement in the campus Black community.

> 7. *In praising* Black on the Block, *Sudhir Venkatesh compares your work to the scholarship of W.E.B. DuBois, E. Franklin Frazer, and William Julius Wilson (Venkatesh 2007). Are these scholars your intellectual inspirations? Are you inspired differently by the scholarly work of men or women? Who else has inspired you over the course of your career?*

I definitely see myself in the tradition of those scholars and can only hope to produce a body of scholarship as full and rich as they have. DuBois's *The Philadelphia Negro* (1899) is just an incredibly vast piece of urban ethnography and demography. I could not imagine coming close to that kind of thoroughness. So I see myself as carving out just one of the areas DuBois did in that book: class stratification. This, of course, is terrain that Frazier has covered as well, and I use him extensively.

Bill Wilson (William Julius Wilson) is really in a different category because he was my dissertation advisor (and Sudhir's), and so while I have only read the books of DuBois and Frazier, I've been able to have conversations and friendly debates with Bill. And I am grateful that he welcomes such debates. My own decision to focus on the Black middle class was because I thought that the sociological cottage industry on urban poverty that Bill helped to create was too narrow in its framing of urban neighborhoods and Black residents within them. But this is no damning critique, and it's one that I think Bill must have shared, because by the time I arrived at the University of Chicago for graduate school, he was launching a study of working- and middle-class Chicago neighborhoods. So he paid for all my dissertation data collection. In this way, WJW is the best kind of mentor: he has staked his claim in his many books and articles, but he does not expect his students to be his parrots. Indeed, his admonition to us when he left the University of Chicago for Harvard was that we should feel free to criticize him, but when doing so, just get his argument right.

My greatest inspiration is actually Zora Neale Hurston. When I read *Their Eyes Were Watching God* (1937) in college I did not know Hurston was trained as an anthropologist. Now, I find it interesting that the writer to whom I was always the most attracted was a social scientist. That book is one of the few that I have read multiple times. I only wish I could write with as much music and life as Hurston.

I know it sounds clichéd but I really am inspired by the people I study. Like Hurston, I love Black English, Black body movements, Black clothing styles, and so on. I marvel at the incredible possibilities of descriptive informal language (including curse words, slang, variable syntax, etc.) to express complex emotions, relationships, and political and spiritual realities. So I am inspired by men and women in these contexts to try to capture these communication worlds on paper.

8. *Your recent book* Black on the Block (2007) *is more interdisciplinary than your first book,* Black Picket Fences (1999). *In what ways has your engagement with African American Studies at Northwestern University encouraged this interdisciplinarity? What benefits do you derive from crossing interdisciplinary boundaries? What challenges do other sociologists, especially more junior faculty, face in doing the same?*

The interdisciplinarity of *Black on the Block*—which includes a little archival research, some legal analysis, some performance studies, and deals with education—was demanded by the research and was not a result of my half-time appointment in African American Studies. I felt compelled to explore those directions to tell the story right. But being in African American Studies (AFAM, as we call it at Northwestern) has very much stretched me as a scholar, and has been especially helpful in opening up my teaching. As a scholar, participating in faculty hiring in AFAM has exposed me to nearly every area of research in the Humanities and Social Sciences—Comparative Literary Studies, Music, Performance Studies, Lit Crit, American Studies, Anthropology, Ethnic Studies, and on and on. It requires me to think about "data" differently. Books and poems are data for literary critics. I had to learn what historiography means (I define it as the preceding historical research and the arguments made in that literature on a particular topic). It even requires me to get better acquainted with works in the social sciences because a PhD in Sociology has just not equipped me to teach students in our new AFAM PhD program. We didn't read Cedric Robinson's *Black Marxism* (1983), Aimé Césaire's *Discourse on Colonialism* (1972), Achille Mbembe's *On the Postcolony* (2001), or Paul Gilroy's *Against Race* (2000) in my sociology PhD program, but my AFAM PhD students have to, and so I have to. So, while I try to stay current on new developments in my fields in Sociology, I am reading some of the more foundational works in AFAM.

If this sounds like double duty, it is. For young scholars considering such joint positions, be clear about this fact. It is twice the work. On balance, *for me*, the pluses of being in both departments outweigh the negatives. I wouldn't give up the signifying we do in AFAM faculty meetings for the world. And I wouldn't give up the opportunity to hear talks on network analysis in our wide-ranging Sociology colloquia either. But be well aware that no matter what anyone promises you, you will have to attend two faculty meetings, two sets of seminar series, two holiday parties, and possibly submit two tenure dossiers to two sets of colleagues with two different standards of excellence.

9. *Of course, we couldn't resist asking a preeminent race scholar an "Obama question." Has the beginning of the Obama era inspired new sociological questions for you? If so, what questions, why, and how will you go about answering these questions?*

Well, if you can't resist asking, I can't resist telling that I know Obama personally. We're not best friends or anything, but lots of Black folks who walked the campus of the University of Chicago knew/know him. My Obama story is the following: I was leaving a downtown event in Chicago and going to get my car, which I had parked in an expensive downtown garage. I bumped into Barack (pre-presidency, so I am using his first name) while waiting for our cars to be delivered. I already knew him from the University of Chicago. Well, my car came, and I realized that I had no cash, and they accepted only cash. Barack lent me $20. I paid him back years later when he ran for the U.S. Senate and I co-hosted a small-invite-list, big-contribution fundraiser for him. It is hard to believe, but we had NO camera at this fundraiser, so I have no picture.

Back to the question: Obama's presidency has inspired many sociological questions for me, but no research plans, for two reasons. First, perhaps I sell myself too short, but I feel like there will be plenty of better-qualified social scientists who will mount rigorous research programs that center on Obama's presidency or the Obama question. Second, I worry about the timeliness of any such research I would do. It takes a long time to collect ethnographic data, and I am also not a fast writer. I know there will be books for decades on Obama, but I always find it difficult to write about a "current event" that seems to change so rapidly.

The Tenth Question
What was the worst (or most difficult, or most embarrassing) interview/ field encounter you've had?

The most difficult interview I've ever had was with a 13-year-old. Since then I've decided that it is not even worth interviewing kids under 16. I know there are plenty of verbose early-teens, but this young man was not one of them, and it made me feel like such a failure as an interviewer, especially as someone who was supposed to be able to connect with young people. I would ask a question, and he would be done with his answer in 30 seconds. I couldn't get any follow-up action either. It was painful. I decided that ethnography is a better way to interact with youth in this age group than interviews.

What did you really want to do for a living? What were you afraid you might end up doing?

Cliché alert: I am doing what I wanted to do for a living. Well, I didn't quite know I'd be a college professor. I went to college planning to become a teacher. But I didn't do my homework and I chose Columbia University, which did not offer a teaching certificate program (Barnard did, but it was too late by the time I found this out). So, Professor Ronald Burt (now at the University of Chicago) asked me if I had ever thought about getting a PhD in Sociology. I hadn't, but then I did, and the rest is history.

While I've always wanted to teach, and I surely think I was always a sociologist, I can't deny that I do have regrets that I'm not doing *enough* towards social justice causes. I think I thought that teaching, and being a college professor, was going to be a more activist experience than it is. I have worked activism into my career, but the need is so great that I always feel guilty for not doing more.

I don't think I had any fears about what I might end up doing. I think that is illustrated in the fact that I, stupidly, only applied to one college. I don't know what I would have done had I not gotten into Columbia, but it suggests that I wasn't working hard to avoid some bad outcome. I do think this casual attitude was born of the middle-class comfort in which I was raised, and the happy ending is surely the product of that privilege as well.

What's the study you never pursued, but always wanted to?

Hey, I'm not retired or dead yet. I still have plenty of time to pursue whatever study I want to. As I write this, I am beginning a sabbatical year and moving to Cartagena, Colombia. I never studied abroad in college and I am happy to get this opportunity now, and to become fluent in Spanish. These are things I've wanted to do. When I get back, I'll be able to do ethnography in Latino neighborhoods. After that, I think I want to re-learn quantitative methodology. Neither of these are actual studies, but they will equip me to do new kinds of research.

2.
SCOTT BROOKS

1. *Your book,* Black Men Can't Shoot *(Brooks 2009), is based on the 4 years you spent as a youth basketball coach in one of Philadelphia's most storied amateur basketball leagues. How did you come to translate what you were doing into compelling sociological questions? What challenges did you confront as both coach and ethnographer?*

I use a grounded theoretical approach, so getting to the crux of what my data say is often difficult. Coming up with questions though, in general, isn't as tough. The data provoke questions. For example, one of the key concepts for my book is "known." Basketball players are stratified into three groups: known, unknown, and scrubs. One day I was speaking to a kid and he began talking about one of his friends in this way, "Jermaine known 'cause…." And it struck me. I then asked him, "How'd he get known?" I then began searching for who was known among my players, what it took to get known, and how did players *know* that they were known. This led me to other things like how far did being known travel? Was it a universal status, what were its limits? I followed kids to games that they played outside of our league (Blade Rodgers) to check this out. I found that some of my players were known on their local playgrounds or in their high schools, but not outside their neighborhoods. In this case, I didn't go into the field specifically with the question, "What terms do kids use in stratifying themselves," but it was definitely something I knew was important when I heard it and then a bunch of questions followed as a result. How did I know that the kid said something important? I think that this comes from what we read. This is where our sociological literature is important. Reading articles and books by ethnographers who also use a grounded approach often helps me. I wonder if some of their ideas are transferable to my study and to determine if so or if not, I compare and contrast our contexts/settings.

As a coach and ethnographer I was in a position to observe and influence the kids I was studying. This was challenging and frustrating, but also rewarding. The research was not separate from my life and when the team lost, I felt the loss. There were times I felt like crying: when I was frustrated by a spat and near-fight with a player I was very close to, or when I learned that another player (not on my team) was shot and killed. There was also joy. One kid graduated from high school and earned a college scholarship, which was unimaginable two years earlier. And we won some big games. My commitment to the man I coached with, Chuck, and the team (as an organization) also meant that I couldn't just come in and out when I pleased. My love for basketball, desire to help kids and marginalized folks, and to win eliminated any feelings of obligation and burden.

Other challenges existed as well. South Philly has a tough reputation. Philly is a big city with numerous "boroughs" so to speak, and the most notorious areas for gangs are South Philly and North Philly. While neighborhood gangs are territorial and adversarial, they come together when their teams play against other parts of the city. Gerald Suttles writes about this in *The Social Order of the Slum* (1968), how neighborhood gangs fight with each other but band across ethnicities to fight outsiders. Moreover, there are intense, long-standing rivalries between teams. My association with South Philly coupled with my desire to speak with non-South Philly coaches was sometimes seen as suspicious. I know that once I was established it prevented some non-South Philly folks from speaking and developing a relationship with me. In one conversation with a North Philly coach about who might take the role of a South Philly coach after Chuck, he told me that I was a

South Philly guy. I told him that I wasn't because I'm not from Philly. *"What you saying?"* he said, "you coach South Philly, you a South Philly guy!"

2. *In that study you describe and explain what two young Black men in Philadelphia "do to go from being good players to great players." What does it mean to be great? Looking back, are these rules the same in the academy?*

For young men, being known as a basketball player is a public identity. One must be acknowledged, recognized by others as a great basketball player. "Great," then, is subjective; it is a distinction made by others. Goffman talks about this in a short essay on deference and respect (Goffman 1959: 47–95). Respect is something that is given by others. Young men who aspire to play in college must be seen, evaluated, and then recruited by college coaches. Others—other players, other kids, coaches—have the power to call a player great. Most of this is beyond a player's control. Yet, there are some things that they do control or at least look to control. They know where people—especially scouts and college coaches—go to watch and evaluate players: tournaments, leagues, and games where there are known players and ranked teams. Certain teams have become known for their winning records and star players. This then can reproduce itself. The best basketball high schools get the best players and scouts and college coaches look for these schools to have talented players that they can recruit. So, players work to get "exposure." They seek to play on teams (and with players) that play in big time tournaments; they work on their reputations and the impressions that they make with coaches and to have coaches recommend them to other coaches; and they maneuver to get the greatest opportunity to play.

Similarly, there is a pattern when one looks at a sample of faculty at R-1 universities. Most faculty come from one of about 20 PhD programs. Going to one of these programs offers exposure. When a graduate student goes to a conference others see her name and affiliation on her tag. The prestige of these programs commands a certain level of status and recognition. These graduate students also reap the benefits of program prestige when they are on the job market as departments with an FTE are impressed by particular schools and advisors. Students from these programs might even be seen as overqualified by less prestigious schools. "She'll never come here. She's from _____ and her advisor was _____. She's gonna have much better offers." Additionally, being a great scholar is a public identity based on peer recognition; it can't be bestowed on oneself. Being great is a function of production: where she has published, how much, and the significance of her work. Our work is peer reviewed, voted on for awards, and recommended to others.

3. *In this volume, Mary Pattillo writes that the visible presence of Black scholars in the academy adds a necessary level of legitimacy to research endeavors. You were on the organizing committee of the Penn Ethnography Conference in 2003. Can you share with us some of the thinking that went into developing the conference? What explicit decisions did you make about how to organize the conference? How was the conference different from traditional academic conferences?*

The organizing committee was made up of four Black people, one senior professor (Elijah Anderson) and three graduate students, one woman and three men. We spent a lot of time figuring out the guest list and who should be invited to be part of the sessions. We brought in scholars from around the country and globe (including England, France, and Finland), different schools, of multiple generations, and studying different topics. Racial diversity occurred almost without effort. I think that for one or two sessions we, as graduate students, spoke about the need for women in sessions, but we never had to talk about including people of color. This is the benefit of working with a distinguished faculty member of color like Elijah Anderson. He had the cultural and economic capital to put together a conference and did not have to worry about inviting "too many" who looked like him. At the same time, our networks were diverse and so we just invited folks whom we knew and whose work we enjoyed. Moreover, the conference had a different tone. It was intimate—we had couches, there was only one session at a time, and we ate together. We did our best to make the conference like a family function across generations, schools, and continents. Ultimately, the connections and relationships have been much more enduring and productive in the long term.

4. *You have received accolades for your teaching and mentoring of graduates and undergraduates. Yet, there is a great deal of pressure for junior scholars at research oriented universities to focus less on their teaching, campus, or community service, and instead to publish, publish, publish. Of course, this often presents a challenge for field researchers, who spend a good deal of time collecting data first hand. How do you manage these competing pressures?*

I often answer, "I'm a teacher," when people ask what I do for a living. Sometimes, it's simply a shortcut. I don't want to go into detail or deal with the surprise or disbelief when they hear that I'm a college professor. But I also say this because teaching is such a significant part of what this job is for me. I take a lot of pride in my relationship with students at the undergraduate and graduate levels. This usually begins in the classroom. I figure if I'm not enjoying the course, my students aren't either.

I manage the pressures of teaching and doing research at the same time by conducting fieldwork in my community. I am currently an assistant coach at a local public high school where I'm researcher and coach. In this way I get to eat where I work, so to speak; research and teaching are within 5 miles of each other. In addition, I also coach recreational basketball for my sons in the community. There's tremendous overlap in all of this.

As a Univeristy of California professor, there's a question of pressure. In sports we talk about "clutch" performers—those who handle pressure situations well—as well as "chokers" who don't perform well under pressure. I feel that pressure is often a mindset. It seems that clutch performers don't generally define pressure situations as pressure situations. Instead, they speak about enjoying the opportunity to do something noteworthy and significant. I felt some pressure in my third year, particularly when a possible book contract fell through. But I relaxed when I reflected on my initial reasons for pursuing a PhD. I decided to take this life path because I wanted to teach, do research and write, and be considered an expert. I asked myself why I felt pressure to do what I want to do and have been trained to do. I know that being a professor is a privileged life. In my previous job as an accountant, I remember making a wrong accounting entry for a month-end close worth nearly $4 million. I realized the error at dinner and barely slept. Now that's pressure!

5. *As field researchers, our multiple identities influence the stories we tell, and how they are received by others. In what ways do your intersecting identities—African American, highly educated, Christian, heterosexual—influence your ability to tell the stories of young Black men and those who try to help them? How does your status position(s) shape your engagement with your respondents, the stories they tell, and, ultimately, the stories you tell about them? Are there moments when you feel constrained in the stories you are able to tell?*

Identity is a complicated thing. It is very difficult to determine how much of one's identity shapes/influences behavior and interpretation. But one thing that matters to the shaping of my identity is the response from people in the field. I was generally accepted as a young, 20-something Black man who coached kids, even by those who knew that I was a graduate student and was conducting research. The academic label was weird and meaningless for most folks. The shortcut was that I was writing a book on Philadelphia kids and basketball. In one home a mother corrected how I pronounced the word *water*. She chuckled and looked at me with sarcasm. She never mentioned that I was educated and should know better. Instead she seemed to feel that she could correct me because I was younger and didn't know better. In another situation she introduced me to her friend as her son's coach, who acted like a big brother to him. With another family, a grandmother needed to sell some silk floral arrangements that she made to make money. Her buyers fell through and she called me in to buy an arrangement. She believed that I had money and could buy the arrangement. I was a graduate student at Penn and didn't live in their neighborhood. She imagined that I was probably doing well financially, or at least much better than she was.

I visited the summer league in which I coached after moving to California two years earlier. One of the league's staff members saw me and we shook hands and hugged. He then asked, "Where you been, Scott?" I reminded him that I had moved to California a year earlier. He acted surprised. I then told him that I was from California and had only been in Philadelphia for graduate school. He said that he didn't remember and thought that I was a Philadelphian. My intersecting identities are mine, but not necessarily how others see me. This means that my story-telling is heavily influenced by how others perceive and accept me. I fit the norm as a coach. Rapport wasn't as difficult as it might have been had I been a woman, non-Black, gay, etc. At the same time, for people like the grandmother above I was perceived as being from a different class, having more opportunities, and some privilege.

In general this dynamic process or series of interactions that reflect how others see me, I see them, and see myself, undoubtedly comes out in the stories that I tell. My perceptions—what I see and interpret as having seen—is shaped by my multiple identities. I don't believe that I have some set hierarchy of identities. It changes. There are times when I'm more of an uncle or a father or a brother. There are times when I'm a mentee or younger person who listens and defers out of respect for an elder. There are also times when I'm a coach, angry coach or a proud coach. These identities and the behavior associated with these roles are different. Which role I take is largely influenced by the interaction and relationship that I see myself as having with individual people. And my sexuality, Christianity, and race, and other identities shape what I know about a role and the appropriate actions that come with it. They are not static.

6. *As an adolescent, you lived for a period of time in the Middle East. How did this unique experience as a teenager shape the development of*

your sociological imagination? How does your childhood contrast and compare to that of the young men you write about in Black Men Can't Shoot?

My childhood was very different from the kids I've studied. I grew up in more heterogeneous communities and therefore experienced privilege and racism firsthand and regularly; I interacted with those who were working class and poor and I went to school with white Americans and other non-Blacks in Saudi Arabia.

In Oakland, California I went to a grammar school that underwent massive demographic change in only a couple of years. We may have moved there at the end of the change. It went from being a mixed school to being a predominantly Black school. It was a neighborhood public school and most kids' families were Black middle class in the Andrew Billingsley (1972) sense—"last hired-first fired" and one paycheck from working class and poor. While we lived in the Oakland Hills, we attended church in "the Flats," the larger more working-class/poor neighborhood that was down the hill from our own. I lived Mary Pattillo's *Black Picket Fences* (1999). We created copycat gangs during grammar school and had gang wars. I boxed, ran track, and swam at a recreational center and boys and girls club in a tough, poor/working-class neighborhood. And, a few of my neighbors became drug dealers and ended up in jail or killed via drug-related violence.

When I was nine we moved to Jeddah, Saudi Arabia, and I entered a school where my brothers and I were a part of a handful of Black Americans. The school was international but mostly white American. I still remember sitting in class and going through the social studies lesson on slavery and Blacks. One kid sat across from me and mouthed the word *nigger*. This was the first time that I can recall being called "nigger," emphasis on the –er. In Oakland, we used "nigga." I knew that there was a big difference between the two words, and I was uncomfortable. I had moved thousands of miles away from America to be called a nigger! I also experienced being gawked at and stigmatized, as well as being called a "darkie" by a British youngster. At the same time, I was embraced by Arabs and other Muslim men of color who asked if I was Muslim, and when I responded "no," I was often told that it was okay because I was Black; skin color was an asset and distinguished me from white foreigners. Jeddah was semi-strict in its religious observance. They closed for prayer times, and religious police were more prominent than civil police. There was very low crime and race and class inequality wasn't apparent. I was struck by the idea that government could come in different forms and wondered about America's form. Was our government tragically flawed in terms of racial and class inequality? There were also horrific myths of non-Arab and non-Muslim women being harassed by religious police who drenched women in red paint who were "inappropriately" dressed. So, Arab government wasn't close to perfect either. I wondered what might strike the right balance. How could a country run best?

My experience overseas had a tremendous impact on how I see the world, globally and locally. I also understand nuances of being marginalized and a person of color. This doesn't mean that interpersonal interaction supersedes structural norms of racism, but it does complicate experience. I feel that what my experience did most was affect my "double-consciousness" and enhance my ability to be the other, take on the other, and comprehend culture.

Does your sensitivity to class relations and effects in any way distinguish your work from that of other urban ethnographers?

Being sensitive to class, gender, and race is not simply academic. We all have unique concerns, interests, and daily demands to meet. To compare ideals, culture, and actions is problematic; instead we as researchers, need to take on the role of the other and understand how people make sense of themselves, their actions, their ideals, and culture: judgment is the end of analysis. I work at trying not to moralize others' behaviors and to understand that culture is complicated. It is not simply what I see people doing or what they say; it is a complex web of socialization, circumstances, ideology, emotions, and resources. I've learned a lot about taking on the role of the other and study- ing culture from reading the work of other ethnographers and scholars like Mary Pattillo, Sudhir Venkatesh, Susan Clampett-Lundquist, Nikki Jones, Patricia Hill-Collins, Mitch Duneier, Alford A. Young, Jr., and Elijah Ander- son. Our goal is to bring the thinking of marginalized folks/communities to light and end the pathologizing. Through the work of these scholars we learn that: gangs and drug dealers provide some protection for neighborhoods; that inner city girls and boys are not simply "ghetto" or "good," and that they are negotiating violence rooted in unemployment and concentrated poverty. The experiences of Black women exist at the intersection of race, gender, and class where they are oppressed by a matrix of domination that operates multi-dimensionally and simultaneously; and Black men young and old are grappling with mainstream standards of masculinity and respectability, yet creating their own standards and culture of decency amid socio-structural impediments. People are not simply good or bad; instead they are human beings doing what they can, with what they have available, what they per- ceive to be realistic, and what they consider relevant to identity maintenance.

In my work, young Black men are not simply athletes; they are thinkers, working at mobility and to distinguishing themselves from others. Mothers want their sons to live beyond 25 years old, and to get an education; they are not simply pushing their kids to be lottery tickets, so that they can live like the "Huxtables" or "Jeffersons." I hope that my work adds to the humanistic scholarship done by other scholars.

7. *In your current work, you explore the importance of mentoring for marginalized youth. Did your last project shape this new research question? In what ways have you benefited from mentoring? Where have you found these mentors, or where did they find you? What is your view of colleges and universities that are trying to institutionalize mentoring?*

Black Men Can't Shoot definitely led to my current interest in mentoring. In working on the book, I found that there were some chapters on the "cutting room" floor. These chapters just didn't fit with understanding the process of athletes going from good to great. Instead they spoke more to the relationships between coaches, players, parents, and others. I've had an interest in youth development for a long time. It is one of my core passions. *Black Men Can't Shoot* indirectly speaks to how youth development programs might improve by illuminating how young men work to turn dreams into reality. Mentoring programs need to address structural as well as individual needs. A major reason that basketball is encouraged and highly regarded is because within it there is a history of Black men's success, accessible networks exist, the process of becoming a basketball player seems transparent, and Black men—marginalized in other areas—have a competitive advantage over other groups, even if the advantage is based only on false constructions of race and athleticism. Successful mentoring in other areas will need to create or illuminate that same record of Black success, have sustainable, accessible, and effective networks that stand in the gap for people to create new opportunities and resources, and inform mentees of the process of becoming.

I have been blessed to have some direct and indirect mentors, inside and outside of academia. My mentors have shared their life experiences and offered support, encouragement, and networks. I have found my mentors in corporate America, the academy outside of my department, and in family members and personal friends. I have asked some folks to be my mentors and other relationships have happened more organically, through working relationships and sustained friendships. For me the greatest impact of mentoring has been to help me understand how to be successful.

What I've found is that there are very few people who step up to mentor Black men. Race, gender, and class, as well as perspective/scholarship impact this for me. There are very few Black full professors on my campus who might be motivated to mentor me because of racial ties. Feminist networks are growing and seem to be an important source of information exchange, support, and collaborative work. But this doesn't exist for men of color. And while I have been given advice and encouragement, it generally comes from one to three people. Colleagues don't share their resources. I typically find out about helpful opportunities late, just prior to the deadline or even after. I haven't received any mentoring regarding writing grant proposals. I haven't had a serious offer or opportunity to co-author, although this practice is somewhat common in my department. Seeing other collaborative efforts—in articles, research centers, labs—leads me to believe that there is a backstage that I'm unaware of.

> *You seem to suggest that professional mentoring can be as consequential as mentoring early on. In academic cultures that don't encourage mentoring (particularly of young faculty of color), what institutional efforts might work to change such practices?*

I've just learned that our campus has piloted an outside mentor program that will be instituted across the campus for junior faculty. This is a wonderful idea. Outside mentors have no stake in the departmental politics, only in helping a young faculty member to understand better the expectations held by more senior faculty and to navigate departmental and university politics. They can also offer a junior faculty access to a totally new network. It is akin to having extended family members. I believe that mentoring efforts that extend beyond the university to local corporations and organizations and across campuses (if at a public university) could be very helpful. Moreover, we know that raced and classed networks exist where people at similar levels across occupations are more likely to interact and develop friendships. Institutions could help faculty connect to other people at high professional levels by inviting young faculty of color to the events, meetings, and conversations between universities and with outside corporations.

8. *Your partner is a talented artist. What lessons have you learned from her artistic point of view? In what ways is the work of an artist similar or different to the work of an ethnographer?*

My partner's talent inspires and baffles me. I've asked her how she knows which stroke to paint or draw. How do the individual strokes become a whole masterpiece? She has helped me to see that ethnography is a craft and taught me a lot about working the "craft." Kara told me that it's not one stroke that she is thinking about because no single stroke is so important. The project is always changing for her as she creates and re-creates. In fact, she rarely, if ever, feels as though she's finished. This takes great patience and she is able to "feel" when things are right, even though it may not seem right technically. This then moves her to reach some resolve, having the feeling match the technical.

Ethnography is both inductive and deductive. Sometimes I enter the field with pointed questions. These new questions may be gut feelings or questions that have come straight from the data. The great thing about fieldwork and putting in time is that I'm not dependent on one interview—one "catch." Instead, we get to enter and re-enter the field and ask more people, test hypotheses, inferences, and speculations. And so, I have learned from Kara to try to juggle the micro and macro, the small and big pictures at the same time. I try to step back and not focus on right and wrong so much, but on the process of getting to something right.

> *How do you communicate this rather intuitive aspect of research to graduate students—or maybe it is something one has to discover for oneself?*

I teach the process of juggling micro and macro by trying to show how I mind-mapped and flow-charted my dissertation data, divided the data into pieces, and wrote ethnographic memos, and then papers and a book. However, it is nearly impossible for students to really experience this for themselves in a 10-week quarter, and not as part of a large research project. I was blessed with great ethnographer friends in grad school; we met and read each other's work, and we gave sincere, critical, and thoughtful feedback. It is very difficult to do ethnographer alone, although the fieldwork is often conducted by one person. An ethnographer needs a key informant and others to help raise questions, as well as their partners, friends, and support systems inside and outside of academia. This takes time in the field as we are doing investigative work and need to turn over many stones, follow leads and dead ends. I needed others to maximize my understanding, comprehension, and reporting.

9. *Why do you do ethnography? What understandings does ethnography provide on its own that might be missed by other research methods? Is ethnography a method, a craft, an art, or all three?*

I do ethnography because I believe that getting with people is the best way to understand them, their lives, their thinking, struggles, expectations, and decisions. I also feel that serving others is the basis of humanity. I tell my students to reserve their judgment of people, because judgment is a roadblock to analysis. How can I really be open to hearing and "taking on the other" if I've already decided what the other should have done and whether it was a right or wrong decision? This is a struggle but it makes me human. I want to understand others' thinking. This is wonderful and unique because it assumes that each person has intelligence, a valued voice, and a story worth hearing. This can only be done through close, sustained, participant observation. It is definitely a humanistic method, craft and art form.

The Tenth Question
What was the worst (or most difficult, or most embarrassing) interview/ field encounter you've had?

Only three girls came to practices over the 4 years that I coached. Of those three, only one played a whole season. I never pursued the possibility of doing deeper research with young women. This wasn't planned initially. I had coached young girls at a Catholic middle school—fifth and sixth graders—while in high school as part of my mandatory community service and enjoyed the experience. However, the possibility of working with young girls in South Philly was very different. The girls, like the boys, were from poor households but carried very different issues because of their gender. They were and had already been taking on the *second shift* that Arlie Hochschild (1990) speaks of; they were mothers to their siblings. They also had experienced violence in the form of sexual harassment and assault from men and boys. One of the girls had been raped. Another girl was harassed by one young boy on the team who made sexually explicit comments about her body and wanting to have sex with her (he was kicked off the team immediately). And the third was regularly approached, gawked at, and commented on by men outside the recreation center.

Just learning and observing some of what these girls dealt with daily was sobering and I came to think about what Black men might represent to young Black girls. My awareness was piqued when I felt that one mother was too aggressive in pushing her young daughter on me. The season was over and the mother said that her daughter needed more help, some "one-on-one" basketball coaching during the summer. I may have just been hypersensitive. I don't know why it felt as though the mother was asking for something inappropriate. It was the way that she insisted on "one-on-one" time. No mother ever asked me to spend extra time with their child, let alone "one-on-one" time. The mother also asked for some shoes or clothes that I/my partner might have. I did get her some shoes but I didn't follow up with the mother about coaching her daughter. The daughter didn't play for us again, although she continued to play.

> *What did you really want to do for a living? What were you afraid you might end up doing?*

I wanted to be a "practicing" sociologist, meaning someone who observed, analyzed, and interpreted human behavior/culture for an organization. I've always liked Harry Edwards, so my dream job was/is to be a team sociologist with a sports organization. I also wanted to run a youth recreation and development program. I was an accountant/financial analyst for 4 years while doing my master's in Northern California, and I was afraid that I would end up an accountant for life. It motivated me to attend school at night while being a husband, father, and working full-time.

> *What's the study you never pursued, but always wanted to?*

I'm still young and don't have a "wish I had, but didn't" list of research yet. At the same time, I'm seeing how one topic/setting can last 10 to 15 years. I still don't feel as though I'm through with basketball, although I don't expect to study it for the rest of my career. I'm very excited about the mentoring and dating research that I've been working on for years but am just getting the resources and time to pursue it consistently and deliberately. This feeds my long time interest in understanding relationships—how they start, continue, change, and end. How and why people enter into relationships and the games involved in interaction, giving affection, and trying to get affection from others.

I would love to understand "shark experts," those persons who claim to know dangerous animals through mere observation, and particularly with the goal of claiming that animals are humanistic (i.e., they don't want to eat us). I love the shows about sharks and shark research, crocodiles, alligators, and bears on the Discovery and Animal Planet channels. It never fails to make me laugh when someone who's been bitten says that the shark didn't "mean" to bite them. Observation, to me, isn't enough on its own to draw the conclusions that they draw and I figure that's why they—shark experts—continue to get bitten: they are making a tragic mistake by beginning with the idea that sharks are rational thinking beings like us. Interestingly, the only shark, crocodile/alligator, and wilderness experts that we see on television are white men. So, this seems to be a study of race, gender, and probably class as well.

3.
ALFORD A. YOUNG, JR.

1. *In your book,* The Minds of Marginalized Black Men *(2004) you write that your analytical approach to the study of low-income African American men "represents a new approach for overturning a long legacy of research that has served to construct the standard and overly simplistic image of the underclass in general and low-income African American men in particular" (p. 13). What is new about your approach? And why is such a new approach necessary?*

What is new about my approach is that I move from looking at the behavior of Black men (a common point of attention for many cultural sociologists), and norms and values (which are commonly deduced from such behavior) to looking at how men construct meaning about various aspects of the social world (what is a good job, whether racial equality is a viable outcome in American society, what role does belief in a higher being have on one's sense of his life chances, etc.). The objective in looking at such seemingly mundane questions is that it allows for Black men to be viewed as practical theorists of the social world and of their own existence in it. By situating men in such a way, they can be regarded as more complex beings than has been the case in considerations of them that focus on presumably flawed behaviors or norma- tive value systems. Furthermore, as I argue that norms and values are rooted in the basic schema of beliefs that people hold about how the world and its inhabitants operate, a better grasp of why and how such men commit to the norms and values that they do comes from a more focused consideration of their beliefs and worldviews. If such men fail to see certain things in their outlooks on society (like why a liberal arts education may matter for access- ing extreme socio-economic mobility) then why such men may not value that kind of education, or otherwise regard education in different ways than other people becomes much clearer. In this case, the value of education is rooted in a system of beliefs about what education does and does not deliver to people, and how those mechanisms of deliverance are read as pertaining to one's life. My focus on beliefs and worldviews is aimed at broadening the terrain of cultural analysis of Black men and marginalized people more generally. This contributes to the modern project in cultural sociology of using cultural analysis as a tool to unpack the complexity of people's lives rather than trying to document some airtight and systematic notion of the culture of a group of people. When Black men are viewed as practical theorists in their own right, they can begin to be regarded as complex people in the same ways that others are, and not simply as culturally backward or undeveloped beings.

2. *In your book, you make an interesting discovery regarding how low-income men make sense of their social position: the more socially isolated
men were, the more likely they were to offer a personal responsibility
narrative for their perceived failures. These men seemed to embrace the
American Dream wholeheartedly; they expressed a strong belief that
anyone can make it in America. Yet, those men who had regular contact
with people outside of the neighborhood, especially white managers or
other professionals—that is, those men who were actively pursuing the
American Dream—did not share this belief. Instead, these men were
much more likely to express a critical analysis of structural barriers and
inequalities, especially racism. Can you describe the process of coming
to this discovery? Did this finding surprise you? Did it make you rethink
any assumptions about race, class, and social mobility?*

The finding greatly surprised me. I assumed that any urban-based Black man would have much to say about the perseverance of racism in American society and in his own life. I came to this discovery by first sharing my frustration with my spouse (then fiancée) being unable to discern what was going on in these moments of complete investment in notions of the American Dream. She encouraged me to go outside of the data, so to speak, to determine whether there was anything about the life histories or present-day circumstances of the men I interviewed that paralleled the kinds of comments they made about mobility and the American Dream. It was after doing so that I saw how much men who were locked into virtually exclusive African American life worlds did not make much sense of race.

In sharing my work in conferences and professional gatherings, I was encouraged to think about whether social connections alone mattered for why and how these men took account of mobility processes. It was thereafter that I began to think more deeply about how different historical periods involve different degrees of public investment in "race-talk," and how much more vacant such conversation has been in the past few decades, for example, than in comparison to the 1960s. I realized that perhaps Black men at that time who had been socially isolated in terms of race would have had a different kind of racial consciousness because race was such an overwhelming part of the public discourse then. Consequently, I radically re-thought my assumptions about race, class, and mobility, and am more committed to the idea that an interplay of public discourses and patterns of personal experience determined the myriad ways in which race, class, and perceptions of mobility opportunities emerge for people who share the same demographic classifications and even live through the same historical periods or experience the same events and conditions.

3. *In "Trying to Go Home Again," a book review published in* Sociological Forum *(Young, 2008), you provide a brief but descriptive account of the social landscape you navigated while coming of age in East Harlem. Looking back, how did growing up in East Harlem in the 1970s and early 80s shape your sociological imagination? How did growing up in East Harlem influence your pathway to becoming an urban sociologist?*

East Harlem was pivotal in that I was born into a highly impoverished neighborhood (and one that many sociologists have documented as being the most violent urban neighborhood in America at the time of my youth) yet into a white-collar professional family (at least in terms of the status of my father, a certified public accountant). This situation allowed me to see others experience urban poverty on a daily basis, while still allowing me access to politicians, business executives, and other high-profile people that were in my father's social circles. Issues of stratification, inequality, and social difference were quite vivid for me throughout my life. Yet I also saw that many people, who by virtue of their class standing would never interact with each other in any sustained way, seemed to hold similar beliefs, attitudes, and opinions, or otherwise struck me as being quite similar. Hence, I entered sociology with a vision of people as not always as different as they seem when thinking about class and race distinctions, and often highly misunderstood when thinking about the racialized urban poor. These and other curiosities kept me focused on the city as a site for exploring who people are and what they do (with and to each other).

4. *Sociologists and policymakers are becoming increasingly interested in low-income African American men and fatherhood. We now hear a lot about encouraging "responsible fatherhood." Can you describe your analytical approach to the study of low-income African American fathers? How does it extend the type of analysis that you provide in* The Minds of Marginalized Black Men? *What are the important questions we should ask about fatherhood that would shed greater light on the topic?*

I desire to know how young men who often have not been raised with their fathers conceive of fatherhood. More specifically, I am interested in what these men conceptualize as ideal fatherhood given that they have not often experienced any such contact with fathers who exemplify that. In asking men to describe the traits, characteristics, and qualities of such fathers, I aim to acquire some purchase on what is not mentioned or considered in their replies, which is where the effects of absentee fatherhood surfaces for these men. That is, whatever they do not include or account for in their explanations, or whatever they cannot elaborate upon in rich detail, is often a consequence of what they were exposed to in their own lives. If they cannot conceive of certain aspects of fatherhood, they will not be able to aspire to it, even if they hold to some general notion of wanting to be good fathers.

> *Does gender figure into your interpretation and analysis of fatherhood in the lives of Black men? If so, how?*

While I have not focused on gender in an analytically rigorous manner, I have recognized that the men that I study fully commit to the notion that a father is supposed to be a bread-winner, and that there is some inadequacy to fathers not being able to provide that service. The men I have studied who are involved fathers do consider services and obligations such as the provision of emotional support and intimate social interaction with their children as important, but they never lose sight of the classic depiction of who and what a father is. Often, the challenges they face in living up to that classic notion is the source of problems in that they sometimes are inclined to withdraw from partners and children when they cannot deliver in the area of material support. Hence, some traditional depictions of manhood loom large in the quest of contemporary African American fathers to make sense of fatherhood.

5. *Beyond your analytical approach, how does being a father yourself shape your approach to the study of fatherhood? What "situated knowledge," if any, do you bring to your study of low-income, African American men that derives from your role as a father and a son?*

Many of my queries about Black fathers and Black men come from my thinking about being an African American father and an African American son. I quite literally think about what I value about both roles and why I do so as bases for developing questions and queries to pursue on issues pertaining to Black men and Black fathers. I take seriously that I am the product of a professional, white-collar family that resided in a highly impoverished urban community. Consequently, much of my research centers on unpacking the varied ways in which men define fatherhood and manhood given the differential access to societal rewards and conditions that they have experienced. I am also aware that men can hold onto the same visions of social reality even if their own experiences differ (and I have witnessed that in my interactions with other Black men and fathers). Hence, my own life experiences and identities matter greatly in how and why I craft research agenda as I do. I maintain in my inner thinking that a great deal of my investment in research is to help me to explain myself, and in doing so I aspire to explain many other kinds of Black men as well.

6. *In this volume, Scott Brooks writes about how important informal and formal mentoring was to his development as a sociologist. He also writes "there are very few people who step up to mentor Black men." Can you describe the role mentoring has played in the development of your career? Also, what key lessons have you learned from your research and administrative service at the University of Michigan, as you are widely known as a leader in developing young scholars of color?*

I was fortunate to have benefitted from the mentoring of three African American male social scientists and other Black men who were professionally or personally committed to serving the interests of African Americans. As these mentors gave me extensive elaborate support, counsel, and resources, I believe that I owe others the same. More importantly, few African

Americans seem to make it to and through the scholarly community without significant mentoring. Hence, preserving and enriching this community of scholars is contingent upon a commitment to effective and dedicated mentoring. The major lesson that I learned from my service at Michigan is that a good mentor provides insight that comes from no classroom experience. It is through mentoring younger scholars that such folks learn how to consider and approach various kinds of career options. Being an African American scholar is a unique situation in the academy, especially because there are so few of such people. Hence, mentoring is the place where young scholars truly learn about how to navigate that situation and find places of comfort in their professional careers.

7. *You are presently spearheading a Ford Foundation initiative on the study of African American men and boys. The initiative is unique in bringing together scholars from the Humanities and the Social Sciences. What insights have you gained from leading this interdisciplinary effort?*

I have learned that the social sciences and the humanities can come together to answer various questions about culture, identity, and public representation. Each of these points of concern are central issues for African American men, and therefore these two domains of inquiry desperately need to be in close connection in the larger effort to advance better understandings of the situation of African American men. Scholars in the humanities have much to say about the possibilities for different images of social reality and different ways of considering the human condition. Social scientists tend to be exclusively focused on the realities that are perceived to exist. In order to improve upon these realities attention to some new, and often unforeseen, possibilities need to be brought into the scholarly conversation. By bringing together such a range of scholars this network aims to achieve this end.

> *Have you been surprised at the degree of overlap or convergence that has emerged during these conversations? What challenges confront scholars who would like to draw on a more interdisciplinary approach within the disciplinary constraints of sociology?*

I was not greatly surprised by the degree of convergence across these scholarly communities because I had some initial sense that scholars who were interested in the plight of African American men were concerned about the same set of issues and conditions. I have always had a strong interest in how race and gender were pursued in the humanities (and I have been informed in my own work by many theoretical efforts on these fronts—particularly the Birmingham School in England, and the work of Houston Baker, Michael Awkward, and various African American philosophers) so this effort allowed me to act upon interests that I developed some time ago. I do think that the professional demands of disciplines prevent more exchanges of this sort from developing, and scholars have to exercise a certain degree of initiative and fortitude to seek them out and engage them.

8. *You have written about the early tradition of African American sociological thought. How do you see your work fitting into this tradition?*

I think that every tradition of inquiry on Black people (men or women) includes some notion of what constitutes a healthy Black individual, and those notions change overtime. My investigations of the early (and later) traditions of Black sociological thought are designed to explore what notions of healthy or positive Blackness were promoted and embraced over time and why. I pursue this work so that in my own efforts to make sense of Black men and Black masculinity in the contemporary world, my work is informed by the idea that these efforts are situated in space and time, and thus susceptible to being re-thought and re-configured in light of later social, political, and intellectual developments.

9. *You have not written extensively on the lives of low-income African American women, yet their lives are undoubtedly intertwined with the men you study. To ask the feminist question: What about the women? Furthermore, how has your research among low-income African American men informed your analysis of gender or Black gender ideology?*

One of my principal objectives in doing social research is to affirm that specificity and precision drive substantive analyses. With that in mind, I commit to the study of men because I believe that remaining so focused allows my work to speak to broader issues of gender relations precisely because I have found so much to say about men. I do not believe that my focus on men affirms the idea that Black women are less important to study, nor do I maintain that the issues confronting Black men are more complex or problematic than those that pertain to such women. In an ideal world, scholars who study Black women and I would meet on a regular basis to share findings and insights. In fact, I do this when time permits, but certainly not in a way that reflects an ideal pattern of idea-sharing.

The Tenth Question
  *What was the worst (or most difficult, or most embarrassing) interview/
  field encounter you've had?*

The most difficult field work encounter occurred for me when I was interviewing low-income African American men in Chicago, and in the middle
of an interview with one young man, a well-known gang leader entered the
community center office that I was using, prompting the young man to stop
in mid-sentence and walk out of the room. The leader then took his chair,
explained that he had heard about me and the research that I was doing in his
neighborhood, and then took the interview protocol from me and proceeded
to answer what seemed to be the specific questions that most interested him.
He allowed me to tape record his replies, but the moment was really one of
his creating his own interview. I never experienced such a moment prior to
or before this occasion. What he offered to me was provocative and informative, but only partially connected to my overall research agenda. It did
inform me, however, of how much certain people may want to go on record
with a researcher so that different views and attitudes about Black men could
be put on the table. In particular, this man wanted to make clear that despite
all he and his associates did that could be seen as problematic in their community they also sponsored social events and other activities that gave life to
the community. He also wanted me to meet some of his younger associates
so that they could have conversations with a college-educated Black man. For
reasons that I would have never guessed prior to doing this research, some
form of reciprocity was realized by my being in this field site.

  *What did you really want to do for a living? What were you afraid you
  might end up doing?*

I am doing exactly what I decided that I wanted to do when I was 20 years of
age. I have absolutely no regrets about my career choice.

  What's the study you never pursued, but always wanted to?

I have been interested in why non-African American scholars commit to the
study of African Americans and the African American experience. I want
to know what motivations and curiosities brought them to that topic, what
vision of race and racial equality they have, and....

4.
MITCHELL DUNEIER

1. *A central, motivating concern in your ethnographic work is document-ing the moral worlds of poor and working-class Black men. How would you describe your interest in the moral order in general and in the moral worlds of marginalized Black men in particular?*

A fundamental theme of my sociological work has been about the struggle to live in accordance with standards of moral worth. I developed this interest in graduate school when I was writing my dissertation, *Slim's Table* (Duneier 1994). My goal was to understand the way that working-class and poor work-ing men struggled to live in accordance with standards of respectability—moral worth—in a world in which they felt those aspirations were devalued. Many of the men who hung out at the Valois cafeteria did so in an effort to form a community with other like-minded people who shared their beliefs and values. They had seen the ghettos change and transform during their own lifetimes as the South Side was ravaged by deindustrialization and the flight of the Black middle class following the Civil Rights Movement.

Sidewalk (Duneier 2000) was also about men living in accordance with standards of moral worth, but they differed from the men in *Slim's Table* because their efforts occurred in a setting much more unfavorable to such behavior. Most of them had come out of prison, and had been basically cast off by the society. In the United States, once you have a felony conviction and you're a Black man and you come out of prison, you can't get housing. You can't get an interview for a job in the formal economy. There are so many ways in which you're blocked from living a conventional life and these are men who live under that burden. How then do you construct a so-called moral life for yourself? It seemed like an even greater challenge for me to understand how someone makes that happen.

2. *You've written an article with a very provocative title: "How Not to Lie With Ethnography." Is "not lying" with ethnography the same thing as telling the truth?*

The article was forthcoming from *Sociological Methodology* with that title, but at the last minute I changed it. I felt that it would lead to too much mis-understanding. But I think the dilemma I felt is worth talking about. The main point of the article is that ethnography is difficult, not only because it requires deep immersion in other worlds, but because there is little agree-ment among its leading practitioners regarding how to do it. While there are a number of ethnographies that are popular among sociologists, the authors of those ethnographies frequently disagree about what constitutes good work and how ethnography should be undertaken. Further, these disagreements are frequently pitched in moral terms. I was trying to think about why this might be so.

The answer, I think, lies in the fact that so much of this disagreement can be summarized as being about transparency. When people read and consume most kinds of documentary work, they feel a need to understand how they have been convinced and more generally, how the effects have been achieved. Howard Becker has argued that misrepresentation becomes a moral wrong in the eyes of readers when they come to realize that an "effect was achieved by means that, [they]…weren't fully aware of and therefore can't be critical about" (2008: 133).

It was on that note that I invoked Darryl Huff's 1954 classic, *How to Lie with Statistics*, the best selling statistics book in the history of the field (for discussion see Steele 2005), from which the title of the paper was to be derived. Huff was an undergraduate sociology and journalism major at the University of Iowa and received his master's in journalism there before going on to become the editor of *Better Homes and Gardens*. Upon his early retirement, he moved to California with his wife and began a second career as the freelance writer of 16 "how to" books including *Twenty Careers of Tomorrow* and *How to Work with Concrete and Masonry* (Steele 2005).

Part of what made Huff's statistics book so successful was his argument that people who used statistics needed to achieve transparency. Like Huff's book, my paper focused on some little discussed problems of transparency, in this case with regard to the ways ethnographic data is used and misused. Huff had a moralistic stance which appealed to readers. He argued that the misuses of statistics he identified were not innocent. It wasn't just that the perpetrators should have known better, but that often they probably did. But in my paper, I did not spend much time distinguishing between untruths, falsehoods, and lies, and unlike Huff, I concluded by looking at the structural reasons that a moralistic tone enters into so many discussions about truth and falsehood in ethnography. For that reason alone, I should not have thought of drawing a connection to Huff's work.

3. *Do you think the kind of moralism that Huff adopted is ever appropriate when talking about ethnographic data?*

We can also examine this in another way, and perhaps one that is even relevant to the concerns in my paper. Huff believed that numbers could be manipulated to support any argument, and he was concerned with the kinds of manipulations that unsuspecting readers would not know to look for. One way of thinking about the voluminous sociological literature on ethnographic method is that so many of its key papers tend to ultimately contain insights that come out of a positivist legacy about how to achieve transparency. While some sociological ethnographers are more akin to those in the fields of anthropology and education in rejecting that legacy (see Smith 1987; Reinhartz, 1992; DeVault 1999; Stacey 1997; and Thorne 1993), many more embrace it and struggle with transparency as part of that legacy.

What unites the methodological writing and the ethnographic work of many of these scholars is a sense that they are aware of how easy it is for a reader to be unknowing about how effects were achieved, but also an awareness that their own greatest personal accomplishments have to do with the way they been successful at being transparent by some standard. I would argue that it is no coincidence that, regardless of the differing styles of those who have written the most influential ethnographies, one thing that has made their work appeal to readers is a sense that they have struggled with this issue. In the work of each of these practitioners one sees a multitude of different approaches to the problem, and in some cases no small amount of moralism in their own writing when there is a sense that someone else is achieving effects by means that are not sufficiently understood.

Among the topics that are covered in such discussions and about which there is little agreement are: how much data and variation are necessary to make it possible for readers to evaluate claims; the necessity to avoid a false objectivity through reflexivity; the need to achieve transparency about all the perspectives or variations that the reader does not learn about; the importance of not influencing the setting of research in ways that are unknown to the reader; and the question of whether theory is a necessity or a contaminant to openness to the kind of conflicting evidence and surprises that a transparent study must contain. In each of these influential methodological statements, there is a pervasive theme of privileging the importance of transparency, but in each case the fieldworker privileges his or her own criteria for how such transparency is to be achieved. Most writers are pretty clear that the criteria they employ come out of their own experience, reminding us of Erving Goffman's (1959) admonition that statements about technique tend to be rationalizations, "and we are in the precarious position of providing them." Yet, for all of these writers, the very things that increase our chances of making valuable discoveries are the same ones that make what we do in representing the world more transparent.

    4. *You mention the question of whether theory is a necessity or a contaminant in ethnographic work. This brings to mind a recent article in* Ethnography *co-authored by William Julius Wilson (2009), "The Role of Theory in Ethnographic Work" in which he weighs in on the debate you had with Loïc Wacquant in the* American Journal of Sociology. *What did you think of Wilson's intervention?*

The piece has just come out and I have only read it very quickly. I hope to spend more time on it soon. But my initial take was surprise. Most of it is sort of a "book report"—this one said this and that one said that, which is not how one thinks of Wilson spending his time. But on the other hand, Wilson has a longstanding interest in the philosophy of science. The article summarized my views in the debate pretty accurately and Wilson comes pretty close to my own view of the role of theory in ethnography, which is that it is an iterative process. (I think this is also the view expressed by Eli Anderson and Katherine Newman in that symposium.) I found one thing potentially misleading. At the end of the article, Wilson concluded that good ethnography is "theory driven." By which I think he means driven by a concern with contributing to theory. This can be misleading because it could be taken by some to mean that you have your theory when you go into the field. Good ethnography results in surprises of all kinds.

Overall, I find the discussion of the role of theory in ethnographic work to be one that has pretty much exhausted itself. The question has dominated methodological discussions over the past 15 years to the exclusion of other more important questions, and one could argue that this has resulted in work that is not as good. There is, after all, only so much you can think about training students to do in 15 weeks and there is only so much they can or should read about method before they go into the field. Alice Goffman, an urban ethnographer who just finished her degree here at Princeton, recently told me that she hadn't paid a bit of attention to any of these debates about theory in ethnography because they had all occurred after so many of the ethnographies she most admired were written. She asked me if there was any reason for her to think about these things when none of those great authors had done so. I think that's a pretty damning question.

5. *This is reminiscent of Dorothy Smith's arguments (e.g., Smith 1987) Social scientists create social categories, concepts, and theories that help us better understand the social world, but in so doing often distort or erase the actualities of that social world. You have said you are suspicious of the ability of predetermined theoretical frameworks to explain what's happening with "the people." So what good are sociological theories if the people repeatedly burst beyond them?*

Ethnographers are on the front lines of a zone of confrontation where theories developed through survey methodologies, experiments, and armchair reflection meet the actual people whose behavior has sometimes already been explained with these other methods. Other times, they confront persons or social situations that have been completely ignored in the formulations of dominant theories. Ethnographers are in a unique position to take the measure of particular people in groups, networks, organizations, and communities and, through their assessment, simultaneously take the measure of disciplines whose neat theories may be out of touch.

There is always a temptation for the sociologist to depict larger social forces as if they manifest themselves independently of concrete human beings. Today's portraits of globalization, racism, and urban inequality are not unlike the images of bureaucracy of an earlier era; so dispossessed of people that they "appear to realize their ambitions apart from human action," as

Gouldner (1954:16) wrote. What is more, even simple portraits of everyday life like Geertz's description of the Balinese cock fight (Geertz 1973) can be produced without reference to even a single fully fledged human being. As a corrective to this tendency, an ethnographer can "show the people," hoping that if social forces are responsible for the outcomes, these forces will sometimes be manifest in the living breathing persons who, one way or the other, do the will of those larger forces.

But, when the ethnographer feels a sense of responsibility to show the people, these subjects frequently burst beyond the sociological identities he or she is tempted to assign in their absence. This is not unlike the experience of a novelist who finds that her character gets away from her. But the difference is that the novelist has no compunction against "exercising ruthless control" over characters, as the literary critic James Wood reminds us in his book *How Fiction Works*. According to Wood, "Nabokov used to say that he pushed his characters around like serfs or chess pieces—he had no time for that metaphorical ignorance and impotence whereby authors like to say, 'I don't know what happened, but my character just got away from me and did his own thing. I had nothing to do with it.' 'Nonsense,' said Nabokov, 'If I want my character to cross the road, he crosses the road. I am his master'" (Wood 2008: 116). By contrast, the ethnographer who truly commits to showing the people is stuck with her actions and should not exercise ruthless control. Once focused on a subject and committed to transparency, the investigator will benefit from following the subject's lead! The people can keep the sociological theories honest.

6. *You've written that "talk can be cheap." What does that mean in the context of your work?*

In the past couple of decades or so, there has developed a view that ethnography is about "giving voice" to subjects. This is a reasonable agenda for certain ethnographic projects, but not for the method as a whole, which has a variety of pivotal agendas.

There are really a few basic things that an ethnographer is looking for when she or he goes out into the field and one of them is people's definition of the situation. How do they understand the world that they are a part of, and the experiences that they are having every day, which can be very foreign to me or to my readers? So, as an example, in the film that I recently made about what happened to the people in *Sidewalk*, the viewer sees that the men go around on hunts for garbage, looking for treasures that they will be able to sell on their tables—books and magazines that they think may have some value. When I first heard the concept of a hunt, that was something I'd never heard before, and the hunt was a category that the people I wrote about had in their minds, which they used to organize their own experience. They told me that they got their books and magazines by going on hunts.

Well, I could have listened to what they said in the form of an interview and written that down and reported it, but as an ethnographer, we're not merely interested in people's definitions of the situations and the concepts that they use to explain the social world, but also in the things that they do. In other words, the ethnographic method is ultimately a comparative method for me in which people's behavior is compared to what they say. We can compare what people say to what they do. So I went out with Ron on a hunt, I followed him through the streets with the camera and we showed him going from apartment house to apartment house as he went about doing the garbage sifting and collecting until he found exactly what he was looking for. It was in the process of doing that for many years on the street in my role as a participant observer that I came to see that there was a close relationship between the concept and what people said and then what they actually did.

The third thing that ethnographers are trying to do within the framework of a statement that "talk can be cheap" is we're also trying to figure out what it is that people *don't* say, don't articulate but take for granted in their everyday life. And so in the film there are examples of the fact that there were certain aspects of their lives that took me years to understand because the men didn't talk about them—like the fact that they urinate in public places because some of them feel they can't get access to bathroom resources and other places to clean themselves. It was things of that sort that would not have come out in an initial interview if I didn't know to ask about them and were not discussed in the everyday life on the street but took me years to find out—they were basic assumptions of ways in which the people out there lived. So that gives a sense of what people say and what people do.

At the end of the film, I asked Butterroll, who seems to have turned around his life by no longer drinking any alcohol and had basically become sober—I asked him how he was supporting himself, and he said that he was now working full-time as a vendor, that he had his own table, and he was making good money. I asked him how much money he had on him in his pocket, and he told me, and I said, "Can I see the money?" Well, that's the kind of thing that you have to do if you're not going to take at face value the things that people say. And it's something that's not always the most comfortable thing to do or something that you can't always do without offending someone. By the time I asked Butterroll this question, he and I had known each other long enough that he gave me a friendly laugh, and he took the money out of his pocket, and it turned out to be exactly the amount of money that he had indicated. This was a nice indication that he really was living the way that he said that he was.

7. *How was making a film from different from doing the ethnography?*

It has been a really fantastic experience. A lot of people who don't know I worked with a professional have asked me if it was difficult to make a film, and the answer is that it *was* difficult, but not because I taught myself a whole lot about film making. Barry Alexander Brown is an esteemed film editor and director who lived on the very blocks where *Sidewalk* was written. He and I originally were introduced by Spike Lee when he was trying to make my first book, *Slim's Table*, into a television series. Barry wrote the scripts with Spike for that series and, though it never went anywhere, we developed a nice relationship. One day Barry asked me what I was publishing next, and it turned out that he lived right off the very section of Sixth Avenue that I had been studying by working as a street vendor. As I started to wrap up *Sidewalk*, we began to talk about doing a film together. This was 10 years ago.

It started out very slowly. We would go out to the blocks and film a little bit every day. The idea was to capture the kinds of interactions that I had routinely observed for years on the streets, and which were heavily documented in the book: Interactions between panhandlers, scavengers, vendors, customers, and local residents. I thought of it as mainly illustrative, but bringing the people to life with film in a way that I was incapable of doing on the page. One of the big differences between a project like this and actual participant observation is that you go into filming pretty much knowing what you are looking for. This is not to say that there aren't any surprises, but they are pretty limited. Another difference is that I asked a lot more questions on camera than I do in normal fieldwork, which is based much less on interviews. I guess this gets back to my underlying ethos that talk can be cheap.

8. *It seems that your work is addressed to a particular audience—liberal, well-intentioned whites who are generally ignorant of the social worlds of poor Black men. Do you see yourself as a sort of interlocutor for this group?*

My audience is not simply "liberal, well-intentioned whites." It is also liberal, badly intentioned whites. It is also conservative, well-intentioned whites. And it is also Blacks, whether or not they are well intentioned. Despite this qualification, I do not feel that your question misrepresents my intellectual agenda.

When you teach at a university like Wisconsin or Princeton, you look out into the classroom audience and notice a few Blacks scattered around. If you talk about the Black poor in a class of this kind, many of the whites will assume that Blacks in their midst come from families like the one you are describing. I always begin by explaining that the vast majority of African Americans are working-class people and that the vast majority of Blacks that students will encounter on the campus also come from working-class families. *Slim's Table* is a similar kind of pedagogy. I don't think it comes as a surprise to many Blacks that there are so many working-class people in their population striving to live in accordance with standards of moral worth.

But if most Blacks are from the working and middle classes, then why should we expect that there would be any more understanding of the unhoused Black men in *Sidewalk* on the part of Blacks than there is from whites? To the contrary, many middle- and working-class Blacks believe that such unhoused Blacks have no excuse for their behavior and have never spent any time trying to understand the social genesis of their pathologies. In writing *Sidewalk*, I was speaking to them, as much as I was speaking to the badly intentioned whites who try to drive them from the sidewalks.

9. *You've said that there's not much new in urban ethnography since Elliot Liebow's* Tally's Corner *and Carol Stack's* All Our Kin. *Do you mean that all ethnographies subsequent to Liebow and Stack are "only" recapitulations? Or, perhaps the statement is more methodological: that* Tally's Corner *and* All Our Kin *exemplify all we need to know about telling a sociological story. If this is true, should the ethnographer keep searching for the "new." How?*

Stack's *All Our Kin* (1976) and Liebow's *Tally's Corner* (1967) stand among the half dozen best ethnographies that we have. One of the things that Liebow understood that resonates with me in particular was the "chain linked fence" that exists between the observer and the observed. I thought that sort of metaphor that he used in the book is something that really should stand the test of time for ethnographers who don't want to lose sight of their white privilege. He wrote that "despite the barriers, we were able to look at each other, walk alongside each other, talk, and occasionally touch fingers" (1967: 250–251). He also wrote, "I used to play with the idea that maybe I wasn't as much of an outsider as I thought. Other events, and later readings of the field materials, have dissuaded me of this particular touch of vanity" (249). He knew that he would never be "one of them," but also wasn't so far distant that he couldn't understand them. He left open the possibility of a white man entering into a serious dialogue with the lives of poor Blacks and producing a book that gave the reader a set of significant interpretations.

Stack's book was a precursor to a lot of contemporary developments surrounding reflexivity in sociological and anthropological ethnography. Stack was certainly not in dialogue with any of the kind of methodological thinking that came about in anthropology during the 1990s in the "reflexive turn," with the advent of post-modern thinking, critical race theory, or whiteness studies. But she pulled off a powerful self-reflexivity about her own white privilege and her own place in the lives of the poor Black women whom she got to know. She also involved her subjects in defining research topics and specific questions for investigation. There was no illusion that she was one of them. She always understood the difference between herself and her subjects. In this way, *All Our Kin* anticipated changes and transformations that would come about in cultural representation, including the value and possibilities of redistributing ethnographic authority. In a sober way, she anticipated many of the best things that have happened in ethnography over that period.

All urban ethnography is a reflection of the particular moment in which it is written, and it is usually hard for the ethnographer to see the political context in which he or she is working with complete clarity because it is impossible to anticipate the changes. Read together today, these two works say as much about their own times as about the vast changes that have occurred since in the lives of the urban Black poor. After welfare reform, in which welfare mothers were forced off public aid into low-paying jobs, the Stack legacy is a new set of questions about how welfare reform would undermine the ability of kin to do for one another those things that had helped them survive all these years. Stack herself would ultimately ask, skeptically, about the grandmothers, sisters, and cousins who had once been able to offer spontaneous child care. As she said in an unpublished talk, "In the serious attempt to adjust to new values of the marketplace, and to the personal responsibility ethic, mothers come face to face with insurmountable dilemmas of adulthood…. And kin—grandmothers, sisters, and cousins who were once able to offer spontaneous respite care might still have the family system as their primary impulse but could no longer accommodate 10 hour child care days, when many of them are in the same boat trying to make ends meet."

Neither could Liebow have predicted how much worse the plight of his subjects would become. In recent decades, the jobs that Liebow says these men rejected have been taken by immigrants who, unlike Americans, are not comparing them to the jobs of other Americans, but to jobs back home. While the job prospects of poor Black men have worsened and welfare benefits have been slashed, the "war on drugs" has led vast numbers of poor

Blacks and Hispanics to spend their young adult lives in prison. Whereas Liebow made frequent reference to interactions between his subjects and the criminal justice system, he says very little about any of them spending time in prison, or about the impact of prison on their lives. It is hard to imagine that any street corner today would not be populated by the casualties of all these transformations.

Building on the powerful insights of studies such as *All Our Kin* and *Tally's Corner*, the next generation of ethnographic books about the urban poor must explain everyday life under these changed conditions. There is a big difference between the context-driven studies of the 1960s and the decontextualized, quotation-driven studies that are becoming increasingly popular today, however insightful they otherwise are. We should be mindful that the most influential first-hand studies have not been produced by interviewing individuals, but by following and showing people in groups and networks, participating in their lives laterally and over time, and then taking into account how local labor markets, policy regimes, and institutionalized racism may affect them. The case for in-depth, context-driven fieldwork may be even more pressing now than in the past because Black men are now less accessible to surveys than ever before. Going in and out of jail, they are more weakly attached to households, though they can be tracked down by ethnographers, just as Liebow found the men who were absent from the survey of the census workers who went door-to-door. The U.S. Census undercount of these men is once again increasing, so ethnographers have even more of an opportunity to fill the gap. There is some irony that many would choose this time to let ethnography mimic survey research based on snowball sampling.

The Tenth Question
 What was the most embarrassing (or most difficult) field encounter that you have had?

I think the most embarrassing moment I have had in the field was when someone I cared deeply about accused me of what I could call exploitation. "When you buy a textbook to read it you pay money for it. Some of these textbooks cost a hundred dollars. If I was a textbook, Mitch would only want to borrow it. He wouldn't want to pay for it. That's Mitch in a nutshell."

 What did you really want to do for a living? What were you afraid you would end up doing?

From the time that I took a course with Howard Becker during sophomore year at Northwestern, all I ever wanted to be was a sociologist, and this was certainly confirmed by my years in graduate school studying with Edward Shils. But while I was at the University of Chicago, I was run over by a Mack truck. Both of my legs were crushed by the front and back double wheels. I spent a lot of time in a wheelchair, and then learning how to walk again. Given the pessimistic predictions I was receiving about a full recovery, I felt that I couldn't afford to take a chance on a career in sociology and went to law school instead. I received an A- in tort (accident) law, but couldn't motivate myself to do more than the bare minimum on most of my classes. Fearing that I would end up as a lawyer, I spent most of my nights in the law school dorms writing the dissertation I had started at the University of Chicago. It ended up getting published during my second year of law school and when the UC Santa Barbara Sociology Department offered me a job in my third year, I officially dropped out and never graduated.

What's the study you never pursued but always wanted to?

I'd like to write a sociological alternative to *Freakonomics* (2005), a book that reclaims sociology from economists *and* sociologists who think that insightful social science comes from more clever thinking about causality, selection bias, and incentives. I'd like to write that during the year that I'm completing my last semester of law school. I think it's time.

SECTION II

GLOBAL ETHNOGRAPHY AND THE STUDY OF TRANSNATIONAL LABOR MIGRATIONS

5.
MILIANN KANG

1. *Your study of Korean nail salons (Kang 2010) is fascinating. How did you come to study them? Was the fact that the site involved women serving women important to you from the beginning, or did this facet of the work emerge along with the rest of the story?*

Many people have assumed that I study this topic because I am interested in beauty and the beauty industry, but if you take one look at my nails, it's pretty obvious that this is not the case! In fact, I was interested in studying Asian immigrant women's work, and this happened to be the niche in which they were heavily concentrated in New York City, where I was attending graduate school. I stumbled upon these salons as I was wandering the streets of various neighborhoods, and I was struck not just by how many were owned by Asians, particularly Koreans, but also how they offered very different services depending on the clientele. I was especially interested in salons in predominantly Black neighborhoods, both because of the innovative nail art that they offered as well as because of what, at least at first glance, were largely cordial relations. Before starting grad school, I had worked on various Korean American community issues, most immediately with the Korean Immigrant Workers' Advocate in Los Angeles in the aftermath of the 1992 civil uprising in which over 2,000 Korean stores had been looted and burned. I had also followed the boycott of the Red Apple Market in Brooklyn, which was publicized in highly racialized terms as a conflict between Koreans and Blacks. Thus, it was fascinating to me that many of these nail salons operated in similar circumstances—that is, Korean immigrants serving Black, working-class communities—yet did not experience overt tensions at the individual or community level. This is where the gender piece of it became more central, as I believed that part of what distinguished these nail businesses was that they involved women serving women, but I also knew enough to be suspicious of any kind of essentialist argument that women "naturally" know how to get along better. So, this is where the project became really interesting to me, trying to figure out the various intersections with gender that shaped relations between diverse women in these salons.

2. *One of the contributions of that work was its complication of Arlie Hochschild's concept of "emotional labor" (2003). Give or take a couple of years, one could say that it took 20 years for her ideas about emotional labor and "feeling rules" to become embodied, gendered, raced, and classed. We are curious as to how you came to the conclusion that the story you wanted to tell would involve such an extension of her concept. What do you think that process implies about the ongoing theoretical dialogue(s) in Sociology?*

I can pinpoint a definite "aha" moment when my research crystallized around the theoretical framework of emotional labor. I was offering informal English language classes in one of the salons as a way of "giving back" to my research participants, but they ended up giving me much more. Basically, they kicked me in the pants to be able to see what was going on in the salons as both an enactment and enlargement of Hochschild's concept of emotional labor (2003). One day, they told me outright that the English I was teaching them wasn't useful. I swallowed my hurt feelings and asked what English they would like to learn instead, and one of the manicurists said, "We want to know how to say, "You look like you lost weight." From that moment, I got it. They knew exactly what they needed to be able to say to meet their customers' expectations for emotional pampering. However, their performances of emotional labor were complicated by the fact that they did not know English, that they were Korean immigrants serving customers of difference racial and class backgrounds, and that they were dealing not only with feelings, but with bodies, and with feelings about bodies.

I love telling this story because it illustrates how important feminist research is to Sociology. I was able to gain a deeper understanding of what was going on at these sites when I stopped assuming that I had all the answers, or even that I could discover them through my own analytical toolkit. Instead, the research subjects were not merely informants but agents in the co-construction of knowledge. They reframed the questions that I was asking as well as the assumptions I had about nail salon work and those who perform it. Rather than passively responding to customer demands, manicurists are strategic in their performances of emotional labor, as they strive to maximize tips but also to exert a modicum of control over the interactions. At the same time, they are constrained by the larger context of beauty culture and the beauty service industry that shape the terms of emotional labor and how it is exchanged and negotiated.

> *We loved this anecdote! One reaction we had is that it might provide the basis for an exercise in a graduate methods class: Think of an example of how your respondents are actual (not just hypothetical) co-constructors of researcher knowledge. What do you think?*

I think it's a great idea—in fact, I have used this example a few different ways in teaching our graduate methods course, "Issues in Feminist Research." First, I've found that sharing my own vulnerabilities and shortcomings as a researcher helps to break down students' defensiveness and a sense of having to be the expert, both of which get in the way of doing good research. When I've shared my own stories of not getting what was going on right in front of me, it opens space for students to think self-reflexively—"What am I missing? What blinders are getting in my way and how can I get past them?" Second, students can then share reflections with each other on moments where they have overlooked, underestimated, or silenced their respondents and then think of ways to incorporate the knowledge of their subjects more fully. For example, one of my doctoral students, Judith Obiero, shared about her research on girls' primary education in Kenya, and how she had to let go of her own investment in emphasizing gender disparities in order to see other forms of inequality. She told of how boys who were nomadic or lived in urban slums were also marginalized in the education system, and how they literally screamed for her attention. In response, she changed her research design to include the boys, and while she was still mainly interested in the girls' experiences, she shifted to a more intersectional argument that did not assume that gender was the sole or main axis of exclusion.

3. *Following the work on nail salons, how have you explored your concept of "body labor" in other places? (We know you have done some work on tattooing.) What additional aspects were made visible by looking at those seemingly different forms of body labor?*

I collaborated with Katherine Jones on a piece for *Contexts* (2007) on tattooing. We were more concerned with the tattoo itself, and the disjuncture between the personal meaning to the wearer versus the social meaning imposed by others, than on the specific dimensions of tattooing as work. Nonetheless, we did find that similar to manicurists, tattoo artists engage in complex negotiations of body labor; that is, they must manage service exchanges involving the commercialization of both feelings and bodies. If I were to do more research on this, I would explore how the intensity of the kind of body service complicates the terms of body labor—obviously tattoos, let alone various forms of cosmetic surgery, are more permanent and invasive than manicures. I did do some interviews with massage therapists that addressed how the increasing social acceptance of certain kinds of body labor changes the ways that it is practiced. For instance, one woman told me that she used to arm herself with very sharp elbows in case her clients assumed that they would be getting more than a massage, but that she has been able to let down this degree of defensiveness as massage has gone more mainstream. Thus, the themes are similar: body labor in different occupations necessitates very sensitive and sometimes thorny interactions which are shaped by larger cultural frameworks, institutional protocols, and hierarchies of gender, race, class, and immigration.

Do you think, then, that body labor is categorically different from other forms of labor?

I would not say that it is categorically different, but it is different enough to pose new questions and to warrant more attention from those who study labor and advocate for more just labor practices. Body labor is an evolving form of service work that involves challenging dimensions that are not part of other labor exchanges, particularly a high level of physical and emotional intimacy. At the same time, it is similar to other forms of work in that it involves selling one's labor often for low wages, under undesirable conditions and for the profit of others. Thus, it would be a mistake to treat it as a totally different kind of beast, but it would also be a mistake to ignore its distinctive permutations.

4. *There is often talk about the strained relations between urban Korean merchants and their African American clients. One sort of salon you studied involved those relationships. Any comment on those dynamics or how they might be changing?*

As I mentioned above, I was initially struck by how intimate and cooperative most of the exchanges are between Korean manicurists and Black (both African American and Caribbean) customers in what I refer to as "nail art salons." However, as I observed more closely, when a service is botched, it can quickly escalate into a heated, racialized exchange, even in salons that have many years of positive relations with the individuals and communities they serve. The conclusion I draw is that the gendered practices of beauty service work can foster appreciation and counter negative stereotypes, but when tempers flare, race and class differences trump gender solidarities.

What lessons would I draw from this for Black–Korean relations, in general, or even for relations between new immigrants and native-born minorities more broadly? Basically, while it is helpful to learn ways to smooth over face-to-face interactions in small-business settings, as long as unequal opportunities for the different groups that meet in these establishments persist, the possibilities for animosity and conflict continue to simmer just beneath the surface. This is not to say that efforts at community outreach are not valuable, but that they need to be accompanied by attention to real disparities in social and economic mobility.

5. *Over the course of the last 10 years, have you come to think any differently about the simultaneous workings of gender, race, and class that you examined? That is, do you still agree with Gilroy (1993: 85) when you cited him as saying, "Gender is the modality in which race is lived."?*

I guess it comes with the territory that the more I learn, the more I must qualify myself, so I would say that gender *can be* the modality in which race is lived, but it depends on the situation. In sites such as nail salons, this quote is more applicable, as the highly gendered exchange of the manicure is central to the ways that these interactions are racialized. However, while I believe that all individuals and social institutions are gendered, I would not say that gender is *the* central axis in all social settings or exchanges. For example, when thousands of people around the country took to the streets on May 1, 2006 in protests about immigrant rights, I would say that immigration, not gender, was the modality in which race was being lived. That is not to say that women did not participate in these protests or that gender does not play a central role in immigration, but it is to say that what brought people into the streets was their common experiences as, or concerns for, immigrants and the racial profiling, employment discrimination, and other forms of marginalization that immigrant status confers.

6. *How does your present study of the struggles of Asian American women to simultaneously fulfill professional roles, as well as a variety of familial roles under the cultural strictures of the "model minority" challenge our simpler notions of what it means to be a second generation Asian American?*

The mythology of the model minority espouses two things. One, that Asian Americans have achieved overwhelming success—supposedly "out-whiting the whites"—through their own hard work and family values, without nursing grievances or demanding government supports. Second, that this success invalidates the claims of other groups, particularly African Americans that racial barriers continue to exclude and diminish their life chances in systematic ways. Much research has invalidated both of these claims, by largely focusing on the struggles of first generation Asian immigrants and their uneven economic and social gains. My research looks at how this discourse of the model minority continues to be both pervasive and erroneous with regard to second generation Asian Americans, in particular, women negotiating the multiple pressures of work and family responsibilities.

Can you see a parallel between the normative aspects of the mythology of the Asian American "model minority" and those normative discourses that scholars (such as Lacy and Pattillo, in this volume) have talked about with respect to middle-class Blacks?

I've learned a great deal from scholars of middle-class Blacks and Black families more broadly and see striking parallels. First of all, the concept of "middle class" is complicated, as many Blacks and Asian Americans have working-class origins and continue to support working-class parents and other family members. This poses challenges in terms of the normative aspects of culture and identity as well as resources. There is pressure to keep up with the upwardly mobile trajectory of peers while also negotiating differences, judgments, and a sense of betrayal by those who have been unable to crack the same codes of educational and professional success. In addition, the ideology of what my colleague Kesho Scott calls "the habit of surviving" is particularly pervasive among both Black and Asian American women, and I would say women of color and immigrant women more generally. This ethic of persistence and resourcefulness in the face of many obstacles carries a high price not just in terms of family and career tradeoffs but also with regard to physical and emotional health.

7. *What does it mean to feel pressure to simultaneously assimilate and embrace tradition—a predicament for many of your respondents? Do you feel as if you understand this plight in your own life? How has the power of the ideology of the model minority affected you?*

I think one of the reasons that the model minority stereotype, like any stereotype, has gained such traction is that there is a sliver of truth to it. It seems to promise the best of both worlds: that Asian Americans can gain success and acceptance in the mainstream while also holding onto ethnic identity, at least in a very watered-down version. Unfortunately, this promise is rarely fulfilled, as despite the rhetoric about Asians being widely respected and accepted, in most cases, the more "Asianness" people retain, the more they experience social and economic marginalization. The predicament for many of my respondents, which I have also struggled with, comes from knowing that the choices can be very stark between individual advancement versus maintaining strong family and cultural ties and political commitments. These choices play themselves out in particularly complicated ways for Asian American women, as the models available both within the ethnic group and in the larger society, are very constraining. For these women, "having it all" is not just about having a successful career, marriage, and children, but they must factor in expectations and needs of parents and community. These competing demands often instill a sense of loss or failure and can make it very difficult to assert coherent and empowering gender and racial identities.

8. *Some of your respondents have "opted-out" (the phrase given to employed women who elect to spend full time on their families), and some have not. How do your respondents frame those decisions in the narratives they offer up? What do you think is the impact of public discourse about mothering on the stories we tell ourselves and others about our work lives in and out of the home?*

What I am finding is that the "opt-out" debate is not relevant for many of the women in my study, or for that matter, most women of color in the United States. Even for highly educated white women, scholars have shown that it is more about being pushed out of inhospitable workplaces than about choosing to stay home with children. This tension between work and family is hard enough when the "family" part of the equation is mainly about caring for young children. However, when you add to this the responsibility of caring for elderly parents, many of whom have limited financial means, do not speak English, and have made many sacrifices to invest in their children's education, the pressure significantly ramps up. Thus, many Asian American women feel that opting out is not an option, as they must consider not only the long-term economic needs of their nuclear family but also those of their extended family, ranging from paying rent for parents to sending homeland remittances. Furthermore, much of the pressure can be emotional, as it is difficult to let down parents' deferred gratification at being able to say that their daughter is a doctor, professor, or other high status occupation. In addition, the child-rearing piece is also more complex, as it involves having to instill positive identities in children who may face discrimination or reject their cultural backgrounds. Thus, while the general standards for mothering for most women are unattainable, for many Asian American women they can be downright crazy-making, as they demand not only inflexible work and family arrangements but also conflicting ideologies and allegiances.

9. *Speaking of impossible expectations, do your Asian American students ask more of you than your white students? And vice versa? What can we learn about race, class, gender, and identity when we unravel the expectations that in many respects make us who we are?*

I wouldn't say that Asian American students ask more of me than white students ask, but that they ask for different things. I teach at UMass Amherst, which is a largely white institution, although Asians are the largest minority group there. The issues for Asian American students and professors are somewhat, although not completely, different from those at a West Coast school with a visible and significant Asian American student body. I have colleagues at schools where the Asian American students are very politicized and the demands on professors to participate in various campus and community events and projects are heavy. These are the kinds of demands I'm more likely to get from white students, especially feminist students—to participate in teach-ins, speak at events, and so on. From Asian American students, especially women, I'm more likely to get requests for individual mentoring, such as help with a personal issue or academic and professional advice. Here, at UMass and the Five Colleges, we're still at the beginning of raising awareness and pulling together a critical mass of Asian American students and faculty to build programs and engage in activism. We've come a long way in the last few years, with the help of some very smart and dedicated student leaders, most notably those participating in Asian Americans for Political Awareness and the 5-Pan student conference. I'm currently working on a pedagogical study with Sueyeon Juliette Lee that focuses on some of these issues. We look at the dynamics of teaching a course on Asian American Women, comparing how feelings of "white guilt" "Asian guilt," and "feminist guilt" manifest in the classroom and impact learning outcomes. What we've found is that while white students may feel a sense of guilt based on their identities as U.S. citizens and the related privileges and historical responsibilities, Asian American students can feel that they are imposters or have betrayed their culture and communities. Feminist guilt also emerges, fluctuating between paralysis and the urge to "fix" problems. All of these emotions can breed both defensive and productive responses to difficult course material that addresses the experiences of Asian Americans in the United States as well as the history of U.S. military, economic, and cultural imperialism in Asia.

What bridges can you imagine being built across these "guilt" divides?

I don't think people feel guilty unless they care about someone or something. The challenge is to channel this latent sense of caring into something more active and effective. Guilt can sometimes be an easy out—it sort of gets you off the hook without your really doing anything. So the trick is to mobilize uncomfortable feelings like guilt that come up in the classroom into more honest conversations, deeper engagement in the learning process, more investment in the issues and ultimately action toward social change.

The Tenth Question
What was the worst (or most difficult, or most embarrassing) interview/ encounter you have had in the field?

There were several very challenging encounters that I had in the field, most of them having to do with my inability to reciprocate as fully as I or the participants would have liked. I struggled with having to decline requests from manicurists and owners, ranging from tutoring their children, to attending their churches, and even introducing me to prospective boyfriends. In one instance, a woman asked me for help in securing a legal work visa, and I referred her to a friend who did immigration law, but she was disappointed that after the initial free counsel, he let her know that he would have to charge her to file her claim. Other difficult moments emerged around inadvertently crossing boundaries of research versus personal life. In one salon, I became fairly close to the owner and she shared various personal concerns. So when she told me that her son was doing poorly at college and she was planning on going to stay with him and cook and clean for him during final exams, I suggested that this might not be the best approach and there were other ways of helping him to get the support he needed. She did not take this well and soon afterwards asked me to finish up my research at her salon.

What did you really want to do for a living? Where were you afraid you would end up doing?

I wanted to write, both as a journalist and a novelist. I had written for school and community newspapers in high school and college, but was often frustrated that just when a story was getting really interesting and I was beginning to understand what was going on, I would have to move on. So becoming a sociologist—particularly an ethnographer—allows me to incorporate elements of those other jobs. I get to focus on building a sustained narrative, somewhat like a novelist, but also on giving voice to real people and problems. I was afraid I would end up doing something soulless, getting pulled into some high-paying, high-status job and having to make compromises that I would regret. I almost went to law school, which would not have been bad if I could maintain a commitment to public interest law, but I've seen so many people decide to go into corporate law with the intention of staying just long enough to pay off their loans and then they find it hard to walk away. I'm not saying that all corporate jobs are evil, in fact, we need more responsible and visionary people in them, but for me, it would have been difficult to reconcile this work with other values and priorities.

What's the study you never pursued, but always wanted to?

In my 20s, I did human rights work related to Asia, and when I became an academic, I wanted to do a more systematic study of the effects of the wars in Asia on immigrants and second generation Asian Americans. I believe so many of our parents' generation lived through horrendous things in World War II, the Korean War, the Vietnam War, the Cambodian genocide, and various U.S. occupations in Asia, and they carry these legacies with them here. I have friends whose family members are Holocaust survivors, and while I would never wish those experiences on anyone, I sometimes find myself envying the public discourse that recognizes their traumas and gives them opportunities to grieve collectively. I don't think Asian survivors of various atrocities have been able to tap into that kind of discourse and instead hold much of it inside. That generation is dying off and their stories, and the inter-generational healing that could come from telling them, are being lost as well.

6.
HUNG CAM THAI

1. *In your book,* For Better or for Worse *(2008) you describe your motivation for undertaking a study of transnational marriage. Could you talk about how personal motivation and sociological design can productively intersect?*

In the book, I focused on a transnational marriage market that emerged in the mid-1990s linking women in Vietnam and overseas immigrant men living and working in the Vietnamese Diaspora. The project started in Vietnam because I was initially motivated to spend time with my mother, with whom I was united in my early 20s, after having lost touch since leaving the country as a child. I had been interested in immigration, but not necessarily marriage migration until I met a group of young local men who thought I was there to search for a wife. The encounter was an unpleasant one, but it led me to pursue the topic. My personal motivation was very important for the success of the project: I was compelled to spend as much time in Vietnam as possible to be with my mother. I was able to immerse myself immediately into Vietnamese culture, despite not having been back for over 15 years since I left the country as a child. That made the project go very smoothly since I designed the project in a way that I got to talk to the women in Vietnam (prior to their migration) as well as the men they married, who were living in the United States at the time.

2. *Your study began as a dissertation and ended up as a book with Rutgers. Would you describe the challenges of that transformation process?*

I was very lucky to have a number of people who helped along the way in terms of turning the dissertation into a book. I think faculty advisors from my graduate days were instrumental, especially my PhD advisor, Barrie Thorne, who talked with me about the process and got me in touch with potential editors very early on. I also think that because I knew I wanted to turn the dissertation into a book, I wrote it very much like a book, and Barrie was very helpful at seeing the early stages of that development.

3. *One of the aspects of your work that people find compelling is the way in which your discussions of large-scale global diasporic movements still convey an individual, human—even personal—quality. Presuming this is no accident, can you talk about what practices produce that result?*

Because I was one of the "boat people" in Vietnamese diasporic history, I find it impossible to ignore the fact that I was part of a larger global process of diasporic movements. Furthermore, I decided in my early adulthood that I would lead a transnational life after returning to Vietnam for the first time since I had migrated as child. So I think that the fact of being a refugee, an immigrant, and then a transmigrant across different stages of my life has had an enormous impact on how I see the world from the angle of different interpersonal relationships and lives across different corners of the globe. Sociology has helped to put all this experience—this transnational life—into perspective, not only because I am able to understand the macro processes involved, but also because I am able to appreciate how I need to sustain my own interpersonal relationships given my constant global traversing.

4. *You have managed to live each year in two places, with nearly 6 months in Vietnam and 6 months in the United States. What difference has that*

made to your professional life, what advantages does it provide to you as a researcher, and what sacrifices does it demand?

As one of the few people in the field who do research on the impact of immigration on the homeland, I find it necessary to split my time between the United States and Vietnam, where I do fieldwork. To take seriously the notion of transnationalism, I think researchers of global migration need to focus more on the homeland of different diasporic groups. I initially devoted myself to splitting my time in Vietnam and the United States for personal reasons, but very soon realized that my research agenda required me to be in Vietnam regularly in order to understand social changes that unfold over short periods of time. The major advantage I have as a researcher is the privilege of living in the field regularly and being able to see social changes taking place without too much time lapse. Besides personal sacrifices, I think that professionally, I have had to scale back on my involvement with professional organizations, like going to professional meetings that happen during the times that I am in Vietnam.

5. *You've been training some talented undergraduates to do research in Vietnam. What advice would you give to white scholars who want to do research outside the United States?*

In terms of guiding my students, what helped tremendously was having a large social network of friends and institutional support from the local university in Vietnam that I developed over a decade. I also began to bring students to Vietnam with me only when I felt I was fully immersed in Vietnamese culture; that is, only when I felt that I considered Vietnam my home just as much as I considered the United States. I am not sure how I would do it otherwise. I know a number of non-Vietnamese scholars who bring students to Vietnam for research, but they often rely on formal organizations to facilitate their students' experience in Vietnam. In terms of research, in area studies and international studies, many non-native scholars, including whites, have done work outside the United States. The experience I had as a bilingual speaker in Vietnam made things go much smoother, something that I think non-speakers of languages in locations where they do research would have to acquire early on. I knew many people in graduate school who had to take several years of language training in order to prepare themselves to do work outside the United States. I think I had that very important linguistic advantage. I also think that a lot of patience—as with any kind of fieldwork—is required, but doing fieldwork overseas requires even more patience. One just must expect to lose some time in doing fieldwork overseas.

6. *In your book* For Better or for Worse *(2008), you describe your fateful journey with your family from delta to delta: in 1979 leaving your small village on the Mekong River in Vietnam to relocate to Mississippi. Your background and your professional path give you a distinctive perspective on the privileges of the academy. How does that affect how you see your students at Pomona? What do you try to impart to them?*

I was born into poverty in rural Vietnam, migrated, and lived in rural poverty in Pass Christian, a small town in Mississippi, then returned to Vietnam as an academic in my adult life. This trajectory has taught me a lot about different vantage points, but I think my experience at Pomona College is shaped mostly by the fact that I have had a parade of wonderful teachers who guided me in various stages of my academic life, from the rural schools of Mississippi to the global community that made up Berkeley, where I attended graduate school. Because I was fortunate to have great mentors throughout my life, I wanted very much to give back to my students the same gift of mentoring that my teachers gave me, which is one of the primary reasons why I returned to Pomona College (where I began my career) from UC Santa Barbara (where I taught for nearly 4 years). At Pomona, I try to assist my students in seeing the world by using the craft of sociology—that is, to see the world with a lens of difference, inequality, and structure. I work very hard to show my students the power of empirical data—however they can collect it—in order to understand the social order. This is important because I think many undergraduate students think that Sociology is often sentimental or reactionary.

In what ways do your students' lives of privilege prove a help or a hindrance to really learning these lessons of difference, inequality, and structure?

When I decided to leave UCSB to return to Pomona College, many of my academic friends and colleagues thought I had made a bad decision because I was leaving a prestigious research university for a small liberal arts college. But I think a major reason why I made the decision was because I strongly feel that it is the sorts of students at places like Pomona—where most of my students come from wealthy families, if not solidly upper class—who most need to learn about difference and inequality. I think many of my privileged students struggle to understand the world in ways that are very different from the ways my students at UCSB struggle to understand the world. The big difference is that many more of my students at UCSB experience in their lives the kind of inequality we teach about in Sociology

7. *Your present research focuses on Viet Kieu (VK), Vietnamese who return to Vietnam to seek employment. What fascinates you about them? What do you hope readers of this next book will gain from your sociological take on the VK?*

Over the past two decades, since they have been returning in large numbers, the Viet Kieu population has been dramatically altering class and gender relations in Vietnam. My current book is about the nexus between return migration and consumption among Viet Kieu visiting or living in Vietnam. Basically, I am examining various patterns of "return" and how different returnees are able to use consumptive power, through spending money and gift-giving, in order to obtain social status. What fascinates me most about Viet Kieu is, I think, one of the concerns that other "homelands" may have about their respective diasporic groups. We know that across the world, immigrants are increasingly returning to their home countries for various reasons (including to live and to work). Many of these home countries are in the developing world, and the immigrants returning are mostly returning from the developed world. The fascination I have is with the ways in which these immigrants can create disparities within the homeland, even among those who work in low wage jobs overseas. They are able to do so in symbolic and pragmatic ways that non-Viet Kieu cannot. For example, a white tourist can travel or work in a third world city like Saigon and certainly have more economic power and status, but that impact is vastly different from when a Viet Kieu returns to do the same. Why? Because the Viet Kieu person generally will have some community, some family members who recognize that gulf in economic power and status, and who will defer to them in ways that are very different from the ways in which white tourists get deference. This process of returning among immigrants worldwide is severely understudied, yet so important because it sheds light on how immigrants, by building ties to the homeland are shaping their notions of belonging, status, and self-worth in a global age.

> *Maybe you could elaborate on the interactional differences in responses to the VK versus to the tourists. In the future, perhaps as people acclimate to the presence of the VK, do you think these interactional styles will change again?*

This is a tough question, one that is actually a chapter in my book—focusing on interactions and exchanges between returnees and Vietnamese locals. Locals tend to have a very obvious kind of deference to VK. For example, it is not uncommon to see local family members carrying the purses and bags for their family members as they walk around town. Also, in the presence of VK, local family members tend to talk less, offer fewer opinions or objections in conversations, and tend to agree on almost everything VK purport. With whites, these sorts of exchanges do not exist. I think this kind of deference will surely change over time as locals begin to learn that VK have very little economic power on the global stage. And over time, I also think that low-wage VK will not be able to afford to sustain the kinds of lifestyles they try to cultivate upon their return to the homeland.

8. *Among male scholars who study global migration and transnational experience, there are few who focus as much as you on women. What would you say about the advantages, disadvantages, and unanticipated insights that came from interviewing Vietnamese women?*

For my first book on marriage and migration in the Vietnamese Diaspora, it was the research design that led to the focus on women; I was attempting to get at the "his" and the "her" side of the international marriage market, and I purposely designed the study to focus on the stage in the marital unions when the internationally married people were waiting for visas for the wives to join their husbands in the West. This research strategy was important to capture not only the different gendered ideals about marriage, but also about migration. I went into the project very much like a sociologist who might study across racial or class lines. I found it more difficult to understand some women in my study, not because they were women, but perhaps because they were from the upper class. On the other hand, sometimes it was difficult for me to connect with the working-class men in my study because they did not see me as working class.

9. *Hung, you are known as an ethnographer who can "talk to anyone," regardless of class, race, ethnicity, occupation, nation, or sex. What do you make of that quality, how do you deploy it, and how do you impart it to students? In other words, what's the secret?*

I don't think there's a secret, but I do think that I constantly have a desire to understand individual lives no matter where I travel, even when I am not doing fieldwork or interviewing a research subject. I always believe that everyone has an interesting story to tell about their lives. I think my childhood has a lot to do with how I am able to cross lines of difference easily and with great interest. I grew up in the housing projects of Mississippi where the boys rejected me in my surroundings because I was not an athletic kid and failed miserably at basketball in particular. I made great friends with the African American girls in the housing projects, who introduced me to the world of cross-gender and cross-racial friendships very early on. In those years, I also got to know many of the adults in the lives of my female Black friends. So I think the fact that I had to cross lines of difference to make friends made it a part of who I am, always interested in the worlds of people who are not like me. In my teaching, I always encourage my students to do projects and study subjects that enable them to cross those lines.

> *So it was class, and not so much gender that primarily shaped the inter-actions you had with men and women respondents?*

I think class probably accounts more for what results from interactions, but gender certainly also matters. For example, in many cases when I interviewed the women in my first book, many of them wanted to matchmake me with their family—and they also had a certain kind of interaction with me that was also very gendered, which I had to react to. I think in interviewing men, I also had to perform masculinity, by being less talkative, for example, or by being talkative about more masculine "stuff."

The Tenth Question
> *What was the worst (or most difficult, or most embarrassing) interview/ encounter you have had in the field?*

I talked about several embarrassing moments in my book, *For Better or for Worse,* but the most embarrassing one was when I was talking to a groom in my study at a restaurant in Los Angeles where he worked as a waiter. I had already interviewed his wife in Vietnam, who was waiting for paper-work to clear so she could join him. When I met him, he was skeptical about my intentions because, I think, he felt that I could not possibly understand his life; we were at that point very different people (he being a waiter and I aspired to be a professor). I had committed myself to tell my respondents the truth about myself if they asked questions about me because I expected them to tell me the truth about themselves. In this incident, the groom asked me how many times I had been to Vietnam. I told him I had been back seven times in a span of 3 years to visit my mother, even though I knew that it was very difficult for low wage grooms like him to go so frequently. Once I told him this, he got very angry, got up, and asked me to leave. I was very ashamed because it was the first time a respondent asked me to leave—in this case, he was quite hostile. I left feeling very discouraged and wondered for weeks why he had reacted the way he did, and what I could have done to prevent the situation.

In the hindsight of some years, what do you think you might have done to make that encounter run more smoothly?

I have actually thought a lot about this incident, and how it shapes my subsequent interviews. I do believe in the principle of sharing your lives with your respondents when they ask, and so I think I would have done the same thing. I think that man took it differently than many others would have taken it. Some men found it impressive that I could live out a transnational journey and encouraged it. In general I think that when we are truthful with our respondents, sharing with them our lives in ways we expect them to share theirs, they will know it and sense our authenticity. I believe this helps tremendously in most cases.

What did you really want to do for a living? Where were you afraid you would end up doing?

As a refugee kid growing up in the housing projects, I had no role model for a professional life, and therefore, I really did not know what I wanted to do for a living until I reached college. I ran away from home when I was 15 years old because I got into a fight with my father. I had to support myself working three different part-time jobs in my last 2 years of high school. One of the jobs was working as the guy who took orders from customers who wanted to refill their medication at the pharmacy of a drug store—I was the assistant to the assistant to the pharmacist. I remembered thinking that ultimately the job of the "assistant to the pharmacist" was such a good one and I aspired to that job! I was very afraid that I would end up doing physical labor—one of the three jobs I did to support myself was lifting boxes at a flea market and I remember hating it. The job at the drug store was so posh and in an air-conditioned room!

What's the study you never pursued, but always wanted to?

I regularly dream of doing a project about African American girls in the housing projects, perhaps about schooling or gender relations. This project would bring me back "home" in the same ways I think that going to Vietnam brought me home to my roots.

7.
NAZLI KIBRIA

1. *For over a decade you have published compelling analyses of various aspects of the Bangladesh Diaspora. What is the nature of your tie to Bangladesh, its people, and their fortunes around the world? Do these connections change with each new project? How do such connections propel your research?*

I am a Bangladeshi (or Bangali, as I prefer to call it) by birth. Many of my immediate family members, including my mother, live in Bangladesh; I have a transnational family life. My ties to Bangladesh are very strong and dense even though I actually spent very little time in the country when I was growing up. My father was a diplomat and so I grew up in the many different countries to which he was posted, such as Indonesia, Iran, and the United States. My parents were fierce Bangali nationalists who talked and dreamed about a free and independent Bangladesh long before it happened (in 1971). So I grew up with this nationalist ethos. I think this background has given me a particular interest in issues of identity as well as migration and social displacement, broadly speaking. And it has also given me a whole range of resources—social, cultural, linguistic—that I can deploy in my research on Bangladesh and the Bangladeshi Diaspora. The book that I am currently writing—on Islam and identity formation in the Bangladeshi Diaspora—has brought these interests and resources together in a powerful way for me.

2. *One of the projects we found fascinating involved interviews with women factory workers in Dhaka, Bangladesh to try to complicate the sense of what attracts them to participation in urban garment sectors. You seemed to have made a decision to focus particular attention on the "sending family household," and by doing this you got new insight into the contexts in which women are pushed and pulled to change their circumstance. Could you talk about how you came to this focus?*

I began by talking to the women workers themselves. These discussions pointed to the importance of the family context in their decision making. Theoretically too, I have always been interested in families and households as collective bodies that provide meaning to the lives of members. That was a crucial starting point to understanding where those decisions come from and how they emerge.

3. *You have withstood great trauma as a result of the recent terrorist bombings and assassinations in Bangladesh, and you have spoken eloquently of what the government must do to ensure justice for those who have been victimized. What has been your experience when you explain these realities to students?*

I have discovered through the years that talking about these issues elicits a range of reactions—positive and negative—from students, as well as from sociology colleagues. While I firmly believe that teaching and scholarship should not be focused per se on one's personal story, I am also committed to exposing the connections between "private troubles" and larger social and political realities. From this standpoint, I have made it a point to talk to students about some of the difficult issues that have loomed large in my own life. This includes my father's political assassination from a grenade attack in Bangladesh in 2005 as well as the autism of my 11-year-old son and the caregiving issues that surround his condition. Some students and colleagues react with discomfort to these discussions, which are perhaps too troubling to them as well as distant from their lives. There is also discomfort with the public display of emotion from a scholar, which is quite different from the on-screen Reality TV emotion that has become routinized in popular culture. There is uncertainty about how one should react. At the same time, I have found my experiences to be a bridge to many students, at times an opportunity for them to explore and perhaps talk about dimensions of their own lives that they have not talked out before. These range from losing a family member in a military conflict to coping with special needs siblings. At all times, my focus is on getting them to think about the larger social and political structures that undergird their "private" troubles.

4. *In this volume Hung Cam Thai talks about his interest in the experiences of returning international migrants to their home country of Viet Nam. Even though the cultural contexts are quite different, do you think there are enough commonalities to speak reasonably of "The returning worker?" Do you think one useful common focus might be the one you stress: uniformly constrained choices?*

Yes, I think it makes sense to think of "the returning worker," provided one also emphasizes the context of global inequality and low-skilled work. There are in fact significant high-skilled global labor flows today where the dynamics of work and return are quite different. But with respect to the low-skilled worker in the North who returns to the South, I think there are a lot of commonalities. That is, whether one is talking about a return to Vietnam as in Hung Cam Thai's work or a return to South Asia after working in the Persian Gulf states, we see how social and economic capital acquired abroad is "converted" to social status in the home country. We also see how these transnational status dynamics help low-skilled third world origin workers to cope with the degradations of their life and work in the industrialized North.

5. *Related to the last question, in your study of returned and returning labor migrants to Bangladesh your analysis disabuses us of the idea that most returnees are "pulled" to a happy, wholly volitional return. Instead, for most, the various constraints of context operate to severely limit choice. How did your interviews delve deeply enough to reveal the litany of all the "pushes" as well as the "pulls" to return.*

It is unfortunately the case that many if not most low-skilled international labor migrants from Bangladesh find themselves in migration regimes that offer few protections and rights to workers. Even though the migrants tend to suffer a great deal when they are abroad, the opportunity to work abroad and to make money is viewed by them as a privilege. Given these circumstances, it was not at all difficult to gather information about the "pushes" to return—the former migrants were more than willing to talk about them.

6. *Much of your research has clear policy implications, whether with respect to general immigration policies, or with respect to the treatment of individuals crossing borders of various sorts. How do you understand the role of your research as a foundation for policy? What do you do differently because your work has this character?*

My hope is to produce scholarship that can inspire and inform policy agendas and efforts. Because of this, I make a special effort to integrate analysis of the policy context into my writings. For example, if I am looking at women in the garment factories of Bangladesh, I also explore the national and international level policies, such as child labor agreements, that are part of the environment in which the women work in garment factories.

7. *In recent years, your work has focused on how people negotiate Muslim religious identities and Bangladeshi national identities. Has this work taken on special meaning in the post-9/11 climate? Do you see your work as responding in some way to larger narratives about Muslims and Islam that have emerged over the last decade?*

I began this project in 2000, a year before 9/11. But there is no doubt that the post-9/11 climate has shaped it in critical ways. Besides the obvious impacts of 9/11 on the lives of those of the Bangladeshi Muslim Diaspora, it is also the case that my work on this topic is being viewed and evaluated in a manner that it might not have been before 9/11. There has been an upsurge of academic and popular interest in Islam and Muslims, especially Muslims in North America and Western Europe. Even as my work perhaps benefits from this interest in terms of received attention, it also challenges what has been one of the central features of this interest—the homogenization of Islam and the Muslim experience. Both in the media and in scholarly writings, there is analysis of such topics as "Muslims in America" or "the Muslim world," often reflecting a premise of unitary identity. In my work I look at the experiences of those who are of shared national origin (Bangladeshi) and shared religious affiliation (Muslim). But I do so without the constrained lens of what has become a widespread assumption—that "being Muslim" is the most important feature of the lives of those who are Muslim. In short, my work highlights the tremendous diversity of experience and understanding among those who are Muslim.

8. *This question follows a bit from the last. In the United States, there is much talk about living in a "post-racial" America. As a sociologist who has studied racial and ethnic identity close-up, what do you make of this assertion? How do you continue to capture the changing dynamics of racial and ethnic identities given these new, widely circulated narratives about what race means today?*

The assertion of a "post-racial" America reflects what I believe to be a misunderstanding of "race" and the place of racial divisions in global and national systems of inequality. It reflects the desire to "pin down" the particular meanings of race, to give stability to race which actually does not exist. As highlighted by such noted events, from the 2008 election of President Obama to the arrest of Professor Henry Louis Gates in his own home in Cambridge, MA, the significance of race can change and vary, mediated by such powerful social structures as social class. My work on the Bangladeshi Diaspora in several different national contexts—Britain, the United States, the Arab Gulf states, Malaysia—has highlighted to me the continuing significance of race in the contemporary global order. Concurrently, it has made clear the difficulties of defining "race" with reference only to skin color. Instead, I see racial divisions reflecting the construction of naturalized and intrinsic difference from particular others, a construction that is reflective of the superior resources of one or more groups over others.

9. *Finally, much of your early work focused on the impact of globalization viewed largely through the family. Since you received your PhD from the University of Pennsylvania in 1986, the world has gotten "flatter," to borrow a phrase from Thomas L. Friedman's best-selling book. It is oft-repeated that students who succeed today must be able to compete in a global world. What, if anything, can sociologists offer our students to help them compete—or just live well—in a global world? What more can the discipline do?*

It is essential that sociologists make a greater effort, in their teaching and research, to move away from the America-centric perspectives that continue to dominate the field. It is definitely true that the discipline has become better in this respect since the mid-1980s. Comparative and non-America focused work is now generally encouraged and appreciated. At the same time, I do think that much of "basic sociology"—the materials that we teach in undergraduate courses—continues to be America-centric. The reference point for a lot of basic concepts continues to be America or "Western" societies. For example, one of the undergraduate courses that I have taught for many years in this country is sociology of the family. It is still the case that the majority of textbooks in this area are organized around an idealized conception of the family life course that is somewhat relevant for Western industrialized societies—childhood, adolescence, dating, marriage, divorce. But I do think that a critical sociological perspective, accompanied by honest and rigorous analysis, can do much to help students deal with the complexities of the emerging world because it makes visible the global context and its significance to their lives.

The Tenth Question
   What was the worst (or most difficult, or most embarrassing) interview/ encounter you have had in the field?

You saved the best for last. One of the worst encounters I had occurred during my dissertation fieldwork, when I was spending time with recently arrived Vietnamese refugees to the United States. I decided to spend some time observing customer interactions at a Vietnamese grocery store and I thought I had developed a polite and professional rapport with the owner of a store, a man in his 40s. I had interviewed him earlier and he had agreed to let me hang out at the store and take notes. On my second visit to the store he pulled out a small ring box and proposed marriage to me. I was utterly shocked and unprepared. I quickly declined the ring and the offer and left the store. Needless to say, I did not continue my fieldwork in that particular store. I also made it a point to not speak about the incident to others in the community as I did not want the store owner to lose face over it. I was able to complete my fieldwork without any such further incident, but it is an incident I will never forget.

   What did you really want to do for a living? What were you afraid you would end up doing?

I really wanted to be a journalist, an international journalist covering events around the world. In rebellion from the prescribed roles of my mother's generation, I was afraid that I would be a homemaker. I must mention that especially since the arrival of my two children, I have since that time developed enormous respect for the work of homemakers and caregivers.

   What's the study you never pursued, but always wanted to?

I'm not sure how to answer that question because the study I want to pursue has changed so much. In graduate school I wanted to pursue a dissertation topic which I ultimately did not for a variety of reasons. I had wanted to look at women political leaders at the highest levels (e.g., Indira Gandhi, Margaret Thatcher) with the particular goal of understanding the paradox of women political leaders in patriarchal societies. More recently, I have wanted to go back and do follow-up observations and interviews with those who have participated in my research before. In other words, I have wanted to "go back" and talk to the same women garment workers in Bangladesh 20 years later to see where they are and what has happened to them. I have carefully preserved the confidential information I gathered on where they were from—their village of origin. So who knows, I may still be able to do it.

8.
RHACEL PARRENAS

1. *You have undertaken three major studies of so-called globalized work-ers. How has that term changed in your mind over time? And has your view of the nature of women's globalized work changed?*

In the past 10 years, I have done two studies that focus on "globalized" work-ers, more specifically migrant Filipina workers, the first being my compara-tive study of migrant Filipina domestic workers in Rome and Los Angeles and the second being my ongoing study on migrant Filipina entertainers in Tokyo's nightlife industry. The other, which is the second study I undertook, did not focus on the workers per se but instead it addressed the situation of the children of migrant workers who have been left behind in the Philippines.

I tend not to use the term *globalized* when I refer to the migrant women who I have studied in the past and present, because I think it suggests that they are somehow free-floating and able to enter and leave countries freely. But if I am to use the term *globalized* to describe them, it is to recognize that they as workers have a consciousness of the multiple destinations that are in need of their labor as domestic workers or care workers. With a consciousness of these multiple destinations and the different levels of difficulty for entry that these destinations grant prospective migrants, Filipino women who pursue migrant domestic work usually follow a path of serial migration: they begin their global journey at a more accessible destination, for instance Singapore, then continue to a less accessible one, for instance Hong Kong or Taiwan, and end at one of the more prized destinations, which include Canada, Israel, and Italy. The same pattern could be said of nurses, who would begin in Singapore in hopes they would eventually land a contract to work first in Great Britain and then in the United States.

I think the globalization of the Filipino workforce has resulted in what I call a hierarchy of destinations. Nations that offer better work conditions, from less restrictive residency visas to better pay, are more coveted as destinations. They are also more expensive and hence less accessible. For instance, a prospective migrant should expect to pay migrant brokers $3,000 to work in Hong Kong, $5,000 to secure a labor contract in Taiwan, and even more to get smuggled into Italy. This hierarchy speaks of the institutionalization of Philippine emigration.

 2. *How important to your analysis of migrant Filipina workers was the "imagined global community"? How did it serve as an analytic tool for you to make sense of workers' lives?*

An important point that I have tried to emphasize in my work is the wide scale of Philippine migration. The large number of destinations of migrant Filipinos makes the nature of Philippine migration unique, especially as migrants from other countries tend to only go to select nations. To account for the wide scale of Philippine migration, I felt compelled to distinguish the international community of migrant Filipino workers from what is known in the literature as a "transnational community." The latter concept only links sending and receiving communities of migrants, which then fails to account for the possibility that migrants maintain relations across various receiving communities in the Diaspora. With the formulation of an "imagined global community," which is a concept that builds from the work of Benedict Anderson (1991) and his discussion of how the circulation of print media enabled the conception of the nation as an "imagined community," I am able to account for the Diaspora as not just the forced scattering of people from a homeland but also show how a community forms and extends from the homeland to tie together various destinations of the Diaspora. I believe the concept of an "imagined global community" unavoidably situates the migration of Filipino workers in a diaspora. As such, it challenges us to (1) account for relations of migrants across the Diaspora; (2) compare and contrast the way migrants view various destinations in the Diaspora (e.g., hierarchy of destinations); and (3) consciously weigh the characteristics of members in each destination of the Diaspora. Hence, in a variety of ways, this concept allows us to further qualify our knowledge and understanding of Philippine migration.

> *This expansion of the contingent meanings of Diaspora makes such good analytic sense. Does it also stretch the limits of the term as meaning a permanently displaced population—"a scattering of seeds?"*

Most Filipino migrants with the exception of migrants in Australia, Canada, and the United States perceive themselves as temporary settlers in the various host societies that welcome them as workers. It is for this reason that most of them leave their children behind in the Philippines. As women who I met in Japan frequently told me, "We earn in Japan so we can spend money in the Philippines." Despite this homebound orientation in settlement in the Diaspora, its very formation—the scattering—inevitably leads to a permanently displaced population. Even though most will return to the Philippines, migration patterns tell us that another group, a newer crop of migrant workers will replace them. Considering this constant flow of migrant workers to and from the Philippines, we must recognize that the presence of a displaced Filipino population living elsewhere from the Philippines is a permanent fixture in our global society.

> 3. *In the first few pages of your book,* Children of Global Migration *(Parrenas 2005) you tell the fascinating story of how uniquely (and only in the Philippines) your bearing and body movement mark you to others as male. You say, "In the Philippines, my gender determined my sex (3). At that point, something "clicked." Can you elaborate on what the lesson was, and why it was important to your analysis of transnational families?*

During the two years I spent in the Philippines, I was often mistaken to be transgender, someone biologically male who chose to perform a feminine gender. Ironically, I am biologically female who was not intentionally transgressing gender by acting feminine. Because abiding with gender normative

patterns did not lead to my social acceptance, I realized that our gender identity also determines our sex. In other words, we are seeing the *naturalization
of gender*. What this means is slight hints of masculinity in my feminine
being—for instance strutting with confidence on the streets, sitting with
my legs apart and squatting—led to my labeling as biologically male. The
logic of those around me was that I could not hide my male identity despite
my efforts to present a feminine gender. This told me that in the Philippines
there is the belief that we have natural gender attributes that coincide with
our sex and that sometimes these natural attributes creep up on us even if we
consciously try to present an alternative gender.

> *So despite the obvious loosening of gender norms, the rigid beliefs about
> "essential" or "natural" qualities remain?*

Yes, the loosening of gender norms is stalled by staunch gender essentialist
views that contest transgressions of gender. This means that we can accomplish a variety of gender practices but these practices must comfortably fit a
box assigned to one particular sex category.

> 4. *We found that the term* nakakabobo *(as you explain, an adjective
> attached to work that slowly drives you stupid), points to the varieties of
> dislocations experienced by those migrant women workers who come
> from some wealth and education and end up in subservience. What did
> you learn about how women cope with such challenges, and have you
> taken away any lessons from their experience?*

The description of migration as *nakakabobo* tells us that migration is not just
a brain drain that results in the depletion of skills and knowledge sources of
one nation by another. It tells us that migration represents the squandering
of skills for an individual migrant worker. Many Filipina domestic workers
do not only have college degrees but had been working professionals prior to
migration. They worked as teachers, accountants, office managers, and bank
workers in the Philippines but pursued migrant domestic work because it
offered greater financial rewards than did their professional jobs. The primary way that women cope with their deskilling is to stress the material
gains enabled by migration. They exchange one form of capital for another
as the increase in their economic capital comes at the expense in the loss of
their human capital. The experience of *nakakabobo* offers a lesson for all of us
as it calls attention to an inequality not recognized in discussions of migration studies or globalization studies. It adds a layer to the notion of the brain
drain. Labor migration does not only indicate that skills are transferred from

a poorer to a richer country (as we see with the case of nurses for instance), but labor migration also involves the removal of skills from a poor country only to be depleted in the rich country. We see the latter type of brain drain in the case of migrant domestic work.

5. *So few ethnographers spend time with, interview, or otherwise include children in their studies. What led you to focus on children?*

I decided to write a book on children because they were glaringly absent in discussions on transnational families. It was important to focus on the children because we need to account for their desires and priorities, which, following the argument of feminist family scholars such as Barrie Thorne we cannot assume would reflect those of their parents. Feminists have long told us that the family is not a collective institution but instead one whose members have different interests, priorities, and desires. Prior to my book *Children of Global Migration* (Parrenas 2005) the perspective of children surprisingly was absent in our discussions of transnational families. I focused on children in order to provide a more holistic account of transnational family life. I wanted to juxtapose their perspectives to those of the mothers I had interviewed for my book *Servants of Globalization* (Parrenas 2001).

How did the kids make sense of you as an interviewer?

Children often constructed me as a reporter or a journalist who had been genuinely interested in their experience. At the same time, they knew I was a "foreigner" and not a local Filipina. For the most part, my status as a foreigner is why they were drawn to me. Many wanted to know about life outside the Philippines. I think their curiosity was motivated by their desire to know about the life of their parents outside the country.

6. *Sociologists often cite their own feelings of marginality as an explanation for their particular (and often peculiar) take on the world (e.g., see Goetting and Fenstermaker 1995; Laslett and Thorne 1997). You note in passing that at the age of 13 you were forced to adjust to a completely new way of life. Did these experiences—surely both exciting and traumatic— foster a sociological sensibility?*

My experience of migration at the age of 13 years old exposed me to plenty of contradictions that without doubt fostered a sociological sensibility in me. If not that, it at least encouraged this strong desire for me to make sociological sense of the contradictions that I saw firsthand in my family. These contradictions included seeing my parents toil as low-wage service workers in the United States, even though both of them had doctorates in education and held high-level occupations in the Philippines. During our first few years in the United States, both my parents worked at the Charles Hotel in Cambridge, Massachusetts. My father worked as a room service waiter while my mother was a hotel housekeeper. Another contradiction was seeing all of my maternal aunts work as domestic workers in New York City, when they all had grown up not only in a fairly privileged family but in the wealthiest family in the province of Antique in the Philippines.

I think the contradictions in the labor market experiences of my older family members have always haunted me. These contradictions are actually the motivation behind my quest to become not just a sociologist, but a sociologist whose expertise is on labor and migration. If I had not become an academic sociologist, I would probably have become a practicing sociologist, more precisely a labor organizer. Seeing my parents and aunts struggle in their low-status jobs instilled in me this strong consciousness to work toward easing the plight of low-wage workers. This led me, for instance, to volunteer at Asian Immigrant Women's Advocate while an undergraduate student at UC Berkeley, I wanted to work with low-wage Chinese immigrant garment workers and Filipino immigrant nursing home workers in the Bay Area.

I think these contradictions exposed me to the various structural barriers that hampered my family's opportunities in the United States, such as the non-convertibility of the educational degrees of my parents from the Philippines and the loss of their networks and access to more secure employment after migration. Even as a child I knew that my parents could not "convert" their educational degrees to comparable jobs in the United States, but of course I could not quite make sense of why that was or what that meant sociologically. One other curiosity that I had as a child was that the *experience* and *feelings* of my parents and aunts doing low-status jobs did not reflect their high-status backgrounds in the Philippines. I think these two curiosities led me to study labor not only as an undergraduate but also as a graduate student. I can say that as much as fostering a sociological sensibility in me the contradictions that I experienced and witnessed as a child have more than anything inspired me to become a sociologist. Perhaps not surprisingly I even devoted an entire chapter to making sense of my parents' and aunts' experience in my first book *Servants of Globalization* and developed a concept which I aptly phrased "contradictory class mobility." I think these contradictions still motivate me a great deal and follow me in my choice of research projects as a sociologist.

7. *In your description of "father-away" families (Parrenas 2008b), we were*
   both struck by the similarity of difficulties men everywhere have achiev-
   ing intimacy with children when they are not present. For whatever
   reason fathers are "away" (divorce, military deployment, frequent work
   travel), they and their children suffer the same sort of embarrassment
   and discomfort you describe. Are there any insights here about what we
   might call the bondage of masculinity?

Your term *bondage of masculinity* aptly captures the predicament of transnational fathers who feel they must demonstrate authority and control and
command discipline in their children in order to fulfill their duties as a father
from a distance. To perform fathering as it is defined by mainstream society
is what they do transnationally. We could thus say that the "bondage of masculinity" culturally arises from what Candace West and Don Zimmerman
(1987) have called "doing gender" Likewise, we could say there is a "trap of
femininity" that subjugates transnational mothers. By mothering from afar,
they "do gender." They not only nurture, but they also exhibit feelings of sor-
row or pain; not being emotionally distraught over being unable to nurture
in proximity would violate gender expectations and render them bad mothers. As good mothers, transnational mothers "do gender" by demonstrating
misery over their inability to nurture up close. The ideas of the "bondage of
masculinity" and the "trap of femininity" are manifestations of the social
pressure to "do gender" in our everyday life.

8. *"[I did participant observation in a club that] employs Filipinas exclu-*
   sively, in a seedy area of Tokyo amid pachinko parlors, soap lands
   (places where men are offered a full service bath), and pink salons
   (where men are serviced with masturbation)" (Parrenas 2008a: 140).
   You go on to say—in some contradiction to the literature—that "Hostess
   work involves care work, sex work (but without penetration or provision
   of sex), entertainment work, and boundary work" (141). In the context
   of these facts, it is so startling to read of all the misconceptions you first
   labored with before you got to know migrant hostesses (and hostessing).
   Are there any general lessons here about sociological claims to validity
   and ethnographic research?

I personally avoid sociological claims of validity because as a feminist sociologist, I claim to at most provide partial knowledge of experiences. At most
I can only present what Donna Haraway (1988) calls "situated knowledge."
As a feminist sociologist, I aim to present the lived experience of individuals
from their perspective. There is a limit to the extent to which I could under-

stand their experience, as I am constrained for instance by my own ideo-logical beliefs. Undoing those beliefs is possible but it is a constant challenge. Because my goal in my research is to present lived experiences from the per-spective of my subjects, I tremendously value ethnographic research and the use of a variety of methodological tools including participant observation and interviews. The key to achieving a successful sociological study is to be open and willing to undo one's assumptions as one gets to know subjects. But I also do see my job as a sociologist as helping us—including them—better make sense of their actions. Hence, as a sociologist, I acknowledge that I label their work, present it using my own interpretation, construct categories to map out their actions systematically, box them and group them according to ways they might not even group themselves.

For instance, my subjects would not personally label what they do as "sex work" and likewise they would not call their action of rejecting customers slyly and not blatantly as "boundary work." By calling them "sex workers" I acknowledge and label their work of sexually titillating customers. It is one I distinguish from prostitution, which they would appreciate, but I do place their work in a continuum with prostitution, which many of them would find bothersome. This latter point tells me that as a feminist sociologist, even though I try to accurately describe the lived experience of people, my depic-tion is one that the people I describe might not think is true. To show that my subjects would disagree with my categorization is one that I try to acknowl-edge in my writings to demonstrate the partial but *grounded* knowledge I present in my work.

9. *From your work we are not only reminded of the central place women's home labors hold in understanding their global condition, but also we learn of your assertion of a "gender revolution" against women's eman-cipation. What future analysis would you undertake—or advise your stu-dents to undertake—to understand these disturbing global dynamics?*

A common question addressed in the literature on women and migration is the following: *How does gender change in the process of women's migration?* The resounding conclusion by most scholars is that women experience some level of gender emancipation. Among other things, their lesser economic dependency is said to lead to their greater power vis-à-vis men. In contrast to the literature, I find that migration does not result in gender emancipa-tion. Instead, I find that men and society resist the gender transformations encouraged by migration. I should note that I am not alone in my views. In agreement with me for instance is Cecilia Menjivar (2006) who found in her study of Guatemalan families in Los Angeles and Salvadoran families in San Francisco the rejection of greater household responsibilities by men who find their wives earning more than them. In addition to my different findings, I pause and question the resounding positive outlook on the achievement of gender emancipation in migration or economic globalization in general because the literature (1) ignores the gender inequalities that feminists in host societies document, regarding the lives of non-migrant women; (2) constructs gender relations in the country of origin as backwards; (3) reduces gender to economics; and (4) supports modernization views of gender. To underscore gender inequalities, I would encourage women and migration scholars to more closely engage with feminist theories and feminist studies in general. I would encourage those interested in studying women and economic globalization to closely examine the significance of women's continued labor market segmentation in feminine occupations. I would also encourage them to examine the income inequalities between men and women. Many inequalities underlie globalization and gender is just one of them.

The Tenth Question
> What was the worst (or most difficult, or most embarrassing) encounter you have had in the field?

When I was doing fieldwork in Italy in 1995, I recall thinking that I must have been transported back to pre-1960s USA. This is because of my unfamiliarity with the racism that I experienced there, which I could only imagine would have been similar to the way of life in pre-1960s USA. This is because the racism that I was subjected to as a Filipino in Italy was quite blatant. Filipinos, for instance, did nothing but domestic work in Italy. I recall telling my friends, "If one were not a priest or nun in Italy, one would be a domestic worker if Filipino." As such, I was often mistaken for a domestic worker, which was a labeling that doubly displaced me because it not only offended me—being a graduate student at an elite university—but made me feel guilty for being offended, because by being offended I was distinguishing myself from all the other Filipinos around me as someone above them, that is, someone who would *never* do domestic work. This displaced identity I had as a Filipino in Italy made me want to leave the field immediately. Additionally, as a Filipino in Italy, one is subjected to an invisible racial line. Before living in Italy, never had I experienced walking into a restaurant where everyone would suddenly stop what they were doing and stare at me. One could have heard a pin drop. Their silence and stares told me that I did not belong there. For sure I did not, as the restaurant was an upscale neighborhood café. Ironically, the café was located in my neighborhood, a mere block from my apartment.

What did you really want to do for a living? What were you afraid you would end up doing?

I always thought that I would be a labor organizer. I even volunteered at the appropriate organizations as an undergraduate student so I could secure employment doing advocacy work for low-wage workers after graduation. Then, a professor during the first semester of my senior year encouraged me to pursue my PhD and become an academic. She told me that the way I asked questions in class indicated to her I would make for a solid academic. She must have known what she was talking about because I have thrived as an academic and thoroughly enjoy what I do. This industry—academia—is one that is closed and unfamiliar to most people, including students. I think many could not imagine spending so many more years as a student after undergrad, and with very little financial compensation. This had been true for me. I lacked the cultural capital to know that a job as a professor was even an option for me. So, now I do what my professor did so many years ago: whenever I have an undergraduate student who I could see thinks like an academic and asks questions like an academic, I always encourage them to consider getting their PhD. I especially get excited about doing this when my student is a feminist. There are not enough of us around.

What's the study you never pursued, but always wanted to?

This is perhaps the easiest question for me to answer because I often think about this study, more like fantasize about it. I very much would like to do a racial comparative study on migrant health professionals in the United States. More specifically, I would like to undertake an ethnography of a hospital and examine the racial incorporation of Black and Filipino migrant health professionals. I would like to see how race is constructed in their job placement, how race shapes their interactions with patients and co-workers, and how racial beliefs are constructed, and change, in everyday actions. I would like to do this study because not only are there not enough works on Black professional migrants but we have yet to do a racial comparative study on contemporary skilled labor migrants. Doing so would expand not only our understanding of migration but also race as a social construction.

SECTION III

STUDYING GENDER, CRIME, AND VIOLENCE IN THE ERA OF MASS INCARCERATION

9.

MEDA CHESNEY-LIND

1. *Joanne Belknap (2004) describes you as "the mother of feminist crimi-*
   nology." At this point in your career, what does this title mean to you? Is
   it something you envisioned for yourself when you began your career?
   Is it something you ever imagined when you were on faculty at a com-
   munity college early in your career?

I'm a bit surprised and honored that someone would think of me in those
terms. Certainly, when I began doing work on women and crime, I was well
aware that there were risks doing the sort of work I was drawn to, particularly if one were looking for an academic job. Some of my closest friends were
being denied tenure for doing what I considered to be outstanding work on
gender. So, actually I went to the community colleges so that I could continue to study women and crime, even though it was a trifle hard, given the
workload.

I also don't know that I can say that I thought much about my "career" as an academic. I backed into teaching in the community colleges to support my graduate studies. Then I got a job, and finally I was able to re-invent myself several times so that I could do the sort of research that blends my twin passions of gender and criminology. I know this sounds terribly accidental, but again, in the years that I was in college, there were so many doors that were effectively closed to us (law and medicine) and what was offered (traditional women's jobs), was poorly paid and dead end, that the academy seemed to offer those of us in my generation some semblance of opportunity. While much of this was, in retrospect, an illusion, we did not quite know that then. We had energy, youth, and the 60s at our backs, recall.

2. *One reason you may have that title is that your work has shaped discussions of sex, gender, and justice significantly, and in pioneering ways. What encourages you most about the development of feminist criminology over the course of your career? What troubles you the most?*

I never imagined that I would see so many young women in the field of criminology and criminal justice. This is just wonderful for the field. In a recent analysis I did of the program of the American Society of Criminology Meetings for 2009, I discovered exactly how powerful the focus on gender and crime has become. The meeting was organized into 137 area/sub-area groupings, with 1,419 submissions in total. The largest number of submissions to any one category on the program came with 52 panels submitted to the area/sub-area entitled "Gender, Crime and Justice: Gender and Offending." Two non-gender topics tied for second with 41 submissions each ("Corrections: Reentry" and "Juvenile Delinquency and Juvenile Justice Policy: Causes and Correlates of Delinquency"). These were followed by "Gender, Crime and Justice: Sexual and Physical Violence Against Women" with 38 submissions. Other areas of the field, even rather significant ones drew far fewer submissions; for example, "Theory and Research on Violence and Crime: Causes of Violence" (12) or "Organized, Organizational and White Collar Crime: White Collar Crime" (15). Essentially two of the top four areas in the entire field of criminology (as arrayed by the panels for the main academic body of the field) were feminist criminology topics. That said, this kind of success can sometimes be a challenge to manage; first, there's just the sheer work involved when we, the women, have to put together a huge chunk of the ASC program. I also suspect that some of our "success" is a function of the fact that these areas are seen as "add-ons" to the important (read "male") criminology, so despite our numbers, we still have a ways to go to be seen as a meaningful part of the field.

Christine Wenneras and Agnes Wold's work, published in the prestigious journal *Science* (1997), explored the awarding of postdoctoral fellowships in Sweden where because of a lawsuit, they were able to review actual applications as well as the score sheets. After a careful regression assessment of nine possible variables (including a number of "productivity" variables such as numbers of publications, citations, and journal prestige), they found that only two variables: "being male" and "knowing a reviewer" affected getting one of these awards. They concluded that a woman would need to be "on average 2.5 times as good" on their measures to be rated as highly as a male by reviewers. Sadly, this did not surprise me, and despite the age of the study, I fear things are not much better today.

Do you think that in some ways, the shift to the study of "gender and crime" has become disconnected from its feminist origins? Or is feminist criminology alive and well?

The Division on Women and Crime of the American Society of Criminology recently launched *Feminist Criminology* as their journal, so that is a good sign. However, the political backlash against feminism (and the word *feminism*) that was launched in the Reagan era has clearly taken its toll. The concept here is semantic derogation, where words attached to groups that are being vilified themselves become problematic (and people want to distance themselves from those words). Think of all the ways that African Americans have referred to themselves over the past centuries from "colored" to "Negro" to "Black" to African American. That said, we have to fight to avoid collusion with efforts to erase the word *feminist* from our lexicon. Being scholars who advocate feminism means that we understand that gender is a fundamental organizing principle of the social world, *and* we are committed to working to make that social world more equitable (Sprague 2005: 3). For feminist criminology, that means working to understand how both racism and sexism interact with (and are enmeshed within) the formal system of social control. That means researching and documenting not just gender, but also patriarchy; studying and explicating not just race but also institutional racism.

Gender has become a relatively "hot" topic in the academy (and this is reflected in the ASC program numbers), and I'm somewhat ambivalent about that "success." But I am greatly encouraged that instead of the "old" days when we had (and I remember those times) one panel on gender for the entire Pacific Sociological Association, we are a huge part of the program, and people want to be identified with this research (instead of fleeing it).

3. *You have written about your life as an academic "on the margins." Since so many feminist scholars speak of their careers that way, what "margins" do you find yourself on? Why is it so important to study the experiences of girls in the juvenile justice system outside of Criminal Justice or Criminology departments? What does a feminist analysis add to these conversations that is otherwise left out?*

Working within a vital Women's Studies Program means that I'm often challenged both theoretically and methodologically. Most recently, I have been teaching our feminist methods class, and I confess that I've learned as much as I've taught. Feminist scholars like Joey Sprague have urged critical scholars to re-think "methodology" with an eye toward epistemology, research methodology, and research methods (2005). More than that, feminists have called attention to the shortcomings of masculinist "science" which is generally unreflective of important issues of power and authority in research settings. Other good ideas that come from feminist methodology include "paying attention to what's missing," the importance of "studying up" instead of "studying down," and working from the standpoint of the disadvantaged.

Feminist theory has also a great deal to offer theoretical criminology. Right now, I'm very much interested in the importance of "theorizing patriarchy" to use Sylvia Walby's (1989) wonderful phrase. Those of us interested in the formal systems of social control obviously need to think about the ways that patriarchy interfaces with the criminal justice system. Much of my early work focused on this, and I'm very interested in returning to that project in my next book.

4. *The 21st century opened with a "mean girl" craze. It is said "mean girls" can be found everywhere. Even in the academy? If so, what does this dynamic say about feminism in general and feminist criminology in particular?*

We know that disempowered groups are always encouraged to engage in what Freire called "horizontal violence," often policing their own members. The social context for girls and women fighting is patriarchy, where men often are the reason women are fighting, the audience for the fight, and the winners at the end. I'm not a big fan of the "mean girl" stuff, because as Katherine Irwin and I said in *Beyond Bad Girls* (2007), the stereotype tracks too closely to the images of women as "manipulative bitches." We also know that covert aggression is not the exclusive province of girls (think Karl Rove). We certainly need to know about covert or indirect aggression so that when it is deployed against us, we know what is going on, and can deal with it effectively.

That said, not all feminists are women and not all women are feminists. Indeed, there are some women, including women in the academy, who pride themselves on being "one of the boys." So, sometimes you are blindsided if you think that you are speaking to a colleague, assuming like values and orientations, only to discover that you have been "played" by someone who is far more interested in male approval than you imagined. That's why I mentioned that *all* of us need to be aware of the possibility of covert aggression coming from a variety of possible sources. Some of the biggest perpetrators, I think, are men, but we can all recall times when a woman disappointed us. But again, there's plenty of reward for women to betray other women to please men, so we just go on. And what gets us through is the friendships between women. They listen to the tales, provide solace, and patch us up, so we can get back into the fray.

5. *You are an inspiration for both scholars and practitioners. Who are your intellectual inspirations? How do you maintain your energy and interests even as criminal and juvenile justice systems continue to expand their punitive reach into the lives of adolescent girls?*

Some of my greatest role models are visionary practitioners who have worked with girls and women in the criminal justice system. I'm thinking here of people like Marian Daniel, who was the author of one of my favorite assessments about delinquency programs. She famously noted that "For years, people assumed that all you have to do to make a program designed for boys work for girls is to paint the walls pink and take out the urinals" (Daniel, 1996: 34). Marian started a female-only probation program in Baltimore, Maryland; it didn't cost a penny more, and it got girls out of detention. Marian has a wonderful sense of humor, and she's a great role model to others in the field, particularly younger African American professionals. I'm profiling her in the work I'm currently doing for the National Institute of Justice. I think we need to forge more professional and person relationships across the professional divides, and that also has the effect of bringing us in touch with a far more diverse group of colleagues.

Of course, as a young scholar, I had my share of mentors and supporters. Here, a shout out to Lee Bowker, in particular, who helped both Joy Pollock and myself when we were students at Whitman College. Lee later went on to do pioneering work on violence against women, and also has served as an expert witness to get women out of prison who are doing time for killing their abusers. Lee was a fighter, not a button-down scholar, and when I first met him (and to this day) he was quite irreverent. I guess I learned from the best!

6. *What exactly does it mean to be a feminist criminologist during a time when many of our students are reluctant to even identify as feminists, since they are told that if they do they won't get a job. What advice do you give students who want to do what you do?*

Whenever I hear statements like this about feminism, I'm always tempted to open with one of my favorite quotes: "I myself have never been able to find out precisely what feminism is: I only know that people call me a feminist whenever I express sentiments that differentiate me from a doormat or a prostitute—Rebecca West, 1913." But seriously, the word *feminist* has been subjected to two decades of demonization by a relentless political backlash, so it is no mystery why younger women shrink from the label. In a misogynistic world, which has not receded despite the recent election, it's still bad to be a strong woman.

Of course, being in Women's Studies I am also aware that the word does not work for many who are seeking justice for girls and women. bell hooks famously noted that we have trouble coming to a consensus about "what feminism is" and she argues for a "shift in expression from 'I am a feminist' to 'I advocate feminism'" in recognition that the feminist struggle is really about ending sexism and all forms of group oppression (hooks 2000: 32).

As to what advice I'd give those starting out, that is a hard question to answer, but I would say that you need to follow your passion. I also think that you need to be committed to more than your "career" to make any lasting difference. Candidly, I didn't start out to have a career, it happened along the way as I was trying to make the world a better place. Fortunately, some folks thought that what I was finding was worth reading. Now, I just wish we could end mass incarceration in my lifetime. I feel as if it happened on "our" watch, and we need to be part of dismantling it.

A number of scholars now argue that the national investment in mass incarceration has undermined the investment in other important social institutions, including higher education. What implications might the nation's shifting priorities have on the critical research and writing conducted by scholars like you?

We held a Teach In on the draconian budget cuts on our campus this fall, and my job was to talk about our Governor's choice to fund prison cells instead of classrooms. In the current great recession, I'm astonished that so little is being said about the enormous costs of our twin addictions to militarism and incarceration. Since I'm wearing my criminological hat, let me talk about the cost of imprisonment. If you look at the data over time, it's very clear that the nation pulled money out of higher education in particular; between 1987 and 2007 the amount of money the State has spent on corrections more than doubled (increasing 127%) while funding for higher education stayed essentially static increasing by an anemic 21% during the same time period (Pew Center on the States 2008). Since the cost of college soared during those decades, most of the increase was born by our students and their families as tuitions soared, and low income youth struggle to pay the new surging bills for even "public education."

Since most states are now struggling to pay the bills, you would think that the failed and demonstrably racist "war on drugs," which has fueled the prison boom, would be the subject of a vibrant discussion (at both the local and national level), and yet with the exception of Senator Jim Webb, most national leaders, including our first African American President, are curiously silent. We need to educate our students that they have been directly harmed by this cost-shifting so that they can put ending mass incarceration on their "to do" list.

7. *As a feminist criminologist, the voices of girls and women are central to your work. What challenges does this commitment pose in the more quantitatively oriented social sciences? What is the benefit of remaining committed to your approach?*

Well, to quote Lee Bowker about the publication bias in what he called "gate-keeper" journals when they received work that is feminist in content: "I think I have found the answer to the question, 'What is the correct methodology for carrying out feminist research?' It is 'Whatever methodology you didn't use'" (Bowker 1988: 171).

As someone seeking to use my research to better the lives of girls and women, I actually advocate a mixed methods approach. That way, the qualitative work we do can't be quite as easily dismissed. But of course, we have to talk to girls and women, and actually you learn an incredible amount when you do this. I also urge us to read the books that are increasingly being produced by the vibrant Convict Criminology crowd, though they lament having so few women in their ranks. But conversations, particularly if they are gathered in a more naturalistic setting where you can also see the context that produces the commentary is very, very important to understanding the "choices" that young people are being forced to make. It would be wonderful if we could all do this the way the "classic" anthropologists and ethnographers did their work, but that often is not realistic. Yet I know of outstanding work that is being done in feminist criminology by emerging scholars that mix advocacy for girls (and gender-responsive programming) with interviews/conversations with girls in those settings. It's hard listening to some of these stories, but very, very important. I also think increasingly about involving young women in participatory action research would be a good goal, so that everyone is engaged in changing and making the world better for young people.

8. *Much of your work—professional and personal—is committed to "truth telling." You've told the truth in your research about girls' experiences with victimization and their subsequent entrance into the criminal justice system. More recently, you've told the truth about girls' violence and the conditions of detention facilities for girls. On your own campus, you have told the truth about seemingly trivial yet insidious displays of sexism and misogyny. Telling the truth is an important feminist ideal but given the popular feminist backlash and increased opportunities for women to be "one of the boys," as you say, is it worth it?*

As you get older, you realize that you have warm and wonderful memories of people who are no longer here. That's very hard, but it also focuses the mind. Our lives are all we ultimately have as our legacy, and you want to look backwards and be proud of what you did and how you lived your life. I've told younger women who speak of the challenges they face as they quit jobs rather than do something demeaning (or put up with harassment), that they will look back on those moments as a badge of honor, even if it is quite stressful at the time. So, nope, no regrets—at least about the things you mention. If anything, I wish I'd done more or accomplished more, especially in my own home town, which runs terrible facilities for girls (and boys). My current project is to document those conditions to try to shame the polite judges that occasionally have to listen to me, to do far better for Hawaii's young people than they have. Of course, that's my beat, but every one of us needs to remember those under lock and key, and not get complacent about what's happening behind those doors. I learned this first teaching in prison, and I re-learn it every decade. The fact that during my "watch" the United States has become the world's largest incarcerator horrifies me. As many have noted, the criminal justice system has functioned really for the past 30 years or so as the "new Jim Crow." Think Henry Louis Gates who was arrested for breaking into his own home.

9. *Recently, your work has extended beyond girls' pathways to detention and incarceration to the conditions in which girls are confined. What do we need to know about the conditions in which girls are held?*

One of the things that struck me looking at the two sides of my town's detention center was the degree to which things have *not* changed in these facilities. Certainly, I'd given talks to workers about girls' needs, but when it came to the place where girls (and boys) are locked up, nothing had changed in the 40 years since I first saw the place. We still have way too much idleness, isolation, and the girls get far fewer programs than the boys. The boys fear the violent guards and other violent boys; the girls are over-policed and over-punished. The girls have far less space, and the boys have a basketball court, but many are in "lockdown" in their rooms. Too much isolation, too little school, and virtually no one visits. I gathered data in the room where the visitors were supposed to come, and almost no one ever showed up. The few parents I did see were visiting boys. I never saw a white girl in the facility, though there were a few white boys. Almost all were kids of color. I tried to tell these stories to the judges who put the kids there, but I was listened to politely and then ushered out. They were very busy in their committee meetings. Again, I feel so frustrated and guilty that I've not done more. We also need to look at ways to work around these issues that are more accessible to those who have the power to change things. I'm not sure academic articles are enough, though.

The Tenth Question
What was the worst (or most difficult, or most embarrassing) interview/ field encounter you've had?

Well, I was teaching in the prison, and the course was Marriage and the Family. One of my worst attributes is that I often speak without thinking. In this case, one of the young women taking my class came up to ask me about a project she wanted to do for the course (the facility, at that time was a mixed facility holding both women and men). She said she'd like to study incest, and without thinking I said, "Why, that's a pretty boutique project." At which point she said, "Well most of the ladies in here have had that experience." I gulped, and said, you should definitely do the project, which she did. That's how I learned about the importance of studying sexual violence in the lives of women in prison. And it's also why I dedicated my first book to Michele Alvey, who taught me that and gave me permission to use her name. So, like I said, it's important to listen to the voices of girls and women; I know that first hand.

What did you really want to do for a living? What were you afraid you might end up doing?

Well, as a girl I never even got interviewed for the jobs we currently dismiss as paying too little (like working in a fast food place or in retail). I ended up not once, but twice, working as a nurse's aide. You can pretty much always get those jobs, because they are pretty grim and awful. So, since I don't have to give folks enemas and change sheets damp with urine, I figure I'm pretty lucky. Even there, I learned as Barbara Ehrenreich did, that there's plenty of unity among the women who work in those settings, so even that wasn't so bad. We were treated badly by just about everybody, but we found our ways to enjoy work and each other. As to what did I really want to do? Well, as a girl I really enjoyed the theater, and I especially liked comedy, so I think that was great training for what I'm doing now. Do I want to do theater now? Nope, too much night work and too much traveling.

What's the study you never pursued, but always wanted to?

I'm a collector of things, people, papers, ideas, etc. I have actually read a study of garage sales, and I'd love to do a study of thrift shops. They are incredibly rich sociologically; they are women's spaces (or were until recently), they are very mixed in terms of social class, and depending on the thrift store, there's a sort of camaraderie that develops among the shoppers, since it's really a treasure hunt as much as anything else. And people enjoy what they find. I did a very early paper on thrift shopping as a graduate student, and much more recently, I spoke at a criminology meeting about the "Thrill of the Gather." I'd like to do more with this idea at some point. Another unanticipated thing has happened to me here in Hawaii much more recently. About a year ago, I figured out that S. Ann Dunham Soetoro (Barack Obama's mother) did her BA, her MA, and her PhD here at the University of Hawaii at Manoa in Anthropology. In fact, she and I were getting our degrees at about the same time and in the same building. Last year, about this time I organized a colloquium on her wonderful dissertation on Indonesian crafts, featuring her dissertation chair, two friends and colleagues of hers that worked with her at different times in Indonesia, and her daughter, Maya Soetoro-Ng. I find myself thinking about her and the life she had here, which was cut tragically short by cancer. I've also been instrumental in helping her dissertation chair and one of those colleagues edit down her 1057-page dissertation into book length. I know that who her son and daughter are is very much tied up with who she was, and there is so much of her and her mother here in the Islands. I cannot do this work, I keep telling myself. I'm a criminologist, and I know nothing about biography, and yet as I told Maya recently in an e-mail, I find Ann popping up in my life in odd ways, so who knows?

10.
VICTOR RIOS

1. *Your book,* Punished: The Criminalization of Inner City Youth, *is drawn from the three years you spent shadowing African American and Latino youth in Oakland, California. What led you to consider a comparative analysis of youth experiences? What did you learn about punishment experienced by youth from different racial and ethnic backgrounds?*

Comparing the experiences of young Blacks and Latinos happened organically. I grew up in Oakland in a traditionally Black neighborhood that had recently experienced a large influx of Latinos. By the time I came of age, I noticed that Blacks and Latinos in my neighborhood encountered very similar experiences with domestic, street, and state violence. As I began my study I decided I wanted to understand how these young people made sense of these experiences. In my fieldwork I learned that race, of course, does matter,

that Black youths often face more dire consequences and heavier criminalization. Moreover, Black and Latino youth respond in very similar ways to
punishment, they resist it, they embrace it, or they find creative ways to survive it.

> *Scholars have written about the role that race or ethnicity plays in build-*
> *ing relationships with respondents in the field, and in how our represen-*
> *tations are received in the academy. In this volume, for example, Mary*
> *Pattillo writes, "While I think there is a certain authority attributed to*
> *those of us who are Black and study Black people, there is also the ker-*
> *nel of skepticism that we are too close to our subjects (i.e., indigenous*
> *ethnographers) and thus not fully objective." How did sharing an ethnic*
> *background with one group in your study but not the other influence*
> *your fieldwork? Was it harder or easier to gain access or build trust with*
> *some boys? Do you feel as if your analysis of the experiences of Latino*
> *youth is given more "authority" than your analysis of the experiences of*
> *Black youth?*

Although I brought my own biography to this study, that was not enough to
give me the insights I needed to develop conceptualizations for understanding the conditions that marginalized young men from Oakland were facing.
Based on my experience of reading theories of crime, delinquency, race, and
punishment, I had my own ideas about youth and punishment in Oakland.
However, these ideas only applied to me. I needed to go beyond my own
experience and talk to people to see if they applied to others more widely.
Experience alone did not guarantee entrée for me; I had to find other ways to
tap into the world of these young people. Some Latino youth never gave me
their trust, while some Black youth trusted me right away. The first questions
in many youths' minds when they first met me were, "Is this guy a cop?" "Is
he a probation officer?"

Colleagues have often wanted me to provide them with something like
a "four food group" analysis of the boys. The expectation has been that I tell
a racial story for each group. However, the boys I studied were more complex than this. Some racial differences did exist but their experiences and
perspectives had more in common than I expected to find. It is important
to accept the fact that many urban neighborhoods in the United States have
become multi-ethnic and multi-racial. In my study, this meant that the boys
shared a common sub-culture and understanding of social control that tran-
scended racial common sense. However, I do realize that not being racialized
as a Black person, I certainly missed some key insights from individuals who
have grown up in the Black experience. I have to be the first to acknowl-

edge that my observation and interviews with Black youth are different from what they would have been if a Black researcher who grew up in Oakland had conducted this study. I believe that after enough time in the field, any researcher, despite his or her background, could find the general patterns that I uncovered in the field: punitive social control, pervasive punishment, the youth control complex, and the need for a "public relations" approach to social control. However, access to certain interactions, more minute patterns, and specific community knowledge may only be grasped by those who are closest in social position to their participants.

2. *In your book, you reveal how your own experiences as a gang-involved youth motivated you to systematically study the punitive social control of inner city youth. You began your research project in 2002 at the age of 24, nearly a decade older than many of the youth in your study. What (if any) similarities and differences did you discover between your experiences and the experiences of your respondents?*

During my time as an active gang member and juvenile delinquent in the streets of Oakland, 1991 to 1994, I witnessed and experienced punitive social control first-hand. However, by the time I conducted the study, I realized that this punitive social control had become formalized, ubiquitous, and systematic. The era of mass incarceration, beginning in the 1960s with law enforcement's repression of social movement activists, and later in the 1980s with disproportionate minority confinement—having increased the U.S. prison population from 700,000 in the 1970s to 2.2 million in 2002—brought about new forms of governance and laws that targeted crime committed by marginalized populations. By the new millennium, zero-tolerance policies in schools, juvenile justice, and criminal justice institutions had become even more punitive and had embedded themselves in the lives of children growing up in marginalized neighborhoods. In other words, my fieldwork taught me that by 2002, mass incarceration policies and practices had solidified themselves and become deeply embedded in the everyday lives of poor urban youths.

3. *In this volume, we've asked other field researchers to consider how our multiple identities influence the stories we tell, and how others receive them. This is something you write about as well. In what ways, if any, do your intersecting identities—Latino, male, highly educated, heterosexual—influence your ability to tell the stories of young Black and Latino men? What challenges do you confront in studying and telling stories about a population and a place that you know well, but are also trying to*

study systematically? What might you say to those scholars who would argue that you are "too close" to tell an "objective" sociological story? Do you see "objective" and "authentic" as fundamentally different?

My work is inter-subjective. The stories of the youth in my study are told through my perspective. My personal background and academic training have an influence on what I choose to represent. However, my obligation is to report on patterns, recurring themes, and systematic findings that anyone who spends enough time in this context will uncover. I believe that acknowledging subjectivity and providing solid empirical evidence are not mutually exclusive. Knowing one's social position and shortfalls is the beginning of the knowledge production process. To conduct empirical work that is replicable, I recognize my multiple identities. I then utilize my subjective strengths and identify my objective weaknesses. I believe that being "too close" to my subjects provides me with an opportunity to reflect on my biases and to learn to separate my own experience from the objective reality of a new generation.

4. *In your current work, you explore patterns of surveillance among gang-associated Latino youth in Santa Barbara, California—a locale that is, at least on the surface, much different from the distressed urban neighborhoods of Oakland. What led you to this new research project? In what ways does this new project extend or complicate the field research you've completed in Northern California?*

Santa Barbara serves as a great case study because of its race and class disparities. Approximately 30% of the population is Latino and working class and approximately 70% is white and middle or upper class. I was drawn to the Santa Barbara research project because I wanted to see if I could compare "delinquent" Latino youths living in relative deprivation with those living in concentrated poverty. In this way we can understand how punishment, race, class, and gender, are experienced and perceived in different contexts by similar populations.

5. *In this volume, Scott Brooks and Alford A. Young, Jr., among others, comment on the importance of mentoring—the mentoring they have received and the mentoring they give students. What role has mentoring played in the development of your career? What are the most important influences (or constraints) on who and how you mentor now?*

Without mentoring I wouldn't be here today. One of my academic mentors was Ronald Takaki, the great historian of multi-cultural America. He was there to hear me out when I felt that I did not belong and he always talked to me as if I did belong. I believe that the greatest challenge to mentors in academia is students' deep belief or disbelief in their own abilities. Many brilliant graduate students find it hard to believe in themselves. I have seen many amazing thinkers drop out of graduate school. How can we teach students to believe in themselves so that they can accomplish the unbelievable?

> *How do you teach students to believe that they have a place in the academic world? Are there particular practices, exercises, or conversations that you find most useful?*

One of the strategies I have found useful with my students has been to provide them with a space of their own. Graduate students and I have organized Friday writing groups where we gather to work on our individual projects. We write for 45 minutes at a time and take 15 minute breaks where we catch up with each other. Another strategy that I have used to mentor graduate students is to involve undergraduates in the research process. This allows the graduate students to serve as mentors to undergraduates and in turn they receive mentoring from me. In the end, we all hold each other accountable for our work. *building community as equals*

6. *You are married and the father of three, including twin girls. How has fathering twins, and twin girls, at that, influenced your sociological imagination? Has being a father encouraged new questions, new lines of research, or new ways of seeing the world?*

During my first week of graduate school at UC Berkeley I found out that my partner, Rebeca, was pregnant with twins. From that day on I realized that all my academic work had to be efficient. Being a father has taught me to let go of my ideas and questions, to allow myself to make my errors and mistakes public. This has produced a collective effect where colleagues, friends, and critics provide me with early feedback that then allows me to produce work already infused with communal feedback. Of course, I had to let go of my ego a long time ago.

> *Have your girls, now 10, made you see the women in the communities you studied—or their children—differently? If so, how?*

Being a father of girls has given me even more drive to maintain a commitment to feminism. In particular, one of the areas I examine in my studies of boys is the ways in which their masculinity has a negative impact on girls in the community. I have also begun to study how some girls embrace masculinity as a self-defense mechanism. My goal is to identify gender practices in marginalized communities that work toward liberation and egalitarianism. In this way, program and policy recommendations can be shaped around strengthening these practices.

7. *You came of age in Oakland after the dramatic shift to mass incarceration. As Meda Chesney-Lind writes in this volume, this shift occurred on "our watch"—that is, it happened even as social scientists researched and published extensively on the consequences of these punitive turns. What hope do you have for the impact of your research in this context?*

I hope that my research enlightens the public, policymakers, schools, and police to change their perceptions, policies, and practices. That it informs us on how punitive social control has failed and how a new form of social control, one that is more egalitarian and productive can be developed.

You do a good deal of applied sociology in Santa Barbara, where you work and where your current research project is based. Can you explain how your field research informs policy and practice in Santa Barbara specifically?

I have made it my goal to become a public sociologist so that my research findings can influence policy and programs. In recent years, I have used my data to inform and advise local school districts and politicians. For example, in Santa Barbara, where I have conducted work on street-oriented youth, I have worked with the school district to devise a "gang prevention" program and to assess its effectiveness. In addition, I have advised private foundations and city and county offices on developing funding that addresses some of the dilemmas exposed by my research. I also conduct staff development with teachers to discuss "best practices" in motivating "at-promise" students to succeed.

8. *You are a faculty member in a department that includes several senior feminist scholars. What role does feminism play in your scholarship? Has engaging with your colleagues challenged or extended your understandings of gender inequality or intersections of race, gender, and class?*

I feel honored to be part of a department that hosts so many groundbreaking and brilliant feminists. I learned about the liberatory power of theory through one of my undergraduate mentors and role models, Elizabeth "Betita" Martinez, a legend in the Chicana/o Movement. I remember reading bell hooks in her course. And the following line always follows me:

...I found a place of sanctuary in "theorizing," in making sense of what was happening. I found a place where I could imagine possible futures...this "lived" experience of critical thinking, a place where I worked at explaining the hurt and making it go away. Fundamentally, I learned from this experience that theory could be a healing place. (1994: 61)

I believe that the feminists in my department, feminists I have studied under, feminists I have read, and feminists in the community, have taught me not just to heal my own personal wounds but to constantly make an effort to help others heal their wounds as well—intellectually, politically, programmatically, and in everyday interaction. My departmental colleagues have played a pivotal role in helping me develop my gender analysis when it comes to studying masculinity. I look forward to developing an even richer gender analysis with their support.

9. *You spent the first years of your career teaching in an institution different from the one you are in now. What advice might you have for young urban sociologists about where they can make the best institutional "home."*

At both institutions where I have taught I have said that I believe that I landed my dream job. The private liberal arts university, University of San Francisco, where I first taught, expected faculty to be committed to its students. I have always felt a deep passion for teaching and mentoring, so I fit in well at USF. My undergraduate students and I would march into marginalized neighborhoods and conduct "community development" programs supported by the university. This gave me an opportunity to teach my students about opportunity, privilege, and reflexivity, and to help young people with job skills, educational information, or youth violence prevention.

When I was offered the UC Santa Barbara job, I thought to myself, "Now I have to publish or perish. My teaching won't be taken into account." However, I have found that teaching at a Research I1 university has provided me with the opportunity to teach beyond the classroom. Being from a Research I university has opened up publication, speaking, and media opportunities that may not have been possible at a smaller university.

I would tell young urban sociologists to ask themselves, "What kind of teacher am I? Am I a one-on-one, quality time teacher, or do I want to teach at a more global scale?" Either way, I have enjoyed my time at both institutions. To graduate students who are headed for academic jobs, I say, "Whether you end up at a teaching university or a Research I university, you picked a great career."

The Tenth Question
  What was the worst (or most difficult, or most embarrassing) interview/
  field encounter you've had?

There have been a few "difficult" field encounters. One of them happened in
2004 in Oakland. I was catching up with some of the boys in the study and
I had not seen this group for a few weeks. The three boys I was catching up
with, I knew well. A fourth boy—let's call him Tony—walked up to us. I had
interviewed Tony once before but I did not know him well. He looked upset,
huffing and puffing. He grabbed a CD case he was holding in his hand, lifted
it high in the air, and slammed it with all his might on the ground. Dozens
of clear plastic pieces scattered over an 8 feet radius. One of the other boys
turned to me and said, "Tony is high man, don't even trip off him." Tony
then looked at me in the eyes and said, "What is this snitch doing here?" At
this point Tony reached towards his hip and over his XXL sized white t-shirt,
sliding what appeared to be a gun to his opposite hip. "I don't like snitches.
Snitches are bitches. I should put my thang [gun] down your throat." He
reached down to his waist one more time, grabbed the pistol, flashed it in
front of my face and put it away. At this point one of the other boys spotted a
police car down the street and told Tony to put the gun away. The police car
approached us and slowed down. Tony turned around and stared the officers
down. Then he walked away. The officers got out of the car and asked the
other three boys and I to turn around. Tony, meanwhile, continued to walk
away. I was caught in a huge dilemma, "Do I tell the cops about Tony and
confirm to him that I am a snitch?" I decided to fend for my life and did not
say a word.

  What did you really want to do for a living? What were you afraid you
  might end up doing?

I really wanted to become an auto mechanic. A few months before graduat-
ing from high school a teacher asked me what I was going to do after high
school. I said, "Celebrate by drinking a forty [40 ounce malt liquor bottle]
every day for the next 2 years and then go to school to become a mechanic."
I was fortunate to have a teacher who connected with some college student
mentors who convinced me that a mechanic could not have as much impact
on society as a college educated person. With their support, I applied to college. The rest is history but I still love working on old cars. It helps me relieve
my stress when I get anxious about tenure. During college, I feared that one
day I would end up working for the "Man." Some might argue that my fears
were certainly realized.

What's the study you never pursued, but always wanted to?

I have always wanted to study everyday acts of resilience among marginalized populations. How do everyday people navigate seemingliy insurmountable obstacles? What skills do those people who survive these obstacles hone? The study would be a comparative ethnography conducted in different parts of the globe where ordinary people are found to accomplish extraordinary acts. How does social efficacy operate in even the most marginalized communities?

11.
MERCER SULLIVAN

1. *You were trained as an anthropologist at Columbia University and have spent most of your research career examining issues of concern to criminologists, criminal justice practitioners, and policymakers. How did you come to focus on youth violence, youth reentry, and gangs?*

My path into graduate school, Anthropology, and the study of crime began during my undergraduate years in the late 1960s when I became passionately interested in issues of social justice and urban poverty. I had started at Yale mostly interested in the Humanities and eventually completed a combined major in Philosophy and Literature. Along the way, however, the world began to look like a very different place. I had grown up in Georgia, in the then still-segregated South. By the time I got to college, I am embarrassed to remember, I had given very little thought to politics, despite having lived through the sit-ins of the mid-1960s. Then, during my freshman year, Lyndon Johnson announced he would not run for another term and the campus erupted with cheers, making me conscious of the draft for the first time. Soon after, Martin Luther King and Robert Kennedy were assassinated.

I met a lot of people who assumed that because I was Southern, I was a racist and a defender of segregation. That bothered me a lot. I grew up in the church and was actively considering entering the ministry. I knew I was not about hate and oppression but I suddenly realized I needed to start asking myself some very basic questions about what I really believed in and cared about. I also noticed that some of my new non-Southern acquaintances would get pretty agitated about the riots in cities in their areas and make comments that led me to realize that reflexive racism was by no means confined to the South.

In the spring term of my sophomore year, I enrolled in a city planning course with the charismatic Alexander Garvin, which was linked to a summer internship in New York City. All the students in the class worked in one or another anti-poverty program in the Morrisania section of the Bronx, a poor, mostly African American area just above the predominantly Latino South Bronx. Some of us sublet an apartment from some Columbia students, in the same little part of the Upper West Side where I have now lived continuously since shortly after finishing college.

My summer job was helping out in a small storefront outpost of Mayor John Lindsay's office. The office was under the nominal direction of a corrupt local politician who was rarely around. Everything that happened there to help the local citizens got done by an underpaid secretary and a young man from the neighborhood named Bill Shuler, who had just gotten out of the Navy. Bill was brash and funny and effective. Everybody for many blocks around was Black, except for me and four elderly nuns who lived in a tiny convent around the corner. Bill quickly bestowed on me the simplest of nicknames: "white Boy," as in "Hey, white Boy, let's go see if we can get the city to clean the trash out of some of these empty lots and put some play equipment in there."

I had the most wonderful time that summer. At work, I managed to finagle resources for a little summer day camp. We would take about 15 children on buses to parks and tourist attractions outside the city. The kids teased and challenged me endlessly and made a regular game of picking my pockets and then giving everything back, but we had a lot of fun and liked each other. That summer I got hooked on trying to save the inner cities. In my own mind, I am still at it even though I have a much more realistic sense of the challenges involved.

By this time my wife, having just finished Barnard, had taken a job as a secretary at Columbia, which carried tuition credits toward a master's degree. Through her, I heard about a research job with Francis A. J. "Fritz" Ianni. Fritz was an anthropologist by training but had been one of the architects of the Head Start program in the Kennedy administration and then became a professor of educational administration at Teachers College. In mid-career, he became a leading scholar of organized crime. He hired me to work on his second organized crime book *Black Mafia: Ethnic Succession in Organized Crime* (Ianni, 1974). Through my contacts at Legal Aid, I did some interviews with men who had been in prison at Attica during the infamous riots. Fritz liked my work and became my mentor. He provided the various research jobs and fellowships that allowed me to complete a PhD. He also introduced me to his close friend Howard Becker. Howie made regular trips to New York to consult on our various research projects, so that I got to know and work with him on a regular basis even though he was at Northwestern rather than Columbia.

Making use of the tuition credits that came with my research job, I decided on Anthropology rather than Sociology, for a variety of reasons, primarily my interest in language and the texture of daily life. I wanted to study the things that I had found so fascinating in the South Bronx and those did not seem amenable to being captured in statistical tables. At Columbia at that time, anthropology seemed the way to go because what I was interested in was not so much the field of anthropology as acquiring a set of tools to study the ways of life in poor, urban neighborhoods.

We still have not gotten to youth violence, youth re-entry, and gangs, have we? But we have gotten to youth growing up in poverty. That has always been my chief interest. I have also always been interested in communities. The Columbia Anthropology Department in the 1970s was a most interesting place to grapple with issues of small communities being swept up into the modern world-system, and the extent to which they were (or were not) isolated tribes. These debates helped me formulate a way of thinking about urban poverty: is ghetto to nation as tribe is to world-system?

My principal professors at Columbia mostly thought and worked in the tradition of British social anthropology where these were the hot issues of the day. George Bond, Lambros Comitas, and Joan Vincent severely challenged my simplistically static and romanticized assumptions about communities and cultures. Then there was the great elder of the department, Conrad Arensberg, who, along with Howie Becker, had the greatest intellectual impact on me in those formative years. I took the last two courses Arensberg taught before he retired. He lectured on Shaw and McKay and the Chicago

School and the latest work in symbolic interactionism. When I went to him to discuss what I was working on, he had me read Herbert Simon on the theory of complex systems. It was from Arensberg that I really learned how to think systematically about neighborhood and community. That was the substantial and original perspective that I was able to bring with me when I finally got to crime.

It would be more accurate to say that crime came and got me. Fritz Ianni had on more than one occasion suggested I might find a nice youth gang to study. He would have loved that, but I was not interested. For one thing, it sounded like scary stuff to mess around with. But my main objection was to studying the bad behavior of poor people. My great insight had been that, once you spend some time with poor people, you realize that they are just like everybody else, except that they have a lot less money. They also have interesting customs in terms of music, food, religion, and speech that are tremendously vital. I wanted to break down the divides between the mainstream and the excluded by accentuating the positive and calling attention to the wasted potential of young lives in excluded communities. Concentrating on criminal behavior was not my first choice.

Then the people at the Vera Institute of Justice found me. They were looking for someone to direct ethnographic studies of youth crime and employment. They called Fritz and he sent them to me and I could not resist. I remember saying something to them like, "I don't know if you understand just how interesting this is or realize that I am the perfect person to take it on." Putting crime in the context of employment worked for me in a way that studying crime as crime did not. Eventually, I took the project over: the ethnographic "add-on" that was intended to add some local color to the original survey became the main project. There was money for that kind of thing in those days.

Arensberg and Becker both helped me connect to the Chicago School roots of modern criminology. I had a very strong sense of working in a tradition. The impact of my book *Getting Paid* (1989) was gratifying. There are some things about it, particularly what we would now call a developmental or life-course perspective, that were quite original at the time and just sort of emerged from the analysis, but other things are quite traditional, even intellectually (though not politically) conservative: I was being an anthropologist, comparing three tribes, albeit in a modern post-Marxian, systems theory kind of way.

Although they get the story, I don't think a lot of readers appreciate how much theory there is in *Getting Paid*. I left a lot of the ideas buried but they are there all the way through. They come mostly from anthropology and they are the reason the story works. There is a tendency sometimes to think of successful ethnographic works as being the products of intuition, good writing, and a talent for description. Good things do get written that way, but that's not sufficient for me. I need for there to be ideas at stake.

2. *As a researcher, you were on the ground, so to speak, during some of the most tumultuous times in the history of the inner city. You've docu-mented some of the consequences of these changes in your research. What was it like to witness these changes in circumstances (i.e., the city) and people (i.e., your respondents) firsthand? Looking back, what do you see now that you didn't see then?*

I sometimes like to provoke people these days by saying I miss the way New York used to be in the 1970s. Take Central Park, for example. Nowadays it's very nicely cared for, but it's just too crowded. You try to take a quiet walk on a sunny weekend afternoon and you get mowed down by feral packs of over-caffeinated stockbrokers racing bicycles. I miss the old days when peo-ple were afraid to go in there; it was much more peaceful. Sure, the old Times Square was kind of creepy, but you have to admit it had a lot of character. New York is turning into Disneyland. I'm expressing a kind of attitude that is called *nostalgie de la boue*—missing the mud. We use the French term because it projects a kind of world-weary yet glamorous persona that goes well with berets and really smelly cigarettes. I don't actually feel that way; not quite.

I've lived in Manhattan since 1971, most of that time two blocks from the largest single housing project in New York City. What I didn't realize in the early years was how bad it was compared to not that many years before. Now I know about the dramatic rise in crime rates during the 1960s. When I arrived at the Big Apple from the sticks I loved everything: the junkies nod-ding out in front of the row of falling down and the grungy movie theaters around Broadway and 96th Street. You could see more indoor movies in that two-block stretch than you could see in the entire town I grew up in. I was accustomed as a child to hearing about big cities in general but New York City in particular referred to as a fascinating but bad place full of filth, sin, and crime—a point of comparison to make us proud of our sleepy, still-seg-regated community. So the squalor and sleaze and muggings and nodding junkies were pretty much what I expected. I took it for granted that all that went along with the music and art and books and ideas that genteel South-erners respect at a distance.

I didn't start studying crime directly until I went to Vera in 1979, and I collected most of the data for *Getting Paid* through the early 80s. By that point cocaine had been getting big but crack was just beginning to appear. *Getting Paid* does not reflect the crack era, but by then I had switched to studying teen pregnancy in the same neighborhoods, right when crack exploded. This was something new and I definitely noticed the change. Whatever level of crime and squalor I had thought to be a kind of baseline for urban life suddenly ratcheted up quite noticeably. Respondents I had known for a while began to deteriorate in front of my eyes. Young men who had been maturing out of crime in a way that seemed consistent with some of the classic criminological theories instead started maturing in the other direction. People who had seemed previously stable died of overdoses or were murdered.

Perhaps the most startling change was in the women attached to our male respondents. The crack epidemic was quite different from the heroin epidemic in the way it affected women. Sisters died. Baby mothers disappeared. I have one longtime contact from those days who is doing well now, but I remember spending months trying to help him establish legal paternity and regain custody of his children from the child welfare authorities after their mother suddenly disappeared.

Then came the 90s and the great crime decline. By this time, I was getting used to the idea that crime could go up and down right in front of my eyes, that economic and cultural changes permeate the texture of lived daily life in tangible, observable ways. By the late 90s, I was studying aggression and violence among middle school students. There was a moral panic over the coming of the Bloods and Crips to New York City that was completely at odds with police indicators of serious youth violence, which showed a continuous decline. Both these things happened together, in many other urban areas besides New York City.

The causes of the decline will continue to be subject to debate for a long time to come. As a citizen and as a researcher, I was witness to the harsh policing tactics of the Giuliani era. Among the junior high students we interviewed in our teen pregnancy study, the experience of being stopped at random by the police was almost universal, including those for whom crime and drugs played absolutely no part in their lives. It was ugly. Did it contribute to the crime decline? Perhaps it did, somewhat, but there was a lot else going on. I think improved economic opportunities also had a lot to do with it and I also think there were cultural changes that are hard to measure but fundamental. Tupac Shakur and Biggie Smalls were murdered during our middle school studies and the shockwaves among the young people were palpable. They saw that the thug life has consequences.

Another kind of cultural change came as a result of immigration. West Indians, Africans, Mexicans, South Asians, and others flooded into the city and transformed the mosaic that had been predominantly African American and Caribbean, and Latino. This process had a number of effects. It blurred previously existing lines of division. While it involved lots of competition, I think increasing diversity has on the whole been a good thing for the established minority groups and the newcomers alike.

The 2000s have been the era of gangs in terms of youth crime, which I wrote about as a moral panic. But a moral panic can be based on some kind of underlying reality and still be panic. That is basically what I think has been going on and what I have been studying most recently, across the river in New Jersey where I work. I've been trying to learn more about how people can be embedded in gangs and yet define themselves as being "inactive" in terms of crime. I am also trying to learn more about how they gradually disengage from groups about which they and others say "in for a day, in for life." These are some issues I am working on currently.

So, what do I see looking back that I didn't see at the time? I knew I was not getting at the relationships between family patterns and crime when I was writing *Getting Paid*. I didn't see the upswing in crime In the 80s or the downswing in the 90s until they were well under way, but of course one doesn't see such things coming. As a result, I am looking forward during this Great Recession with considerable apprehension.

3. *In addition to your work on drug markets, youth violence, and youth re-entry, you have also written several articles on fatherhood. What led you to this topic? In what ways does it complement or extend your other research interests?*

The transition from studying youth crime to studying the male role in teenage pregnancy and parenting was seamless both practically and intellectually. From a practical standpoint, I was in a good place at a good time. I was working in a research institute that had longstanding ties to a funder, the Ford Foundation, which had already been supporting research on teenage pregnancy, with almost all the focus on females. Getting a little money to start was easy. The very early results in terms of visibility—a lead editorial in the *New York Times* on Father's Day, 1984—were spectacular. Then other resources followed. I just kept doing interviews and observations in the same neighborhoods but now focused on a different topic. I also began reaching out to younger and to less criminally involved young men in those areas, acquiring in the process a more rounded perspective on the range of life-course trajectories within poor neighborhoods.

Intellectually, the transition was more than easy. It was a welcome opportunity. My interests from the beginning were in how young people grow up in conditions of urban poverty. I had the chance to write about something that had many positive aspects to it, along with the social problem aspects. By looking at family life, I could also extend my essentially functionalist analyses of neighborhood-level social interactions to deal more explicitly with issues of the social reproduction of poverty.

There are three basic similarities between the early work on crime and the subsequent work on teen pregnancy in terms of the way questions and findings were framed. First, there is the effort to interrogate stereotypes, such as "criminal" and "deadbeat dad," by examining more holistically the individual lives and social contexts in which crime and out-of-wedlock parenting occur. Second, there is an emphasis on adaptive responses to structural disadvantage, the old notion of the inappropriateness of trying to understand the behavior of structurally disadvantaged people by using a "middle-class measuring rod." Ethnographic data show people moving in and out of criminal behavior and confronting unexpected pregnancy in a whole variety of ways. Viewed up close, a lot of puzzling deviant behavior gets de-mystified as we see people who lack conventional means trying to achieve conventional ends in unconventional ways. Both these approaches are, I think, fundamental to a lot of classic ethnographic work, ways of seeing things and thinking about them that I learned from reading books like *Street-Corner Society* (Whyte 1965), *Tally's Corner* (Liebow 1968), and *All Our Kin* (Stack 1979). Gordon West's work on "serious thieves," which Howie Becker brought to my attention, also had a profound proximal influence on *Getting Paid*.

The third similarity, the comparative method, has fewer antecedents in the field of urban ethnography, and it remains pretty rare. I think it is the most original contribution I have made. The people who hired me at Vera already had the idea of picking two or three neighborhoods to study, but I sort of stumbled onto something that I could run with and ran with it beyond what anyone had anticipated, myself included. There were precedents. Cloward and Ohlin's work (e.g., 1960) has been enormously influential, for some good and enduring reasons, but their conception of neighborhood differences was highly theoretical. As Irving Spergel later showed (1966), it did not work very well when fitted to carefully observed social dynamics of actual neighborhoods. A lot of my training in graduate school consisted of sitting down with individual ethnographies and picking them apart to see in what alternative ways they could be interpreted and how well evidence internal or external to a monograph supported contending interpretations. I tried to apply this approach to the task of systematic cross-case comparison of social processes at the level of neighborhood and community. When we are able to examine and compare both the similarities and differences in the ways that delinquency and early, unplanned childbearing unfold in different disadvantaged communities, we learn more about these processes and also more about how local communities are embedded in complex systems of city, state, and world.

4. *In some ways, your scholarly career has been atypical—you worked in senior research positions at the Vera Institute of Justice for some time before taking your current faculty position. How has this trajectory influenced your work?*

The opportunities I had at Vera to work full-time on original, basic research were wonderful. I lived grant-to-grant but I was very fortunate in the nature of these grants, in that they were fairly open-ended and provided multiple years of support. There was a lot of money and a lot of un-surveyed territory to explore. I had one foot in academia and another in the think-tank world and I got to make it up as I went along. Those days are past. Funding procedures and career trajectories are far more routinized now and becoming more so all the time. For me at the time, it was kind of a high-wire act and I am lucky I didn't fall. It allowed me to be original and to take chances.

There was a downside. I did not get fully socialized into academia as a young scholar and I still am not, though I keep working at it. When I've made contributions, it has been from some kind of outside or least some kind of betwixt-and-between. I have intellectual roots but they don't fit into any tidy disciplinary slot. Sometimes people ask me where I came from, meaning intellectually, and it's so idiosyncratic that it is difficult to explain. I certainly didn't plan my trajectory and I'm not entirely delighted with it. When my students ask me about working in think tanks, I try to give them an idea of the pluses and minuses. It certainly beats teaching four courses a term right out of graduate school, but it can be a position of insecurity or, the obverse, you can get stuck. It suits some people on a long-term basis, if they enjoy and are good at grant and contract work, but it can also be constricting if you want to define your own agenda. I got to define my own agenda in that world for quite a while and I was lucky.

5. *Much of your work requires you to cross boundaries of race, culture, and class. In what ways has your own status position helped or hindered your access to the people and the stories at the heart of your research? How do you train graduate students in criminal justice to manage these issues while they are in the field?*

The first thing I would say is that if you don't believe that anybody can communicate with anybody else, and if you don't think communicating across social and cultural barriers is not only possible but also interesting and enjoyable, then field research is not your best career choice.

Facing the racial "other" was a central existential task of my youth. I moved to the North from the still-segregated South at almost the exact time when the non-violent Civil Rights Movement morphed into the Black Power Movement. I started to understand the greatness of Martin Luther King just as the younger militants were starting to call him an Uncle Tom. The moment had passed when I might have been able to blend into the movement. Fortunately, I have always had a pretty good sense of irony, so I tried to take things in stride and go about fighting the good fight without getting too upset if someone accused me of bad faith. Bill Shuler's addressing me as "white Boy" every day all summer long back in the South Bronx and my getting teased by those kids I worked with turned out to be very valuable training for what I ended up doing. I'm still negotiating these things today, by the way, getting to know some local activists here in Newark.

Still, I was indeed nervous and self-conscious when I first started interviewing young people from the inner city and asking them all sorts of personal questions. I had to learn how to do it and it took a while. Part of it I learned just by trying different approaches and trying to be honest about what I was doing. I learned to accept failure if an interview did not work out and go on and try another one. I also got some wonderful advice and help from a number of sources. Howie Becker used to tell us many amusing stories about field relations. I remember one time asking him if it made sense to leave the potentially tense questions until the end. He said something like "Why don't you try asking them at the beginning so you don't worry about it? If you know you need to ask them how often they masturbate, just do it." Looking back, I don't think he had any opinion one way or the other about which is the "right" way to do it. I think he was trying to disabuse me of the notion that there is any such thing as a right way. He's like that.

Another person who helped me a lot was a guy named Tony Valderama who worked with me at Vera. Tony was a Brooklyn Nuyorican and introduced me to some of the first guys I interviewed. He taught and demonstrated to me how to kind of act tough in a non-threatening way. For example, if somebody schedules an interview to get asked questions about his criminal activities and doesn't show up, don't be polite about it and don't get mad. The next time you see him, call him a piece of shit with a relaxed smile on your face. That way you are not a wimp and not an arrogant jerk. You are acting like a regular person who might possibly be someone the guy could conceivably talk to. You don't want to try this until you can do it with confidence.

Working out your own way to do it, whatever that is, is the key. My punch line on this topic is always: "In field research, your research instrument is your personality. You only have one and it's not like anybody else's, so you have to experiment until you learn how to use it in a way that works for you."

6. *In addition to publishing articles and books on youth and crime in inner city settings, you also examined a school shooting in Rockdale County, Georgia—a wealthy suburb of Atlanta that is a far cry from Brooklyn. How did you come to that study? What did you learn about violence that you hadn't already learned from your research in New York?*

I had been working with a committee from the National Research Council on a report about the state of juvenile justice in the United States when the NRC received a request from Congress for a study of the mass school shootings that had been rocking the country in the previous few years. When it came time to decide which member of the research team would study which incident, I immediately asked for the site in Georgia. After many years of studying deviant behavior in Northeastern inner city neighborhoods, I was fascinated by the opportunity to study crime in a community and social stratum rather like the one where I had grown up just a few dozen miles away. One of my uncles had served as an Episcopalian minister in a community very close to Rockdale. I wanted to explore any similarities as well as any differences between the social forces leading to two seemingly very different patterns of violence. I wondered if I might understand something about my own roots by bringing my scholarly training back home. At the same time, I wondered if studying youth violence in a different kind of setting might open my eyes to new aspects of what I had been accustomed to studying.

As it turned out, Rockdale County was quite a bit different from my hometown of Rome, Georgia, in complex ways that would take more space to describe than would be appropriate here. We are talking about the difference between Rockdale, a wealthy, relatively homogeneous suburb and the small city of Rome, with a full spectrum of social classes from Main Street to industrial ring to hardscrabble agriculture.

The differences between the Rockdale incident and the routine youth violence of the inner cities were so numerous and striking that it almost felt like studying an entirely different sort of phenomenon. In Rockdale, as at Columbine and several other places around that time, a youth with no previous history of violence used deadly force against multiple victims who were selected seemingly at random. Individual pathology appeared to trump social ecology by a wide margin. Yet, with sustained development of the evidence by means of extended case method, I saw some equally striking similarities beginning to emerge. One was a culture of guns and the importance of using, owning, understanding, and valuing guns as a source of personal identity. The other strong similarity appeared to be the importance of reputation and peer group for adolescents. Even though the delusional Rockdale shooter was withdrawn and had no close friends, one of his few sources of pride and respect in the eyes of his peers was his deep knowledge about guns. His anger and despair were rooted in a pathological set of family relationships, but he acted them out with guns against his schoolmates in the local high school cafeteria. I concluded that the main link between the "extraordinary" violence of the Columbine-type incidents and the all too "ordinary" violence among inner-city youth is the overwhelming importance of reputation and peer group in adolescence.

7. *Ethnographic work like yours regained popularity in the 1980s and is now often integrated into large-scale quantitative projects. "Mixed methods" is certainly gaining in popularity. What do you make of this recent embrace of ethnography? What can ethnography do for larger "N" projects? Is this change good for ethnography? Is it good for social science?*

I am all for mixed methods when possible and appropriate. In my comparative neighborhood work, I have always looked for and presented small local area statistics on things such as demographics, crime rates, and birth rates, to complement and support my ethnographic data. If the numbers are there and help establish the findings, why not use them? The findings are the important thing, the methods important only as a way to them.

As there can be no up without down, right without left, so can there be no *quanta* without *qualia* and thus it has been always. Even though the explosion of the use of quantitative methods in social science in the last half of the 20th century may have seemed to eclipse ethnography, field research was never in danger of disappearing. The methodological underpinnings needed to be explicated and that has happened, with a vengeance. In fact, I rather wish we had fewer books about qualitative research methods and more high-quality examples of their application. Howie Becker used to tell us: methodology is too important to be left to the methodologists.

That is also my attitude toward mixed method research designs. Overall, I think greater reliance on mixed methods design is a positive trend, but not because mixed method research is in any sense valuable for its own sake, any more than was the use of structural equation modeling in criminology during the period just a few years ago when I was editing the *Journal of Research in Crime and Delinquency*. It all depends on what you are trying to find out. Since many questions of interest have unknowns in terms of both *quanta* and *qualia*, the increasing use of systematic mixed method designs makes a lot of sense.

This trend, if it endures, will only be "good for ethnography" to the extent that both ethnographers and their research partners understand what good ethnography is, what it is good for, and what it is not good for. If field research is used to provide interesting illustrative anecdotes for the "real" researchers who are crunching numbers, it is largely wasted. If a serious, in-depth case study is categorized as an intriguing single case awaiting quanti-tative corroboration before it is of general interest, then ethnography is being kept in an intellectual ghetto. On the other hand, I find it wrong-headed to try to fashion some sort of post-modern rationale for treating ethnographic work as a kind of alternate scientific reality that can compete with, say, large-scale survey research on its own terms, producing the same kinds of results by different means. Ethnography in my view is a way to study social context, social process, and social meaning, in detail and with precision. There are other ways to study these things, but ethnography comprises a powerful and enduring set of tools for getting at them. The best advertisement for ethnog-raphy, undertaken for the right reasons, is always going to be good original work.

8. *As a discipline, criminology and criminal justice has expanded (or bulged) right along with the dramatic rise in incarceration rates over the last several decades. This shift to mass incarceration occurred even as social scientists have published extensively on the consequences of these shifts. What role does/can your work (or the work of other ethnogra-phers) play in this confusing time? What can ethnography contribute to policy, if anything?*

The disjunction between criminal justice policy in the United States and good criminological research of any kind is deeply troubling. Crime is always an emotional issue ripe for political exploitation. I think David Garland (2001) has given us the most penetrating analysis of the relationship between crime and social policy in an historical time of "late modernity" under political regimes of "neo-liberalism."

Ethnography can and does contribute to policy. As journalist Nicholas Lemann, among others, has shown, Cloward and Ohlin's once paradigmatic work on blocked opportunity structures, based on their second-hand read-ing of classic ethnographies, provided the basic intellectual rationale for the Great Society and War on Poverty in the 1960s. As I mentioned earlier, Cloward and Ohlin got the street-level details wrong, but they also got a lot of the big picture right.

Will such a time come again? I cannot predict. I can think of three ways that ethnography can affect social policy. The first is the big hit publication, usually a book. William F. Whyte's *Street Corner Society* (1965) or Cloward and Ohlin's *Delinquency and Opportunity* (1960) can change the terms of public discussion. The closest I have come was probably my work on the male role in teenage pregnancy and childbearing. I don't claim sole credit, but there were two national demonstration programs reaching out to young fathers after a few of us did some early work on this in the 1980s and there is now an ongoing if still fragile infrastructure of fatherhood programs. The second way in which qualitative research contributes to policy is through the mixed-method studies. The two organizations that ran the fatherhood demonstrations I mentioned—MDRC and Public/Private Ventures (P/PV)—are good examples of high-profile policy research organizations that systematically incorporate qualitative work in many of the projects they undertake. The third avenue of influence is through higher education. When practitioners of all kinds—doctors, lawyers, teachers, social workers, police officers, and others—deal with client populations beset by problems that are in important ways social in nature, they are going to do better jobs if they have some understanding of the social processes underlying the presenting circumstances.

I should not leave this question without mentioning the fun we all had when Loic Wacquant depicted those of us who try to understand poor people on their own terms as being spies and collaborators with the oppressive neo-liberal state (Wacquant 2002a). Much as I love a piece of inspired provocation, that is not my own view. I always try to do good scientific work, knowing that I cannot control how it gets used, aware that most of it will not have a big effect on anything, yet still clinging to a musty Enlightenment belief that more good science is better than less.

> *Given your perspective on criminal justice policy changes over the last 30 years, and in light of the potential for change fostered by the Obama administration, do you think we will see the dismantling of the "tough on crime" legislation that has deeply affected poor people's lives and communities, especially in urban settings? How can political climates set the stage for significant policy change, if at all?*

The first part of that question sounds like an invitation to engage in political punditry, which is not my main line of work. With that disclaimer, I certainly agree with your premise about the effects of the last few decades of crime legislation on poor communities. You may assume that I also think those effects have been harmful, which, on the whole, I do. Not every informed person would or does, however, especially in light of the dramatic crime drop during the 1990s, which was concentrated in the same poor communities as the preceding crime/crack epidemic which it reversed. Poor communities became less dangerous in the wake of the legislation we are talking about and I think we have to take that seriously if we are to articulate a convincing case for how overall the effects were harmful. We need to understand just what kind of harm was done and how it happened before we can begin to prognosticate about what might happen going forward.

A necessary first step is to expand the discussion beyond legislation to include policing and corrections, the entire criminal justice system apparatus. A useful second step is to look separately at justice system responses to guns and to illegal drugs. Getting guns off the streets has been and is crucial for public safety in poor urban neighborhoods. Accomplishing this has also meant steady harassment for young, inner-city males, a routinization of indignity for the practice of "walking while Black." I am a signatory to an amicus brief in a lawsuit to compel the New York City Police Department to release its full "stop-and-frisk" dataset so that we can better understand what has gone on. I believe in the necessity of getting illegal guns off the streets and I support aggressive policing that is properly designed, implemented, and monitored for achieving that purpose. This has been done better in some places than in others.

Crime went down all over the country in the 1990s, for a whole variety of reasons including but hardly restricted to or necessarily even dominated by justice system policies and practices. I saw what happened in New York City during the 1990s both in my daily experience as a citizen and in my fieldwork in poor neighborhoods. There was an ugliness and punitiveness to it that was out-of-control, unnecessary, and, in my opinion, undercut some of the positive, technical accomplishments represented by innovative crime-mapping and related management techniques.

With drugs, it is a very different story, one that is national in scope, not just in terms of geography but also in the sense of our idea of nationhood. It is not necessary or even a good idea to arrest and incarcerate people for using illegal drugs. Nobody gets healthier or safer that way. The burden of that policy falls on poor people and communities in a hugely disproportionate manner. The war on drugs has been a disaster both for poor people and for the social fabric generally. Here we are squarely in the realm of Durkheimian punishment-as-public-spectacle, a symbolic drama that society enacts for itself as a whole using the real bodies and communities of the urban poor as props and sets.

Given my analysis of what has driven past policies—a necessary concern with actual violence perverted by a symbolic appropriation of the problems of poverty for ideological and political ends—what do I think are the prospects for a change of direction? The hopeful thinking I run across these days tends to weave together two curiously dissimilar strands, the apocalyptic and the technocratic. The apocalyptic narrative talks about how the time for playing political games with crime and drugs has run its course. That way of getting people stirred up has gotten stale. The public is worried about terrorism and the recession now, not locking up crack heads and petty drug dealers. The linked technocratic narrative says, rather wistfully perhaps, that people are starting to understand, finally, how much mass imprisonment costs and how counter-productive it is. They want the money spent on schools and are finally starting to get it.

These are nice stories. I like them and hope they develop. I think there is a reasonable chance, but, if we have a tea party president next term, I plan to be prepared to deal with that also. While I wait, I'll be doing the technocratic, amelioristic academic work that is expected of me, evaluating youth re-entry and development programs, looking for incremental ways to help increase sorely needed social supports, and document better ways of doing things. This is honest work that I like. If it becomes part of a whole new way of doing business, a re-orientation of national priorities toward investing in all children and young people, and the expansion of access to dignified work for everyone, that would be marvelous.

For that to happen, though, I think the political climate will have to change in a lot of ways besides the recent presidential transition. There need to be some new narratives, and you never know where those are going to come from. Cloward and Ohlin's sociological theories about juvenile delinquency apparently played an outsized role in shaping the last great round of anti-poverty policies, in the 1960's. That's why I hope we academics don't become entirely hostage to the otherwise eminently worthy search for "evidence-based practices and policies." We need more sociological imagination as much as we need anything.

9. *As an ethnographer, you were influenced by the work of Howard Becker, author of the classic* Outsiders: Studies in the Sociology of Deviance *(1963) among other important works. How did/does Becker's approach to field research impact your work exactly? What lessons have you passed on to your own students? Who else has shaped your approach to field research?*

Since I found it difficult to respond to some of the earlier questions without invoking Howie's lasting influence on me, I have a head start on this one.

First of all, you should understand that he could well take issue with any- or everything I say about what he stands for, but here goes anyway. When it comes to how to do field research, Becker is the primary source. I have seen him only a handful of times since I finished graduate school but his ongoing writings have been a constant source of inspiration. "Inspiration," however, is terribly fuzzy, not the sort of term he would encourage. In more concrete terms, I suppose I would point to his emphasis on the study of patterns of social interaction and his regard for craft in all forms of endeavor. Stylistically, he has been doing "keep it simple, stupid" since long before it became an acronym.

Becker's central dictum is that "society is people doing things together." We are always studying activity and it always involves more than one party. Whatever kind of social activity we might want to study, the central "trick of the trade" (to borrow from the title of one of my favorite of his books [1998]) is to discern the roles and routines of patterned behavior, to unearth the hidden assumptions that make any social system possible but that must of necessity remain at least partially hidden if anything is to get done. This also quite usefully entails learning to view chronic conflict and troubled institutions not as imperfect versions of some idealized norm but as actively produced and reproduced patterns of interaction. Dysfunctional schools and gang-ridden neighborhoods are social systems not reducible to the demographics or individual psychological attributes of those who participate in them. They are the outcomes, not the precursors, of shared participation.

When it comes to how to conduct studies of this sort, the main thing to realize is that there are no recipes, no one set of techniques to be used. There is, however, craft. Crafts exist within traditions but they are applied to specific projects by individual craftspersons. Just as what we study is human activity, doing the study is also an activity, an unfolding process that cannot be nailed down in advance. Ask Becker how to dress to go into the field. Ask him how to reconcile conflicting interpretations of some piece of data. Ask him how to present a controversial finding to a potentially hostile audience. He will then ask you how you have thought about doing whatever it is. You tell him something. He may have a comment or two about how that approach might turn out. These may be brilliant comments or just an "uh huh." At the end of the conversation, though, he is likely to say something on the order of, "Well, why don't you try that and see what happens?"

I have read about Zen masters torturing their followers with the seemingly unanswerable questions called koans. Becker is the Zen master of social science. Learning how to solve problems from him is like trying to solve a koan, with the important difference that you must afterwards be able to describe how you did it. Like a koan, a social science problem is something you solve through application, drawing on received craft traditions but ultimately coming up with your own original solution. It's like other Beckerian pursuits such as playing the piano or taking photographs. If you want to do it well, you keep trying over and over again until you get results.

I teach a graduate course in qualitative methods every year and it is my favorite course because every student has to do an original piece of field research, from start to finish. This comes straight from Howie who always maintained that the only way to learn field research is to do it. Of course we learn about grounded theory—as an activity for making theory. I also usually use James Spradley's book *The Ethnographic Interview* (1976) to introduce ideas of cognitive taxonomy drawn from linguistic anthropology. I use whatever the latest version is of Robert Yin's *Case Study Research* (2002), to help them get over the idea that an N of 1 is an automatic impediment to conducting scientific research. The extended case study approach, as championed by Michael Burawoy (1998), drawing from his anthropologist mentor Jaap Van Velsen (1967), is also very important to how I think about and teach qualitative research. Learning to put and present a case in hierarchical levels of context is the key to resolving the worries about generalizability that many students come in with from their introductory research methods courses. Why have we forgotten about the ecological fallacy? It is the equal and opposite fallacy of inappropriate generalization from small, non-random samples. Errors of generalization, from the general to the particular as much as from the particular to the general, are serious. We need a more balanced focus on both kinds.

The Tenth Question
  What was the worst (or most difficult, or most embarrassing) interview/ field encounter you've had?

There was one particular individual who deteriorated on crack while I knew him, until he eventually died. I liked him and thought he had some admirable qualities. He was a valuable informant whom I interviewed several times over a period of several years, first about crime and then about fatherhood. We both enjoyed the interviews and he used to take copies of my reports and show them to his girlfriends. He told lots of detailed and interesting stories, and they checked out with other sources. He had been finished with crime and steadily employed for 2 or 3 years before he got caught up with crack. Then he started getting extremely unreliable. He still told very interesting stories but I no longer knew what to believe. When I heard he had died, I felt a loss.

What did you really want to do for a living? What were you afraid you might end up doing?

Music, always. When I was in graduate school, I was also studying to be an opera singer. I still keep that up on weekends as a paid singer in an Episcopal Church in New Jersey where I have been cantor, tenor soloist, and section leader for the last 20 years. I also like to play jazz on the guitar with friends in a network of like-minded amateurs who come from many walks of life.

I was afraid I would end doing something I found boring, just to make money. Now I worry I should have made the money.

What's the study you never pursued, but always wanted to?

I think Loic Wacquant is essentially on the mark when he asserts that we disproportionately ethnographize poor people. I would like to help redress this imbalance in the ethnographic record by conducting a participant-observation study of the decadent lifestyles of the rich and famous. This could add a new and valuable comparative dimension to my work, but I have not yet found a funder for this important and neglected line of research.

I can't say I have enduring frustrations about not being able to study a particular thing. I could be interested in doing any number of different things, including musicological studies of the jazz world and studying changing sex roles and behaviors. What I am interested in lately and starting to do some work on is learning more about how gang members distance themselves from gangs over time.

12.
VALERIE JENNESS

1. *What led you to do this transgender study?*

Perhaps it began in graduate school when I developed a sociological interest in processes of marginalization and how those who live in—or at least move in and out of—the margins manage, make sense of the world, and occasionally change it. Studying the prostitutes' rights movement as a dissertation project that resulted in a first book (Jenness 1993) only fueled this interest, effectively raising for me many more questions than it answered about the social production of cultural and legal boundaries and the profound consequences attached to both. Likewise, years of thinking and writing about hate crime (e.g., Jenness and Grattet 2001) has further nurtured my interest in how we routinely divide ourselves along some axes of differentiation (and not others), normalize those differences, and use them as a reason for domination. The power of essentializing—rather than complicating and appreciating—social difference ignites my sociological imagination.

Apart from my training and work as a sociologist, it is probably useful to acknowledge that I have always been moved by Horatio Alger stories of a particular sort. For me, it's less about rags to riches and more about margins to center—and back again. This kind of travel never fails to reveal the contours of the social fabric so often taken for granted, but nonetheless is used as the materials from which inequality is built. And so it has been with my research on transgender inmates in California prisons. The transgender study is first and foremost a study of a particular type of social fabric that implicates our essentialized differences, most notably gender and sexual orientation, in a highly institutionalized environment defined by intense formal and informal social control, a consequential distinction between captors and captives, and a host of inequalities that can also be found in more mundane settings. A Mexican American transgender inmate I interviewed in a maximum security prison described the scene to me this way:

> Prison is an alpha male community. It's run by alpha males. So, we're perceived as punks—just women. No one is going to come up to me and give me the respect they give my old man. They see me as his property. And I guess I am. We're seen as weak—a lower species. In a sense we are. But, people should not be taken in by the illusion. Don't forget: we're men. We're just trying to get by in an alpha male community. You women—*you* are a woman—you have it easy. I don't have it easy.

I've reread this quote more times than I care to admit. Each time I do, I wonder: What makes something an alpha male community? Who's a punk and what does it mean to be "just women"? And how does all of this relate to respect, weakness, illusion, and having it easy? Finally, is this unique to carceral life?

The practical origins of this study began with an invitation to meet with Acting Secretary of the California Department of Corrections and Rehabilitation (CDCR), Jeanne Woodford. Ms. Woodford is a well-known advocate of prison reform and a highly visible administrator unabashedly committed to the rehabilitation of inmates. For example, she is credited with—and condemned for—bringing yoga and gardening to San Quentin State Prison, the oldest prison in California and home to California's death row inmates and California's only gas chamber. She expressed a commitment to fully implementing the Prison Rape Elimination Act of 2003, which mandates social science research, and promised me unfettered access to official records (for data collection) as well as any prisons in the state from which to collect original data from a random sample of inmates. More importantly, she promised the CDCR would not interfere with the research or in any way attempt to control the findings. She was very persuasive. And, I must admit, I liked her immediately and she made the pull of the policy audience compelling.

Still, I had other research to do that was more in alignment with my well-formulated "basic research." One of my University of California colleagues said: "Val, you don't have to do this kind of research, you have a perfectly fine academic career." True or not, this comment provoked me to think about something I think about often: "What contributions beyond research have I made?" One of my many laments as a researcher is the thought that my research has produced more presentations, reports, and publications than it has social change or justice. On the more mundane side, this questioning transpired at a time when I was in the midst of an all too familiar grind: responding to comments on an article from reviewers that both enabled another publication and increased my tally of "milquetoast and boring." Finally, I was feeling increasing pressure from my Dean to bring in grant money to support graduate students, and truth be told, I wanted some summer salary. Heartfelt advice and external pressures aside, I wondered if the largest correctional system in the western world—the California Department of Corrections and Rehabilitation—would really let me see ground zero: their much-criticized prisons. And, if I could see them, what would I see? How would it look different from the prison movies I've seen, the "lockdown" shows on television, and the lore that so often surrounds prisons? How could I, a self-respecting sociologist of deviance and social control, resist an opportunity to take a peek? I'm a sociologist with little self-control along these lines. I said yes. And a team of us proceeded to do the work.

Since then, Jeanne made good on her promise and we—my research team and I—conducted the research and delivered the obligatory report to the CDCR on time and under budget. One of the findings in the report is that, in the aggregate, transgender inmates are considerably more vulnerable to sexual assault than other inmates—by a factor of 13, according to our statistics. That is, slightly more than 4% of 322 randomly selected inmates from the general population in California state prisons reported being sexually assaulted, with 59% of transgender inmates reporting sexual assault while in a California correctional facility (Jenness et al. 2007). This finding, based on a comparison between a random sample of 322 inmates and a convenience sample of 39 transgender inmates, proved newsworthy in unanticipated ways and was entered into evidence as "Exhibit 1A" in the highly visible "Giraldo" case (*Alexis Giraldo v. CA Department of Corrections* 2007) in San Francisco Superior Court. With this, I was placed in the intersection where research and real (legal) life collide. By the time this research was completed and I had served as an "expert" in the Giraldo trial, I was walking a tightrope that required balancing my much-valued outsider status (as a professor) with my undeniable insider status (as a researcher for the CDCR). The invisible gate in the wall between academic and correctional institutions had been opened; and I walked through it.

I found myself well-positioned to make the case to the CDCR that now— post-first report and post-Giraldo trial—what really needed to be done was another piece of research that focused exclusively on transgender inmates. I emphasized that the previous study treated transgender inmates as a secondary concern, relied upon a convenience sample of only 39 transgender inmates at just one prison, and was terribly flawed. In addition to problems with generalizability, I explained, the previous research did not attend to crucial considerations related to prison violence, including the relationships among the physical, social, and interpersonal environments in which transgender inmates are housed and their vulnerability to violence (sexual and otherwise). This time, it was I who asked them to support another study. I did so by anchoring my arguments in a critique of my own work, something academics are not terribly rehearsed at doing. The CDCR provided funding for my study of transgender inmates and once again gave me access to all their prisons.

The transgender study can be described as a "prison lifestyle" study. As such, it required considerable fieldwork in California's many prisons at a time when others lament the demise of "in prison" research (e.g., Simon 2000; Wacquant 2002). Collecting data required securing three layers of institutional approval—from UC Irvine's Institutional Review Board, the CDCR's Office of Research, and the California Health and Human Service Agency's Committee for the Protection of Human Subjects—to collect official and original data on prisoners, identify transgender inmates in California's prison, train a team of eight interviewers to conduct face-to-face interviews with transgender inmates, and travel to 28 prisons in California in less than 8 weeks to collect original interview data from over 300 transgender inmates. In the process this study took me back to what for me are sociological basics: social processes related to the production and maintenance of social boundaries and marginalization, normalization and deviance-making, as well as inequality and social control.

2. *What assumptions about transgender did you bring to your study of this group? How were these assumptions shaped by your previous work?*

Emil Ludwig, a German author known for his biographies, once commented: "The decision to kiss for the first time is the most crucial in any love story. It changes the relationship of the two people much more strongly than even the final surrender; because this kiss already has within it the final surrender." It comes to mind here precisely because it applies to my experience in the first and second rounds of interviewing transgender inmates in California prisons.

Prior to the first study, I was someone with very little exposure to people I knew to be transgender. To my knowledge, I do not have any family members, close friends, or co-workers in my immediate workplace who are transgender, and I certainly had never met a transgender prisoner until going into prisons to collect interview data. Unlike other researchers who go into the field and study social arenas and identities with which they are familiar and to which they relate, the first study of transgender inmates constituted foreign social terrain to me.

For the first, smaller study everyone on the interview team agreed that interviewing transgender inmates was, in many ways, more interesting than interviewing their non-transgender counterparts. But why? Certainly, they had more sexual assault to report. Certainly, they were more talkative in general. And certainly, they provided some of the most memorable interviews, in terms of process and content. But, there was something else. I think the social and cultural distance between members of the interview team and the "human subjects" made the transgender inmates all the more exotic and their reports all the more intriguing and often awe-inspiring.

For me, the intrigue was no doubt born of social distance and the awe born of observing—through first person accounts—considerable human pain and suffering suffused with charming *joie de vivre*. This strange combination was downright distracting at times when the name of the game in the field was to "get the data" in accordance with the interview schedule and protocol designed to ensure the data were collected in a systematic fashion across interviewers. Often I found myself considerably less preoccupied with the validity and reliability of data; than I was consumed with thinking about how best to interview transgender inmates without conveying judgment, to interview them in a way that was respectful and affirming, and to learn how to absorb what transgender inmates told me in a way that would shed insight into a world so utterly different from my own. For reasons that are less about me as a researcher and more about me as a person, I immediately liked the transgender inmates and, much to my surprise, found myself wanting them to like me, enjoy my company, and otherwise affirm my work, identity, and ways of being in the world. The flip side of this sentiment was that I did not want to be "hustled" by my subjects—a concern other field workers have addressed in detail (for discussion see Wacquant 1998; Venkatesh 2002).

In was in this context that I devised the second study—the study that focused exclusively on transgender inmates. The second time around, I was more familiar with transgender inmates, more rehearsed at engaging with them, more confident that they would participate in the research, and more committed to doing work that treated them as a special population rather than as a convenience sample. For *me*, *they* had moved from margin to center as I determined how to do better in the second round. "Doing better" required training interviewers differently, developing an interview instrument that better captured prison life for transgender inmates (as opposed to a random sample of inmates), and utilizing consultants who knew more about transgender people and transgender prisoners than I did.

Unlike in the first study, interviewers on the second study were required to watch *Cruel and Unusual*, an award-winning documentary on transgender people who have served time in carceral environments, as part of their training. The goal was twofold: to expedite their familiarity with transgender inmates prior to entering a prison to conduct interviews by providing them with some exposure via film. For the first time in my career, art directly and purposely informed training for data collection. In this case, film was used to ensure interviewers going into the field in the second study (who did not participate in the first study as interviewers) got to "see" and "know" some version of the human subjects before meeting them in person for purposes of data collection. In retrospect, I wish I had seen and known them before the first study. Even so, I find the transgender people in the film less moving and informative than the transgender inmates I interviewed. This reminds me that "live" is always better.

I worked under the assumption that transgender inmates would have a lot of sex and relationship stories to tell just as they would tell us terrible accounts of victimization. I also operated on the assumption that they were not going to be boring interviews to conduct, in large part because of the content of what I anticipated hearing and the way in which I anticipated they would tell their stories—with intensity, with flair, and with sadness. And finally, I made the assumption that they were entertaining and endearing human subjects with whom to engage. All of these assumptions were born of the previous study, and my experience in the second study validated these assumptions time and time again.

These were not boring interviews—not at all. I conducted 50 interviews with transgender inmates (out of the 315 conducted by a team of eight interviewers). My shortest interview lasted 30 minutes, my longest interview lasted 2 hours and 25 minutes, and my median interview time was 1 hour and 12 minutes. I wasn't bored because I grew to like "the girls" (as I and others on the interview team came to affectionately refer to them). Unlike anyone else on the interview team, I gave myself license to purposively go "off protocol" if and when doing so might serve to unearth new understandings or appeal to my curiosity. The privilege I had was to treat the structured interview schedule as semi-structured or not structured at all. Doing so evoked informative commentary from the transgender inmates, which in turn generated insight for me. It also reminded me of the tradeoff between working with an instrument that is structured versus one that is not so structured. And, it is a tradeoff.

I came to know the transgender inmates as a likeable group. It would be too easy to say that I went "native." It is fair to say that I was easily charmed by many of the transgender inmates I interviewed. They were pleasant people with whom to engage—much more so than some of the people with whom I interact in my daily life! In the main, they were well rehearsed at social niceties, including asking how I was, saying please and thank you in expected ways, and otherwise lubricating the social interaction in a way that makes chatting easy. Sometimes, they freely offered me beauty tips: for example, how best to get rid of cellulite (which they apparently could tell I have), what color hair might look best against my aging skin (recognizing that I do color my hair), and how best to shape my eyebrows (to achieve both a professional and a sexy look). As someone who does not receive beauty tips often, I was always caught off-guard by this effort to help with my appearance in obviously gendered ways. I secretly enjoyed their sisterly advice, even as I sometimes perceived it to be part of their hustle. Hustle or not, it made me feel like we were bonding over girl talk in a way that, well, I wish I had more of in my life. (Now that I think about it, it is odd that I have to get that in a prison.) Also, they often wished me well with "the little project," feeling free to add suggestions for improvements related to the instrument, how to encourage transgender inmates to participate, and what to write in the final report.

Our interviews and their niceties combined to provide me with something I didn't anticipate, something—I'm embarrassed to admit—I didn't assume early on. I came to appreciate the many ways their humanity is more similar to than dissimilar from my own. From the first study, I gained an understanding of the importance of respect for inmates, transgender or not. But it was through the second study that I came to more fully understand the fragile foundation upon which self-respect and respect from others rests for transgender inmates in prison, as well as the fierceness with which they claim gendered identities that routinely threaten that foundation. A biracial, bisexual transgender inmate summarized it this way:

> I've been in both worlds (transgender and bisexual), so I know. We as bisexuals and tgs can make it in here. If you can make it in here, you can make it anywhere. Who said that? A star? It's true.... We're surrounded by men, real men, with short fuses. It's not easy. It's worse than being on the street. Here they are locked up and they don't have women, even women they can buy. We're the best they got and they hate that.

Finally, on the topic of "assumptions that are 'way off'," here's a tidbit: When devising the instrument for the second study, we were contemplating response categories for a question about why a respondent was in a relationship with another inmate (i.e., "What was the main reason you were in a relationship with this person?"). In the name of being exhaustive, a research assistant who had never interviewed inmates suggested "love." An RA who worked on the previous project and interviewed many transgender inmates and I cracked up laughing. We were sure that "love" would not be an answer to the question. Still, we put it on the interview schedule as a possibility, in part to humor the person suggesting it. We were wrong. Dead wrong. They get involved with each other for a number of reasons: boredom, protection, commodities, sex, comfort, and yes, love. As one of the first transgender inmates I interviewed, a particularly beautiful person, explained to me: "I have a whole waiting list of folks [in here] who want me—people don't care that I'm HIV cuz I'm pretty and I know how to please men." She went on to explain her institutional marriage: "I love him. I really do. He's the first person who makes me feel like I am worth something. He tells me I'm beautiful and I believe him. I love him, just like you love whoever you love."

3. *In the original CDCR report, you had to be rightly circumspect in what you were able to generalize from a non-random sample of 39 transgender inmates. So going into the follow-up study, what was your gut feeling about the general problem of the sexual assault of transgender inmates? Did that hunch make a difference to the character of the interview protocol?*

Given the findings reported in the first study, my gut feeling was that in the second study we would once again hear similar reports about consensual and coercive sex, a range of types of assault, and the lack of effective redress for victimization. I was right. We did hear more along these lines, in part because this time we had an interview instrument that was more attentive to the specifics of being transgender in prison as both a lifestyle and a magnet for violence. Enacting the interview protocol was, for me, also a different experience in this project. For whatever reason, I was more emotionally engaged in the process of discovering, documenting, and understanding the contours of transgender inmates' lives. Contradiction and inconsistencies fueled questions. Questions fueled data collection. And data collection inevitably revealed more contradictions and inconsistencies. For example, time and time again when we asked how a transgender inmate gets respect in prison the immediate response was "act like a lady." In one case, a transgender inmate I interviewed explained that she has a poster behind the toilet (where she sits to pee) in the cell she shares with a man she calls her husband that says "act like lady." Often transgender inmates were not able to articulate what, exactly, it means to "act like a lady." When they could describe in detail what it means, their descriptions were often anchored in images of Victorian era traditional gender roles that would eschew any connection between femininity and violence. Nonetheless, this "act like a lady" mantra was often coupled with stories about being tough and strong, and some version of standing up for yourself, not taking shit off anyone, and being willing and able to fight even at your own peril. For example, a very soft-spoken, African American transgender inmate who was a gang member from LA prior to coming to prison and who struck me as one of the more classically beautiful girls I interviewed, explained to me that she prides herself on her feminine appearance, especially her large breasts and soft skin, just as she prides herself on being able to fight like a man. In her words:

> I was a gang member and tg. How strange is that? Can you imagine? I had to portray a certain image. I boxed for two and a half years at [name of another prison]. And I was good. I don't like to fight, but I will. And, I've won. Not always, but a lot.

Another transgender inmate explained fighting as "dyke-like" behavior:

> I'm a dyke, but not a dyke dyke. [Interviewer asked, "What's the difference?"] A dyke is a lesbian. You know, I have male parts. But, I really like men. I really like men, so as a girl that likes men, I'm not a dyke. But, I'm a dyke because I fight. I'm tough when I need to be. But, I don't want to be tough. I prefer to be a girl. I don't like to fight, but I will.

We heard stories time and time again that revealed a plethora of ways in which transgender inmates are at once feminine and masculine, passive and violent, manipulated and the manipulator, the victim and the predator, the subject and the object. Indeed, these dualities are rendered problematic in light of what we learned about being transgender in prison from the girls. Their lives, as experienced and reported by them, are replete with contradictions, which in turn effectively intrude upon the sanctity of our social, criminal, and analytic categories. This is certainly not the first study to reveal that our analytic categories, arguably the most important tools in the sociology toolbox, are social constructions that may or may not fit lived experiences.

The problematic nature of our analytic categories, which of course were based on a whole host of assumptions, was most consistently revealed when we asked the so-called money questions for this research. For example, when I asked "Have you ever had to do sexual things against your will with other inmates while incarcerated?" sometimes an inmate would say "no." Then, I would ask the follow-up question—"Just to be sure, have any of the following things ever happened to you with other inmates while incarcerated: groping or fondling, kissing, genital contact, oral sex, or penetration against your will?"—and she would say "yes." And, finally, to capture coercive sex that is arguably not against one's will, I asked a question designed to allow for the possibility of "prison prostitution" and "protective pairing," with the latter being a situation in which an inmate willingly engages in sex with another inmate with the hope or promise that that inmate will provide protection from other (more) predatory inmates. With these concerns in mind, I would ask: "Well, what about sexual things [with other inmates while incarcerated] that were perhaps not against your will, but you would have rather not done?" The range of responses to these questions rendered problematic generally accepted notions of "consent" and "coercion." So often this distinction was just not meaningful for transgender inmates. Even more problematic, I often was greeted with responses to questions that made me re-think even the category of "sex." For example, when I asked about "sex against your will," one transgender inmate said "do you mean with my clothes off?" In another interview, when I asked a transgender inmate about sexual relationships, she said "do hand jobs count?" I said "yes" and she said "but we didn't have sex." I recalled the Clinton era discourse on sex, but resisted the urge to reminisce about it!

4. *You've got stories about how prison officers "helped" you find, distinguish, and understand transgendered inmates. The perceptions of officers throughout the transgender study suggest a fascinating counterpoint to how you and the research team saw your respondents. What insights about the confusing nature of sex, sex category, and gender reside in the officers' more "down-home" understandings?*

This focus on transgender inmates as the target population immediately raised a dilemma best phrased as a question: "Who is transgender" in prison and how can we identify transgender inmates in California's prisons? Answering this question is not made any easier for numerous reasons, including: among the public, activists, medical experts, correctional officials, researchers, and transgender communities, there is very little agreement on what it means to be transgender; there is no agreement on what transgender means in a prison setting and by what criteria an inmate should be classified as transgender; and the CDCR does not have an agreed upon definition of transgender that is used to identity and classify inmates.

I presented an overview of the research plans to wardens and other CDCR officials in attendance at a wardens' meeting in Santa Barbara, California in February 2008. During and after this presentation, I solicited the assistance of the wardens to identify all transgender inmates in their respective facilities. After delineating four criteria by which we hoped to identify transgender inmates in California prisons—anyone who self-identifies as transgender (or something analogous), presents as female/transgender/feminine in prison or outside of prison, has received any kind of medical treatment (physical or mental) related to presenting as a gendered being (e.g., hormone treatment), or participates in groups for transgender inmates—the first warden who asked a question said: "So you want our homosexuals?" Sincerely delivered, this question came off as reasonable and attentive as he was trying to ensure he understood who should and should not be on the list produced at his prison. It also signaled to me that—for this group of professionals—"transgender" and "homosexual" are conflated social types in a perceptual scheme that sees very little distinction between the two. I politely explained that, "Well, some transgender inmates might be homosexual, but some might not; and, in any event, we want to select transgender inmates, not homosexual inmates." This response evoked a blank stare, and when it occurred at other moments in the field it evoked a discussion about the nature of the difference. The one rare exception to this pattern occurred when I went to a prison to take pictures of transgender inmates and the lieutenant with whom I was working brought his camera to assist. As we were walking through the administration building and toward the yard, each of us with camera in hand, the following dialogue unfolded:

Lt.:   How will we know who to take pictures of? Do you think you can tell?
Val: Yes, let's just look for the female looking inmates.
Lt.:   But what if they are just gay?
Val: Let's just look for [plucked] eyebrows and makeup.
Lt.:   But that might just be the gay ones.

Val: Okay, let's look for breasts.
Lt.:   Really, are you serious?
Val: Yeah, I think that's our best bet.
Lt.:   I think you're right. Let's go to the yard first.

Touché! I appreciated the lieutenant keeping me honest in the field.

On the heels of the wardens' meeting at which the project was described, the Director of Adult Institutions (i.e., the person to whom all the wardens report) sent a letter to the wardens to formalize the request for assistance and to remind them of the criteria by which transgender inmates were to be identified on a roster for participation in the study. As we worked with wardens and their delegates, we emphasized that it is better to put someone on the list who might not ultimately warrant inclusion in the study than to forego putting inmates on the list who should be given an opportunity to participate in the study. The rosters submitted were combined to create a master list. Finally, we asked for inmates on the master list to be scheduled for confidential interviews and, once we were face-to-face with them, we asked them if they are transgender. If they met our criteria, as described above, then we proceeded to invite them to participate in the study.

Notice that I described that entire selection process without once using a gendered pronoun to refer to inmates. Such was not the case in the field. Again and again, CDCR officials referred to transgender inmates in men's prisons as "men," "he," and "his." We either tried to avoid gendered pronouns when we were with CDCR personnel with whom we had to work collaboratively or we used "her," "hers," and "she" when we were with our "human subjects" and cognizant of the politics of showing respect in ways that mattered to them. Of course, this was often problematic when we were with both transgender inmates and CDCR personnel. This was illustrated most vividly when I was walking across a prison yard with two other interviewers and the lieutenant with whom we had been working for days. A very "flamboyant" transgender inmate was "sauntering" across the yard, rubbing her butt, and announcing to anyone within earshot that she had just had a hormone shot. She made it clear the shot was both painful and welcome. As other inmates on the yard made note of her visibility on the yard and directed what could be perceived as playful or rude comments her way—for example, "Hey, aren't you looking fine, I'd like a piece of that…"—, the Lieutenant amicably and matter-of-factly told the transgender inmate to stop drawing attention to herself. He said: "okay, *Mr.* Hernandez, that's enough." (All names are pseudonyms.) She smiled and quickly retorted: "that's *Ms.* Hernandez." The officer called her Mr. again and she corrected him again. This exchange happened three times, with Ms. Hernandez and the lieutenant finally just walking off in different directions. Once inside, I respectfully asked the lieutenant if that kind of exchange is typical and he said "Yes, but we try to keep it to a minimum." I then asked: "Why not just call her Ms. Hernandez? What does it cost you?" He respectfully explained that Mr. Hernandez is in a male prison, he's a male, and policy requires foregoing the use of aliases. It was that simple. That declarative. But, of course, it wasn't. It gets even more complicated when I acknowledge that this lieutenant proved to be one of my favorite officers to work with in the field because he exhibited respect for the transgender inmates and care about their welfare.

For our face-to-face interviews we operationalized "transgender" for interviewees by saying: "Knowing that different people use different terms for things, I want to clarify that, during this interview, when I talk about transgender inmates, I am referring to those inmates who identify or present as female in men's prisons." This seemed to do the trick. Those who identified as transgender, those who identified as female, and those who identified as something else—for example, "two spirits," "transsexual," "a queen," and "normal"—were able to relate to the interview questions and proceed as someone in prison who identifies or presents as a woman.

Even more telling than the linguistic dilemmas we faced constructing and utilizing an interview instrument, I thought, were the hundreds of informal discussions among research team members that accompanied this project, especially that portion of the project that counts as "life in the field." What I did not anticipate was when we "slipped" and, in the process of debriefing among ourselves, referenced a transgender inmate in our study by using a masculine generic pronoun. We all did it more than once. The "slip" usually took the form of saying something like "well, he said….," "his situation included…," "the guy I interviewed…," "I told him…." These slips occurred despite our commitment to enact the interview training which dictated referring to transgender inmates as they would like to be referred to (i.e., as transgender or female) and despite a genuine desire to be respectful of their self-designations and gendered identities. Sometimes these slips were followed by immediate self-correction, such as "uh, I mean her…,"or "I mean she…," but sometimes they went unmarked. We very much wanted to get it "right" from a research point of view, from a humanist point of view, and from a political point of view. Without malice, and despite our best efforts, however, we sometimes re-inscribed a seemingly intractable gender order on "the girls." We did so even as we (sometimes self-righteously) adopted a critical stance toward CDCR officials for doing the same. We take comfort in the fact that we did it less frequently, with more reflexivity, without contempt for transgender inmates, and without orienting to them as "freaks of nature" or "men who won't act like men" (to quote officers in the field).

5. Are you a real woman?

I just love this question. I really do. It gets at the heart of the matter: What is a real woman? What is a real anything? As I write this, sitting on my desk is the beginnings of a paper I've been toying with for months, tentatively titled "The Olympics of Gender Authenticity: Agnes Goes to Prison." (To give credit where credit is due, Sarah came up with the subtitle over lunch while we were discussing this project.) Who knows how the paper will ulti-mately evolve, but right now it focuses on the palpable and well-articulated competition among the transgender inmates I interviewed for standing as a "real girl," "the best girl," and the most convincing "Memorex" (a facsimile that cannot be distinguished from the original). Through them, I've been trying to discern what constitutes a real girl (in some abstract way), what constitutes the empirical markers of being a best girl (in an observable way), and how being a Memorex is experienced (in a lived way).

The more I ask, listen, contemplate, the more confused I get. Consider a few examples of what the girls have explained to me. An outspoken transgen-der inmate serving a life sentence who I've interviewed twice and with whom I've established considerable rapport said the following to me out of the blue during a lengthy second interview:

> "Val, you're a biologic, right?" [note: earlier she explained that being a biologic means being born biologically female] After I said "yes," she said, "I figured. We have the utmost respect for biologics. You are perfection. I am Memorex. You are what I can never attain. But, like all good Memorexes, I try to get close. Always a copy. Never the real deal. But a damn good copy. People can't tell the diffe-rence between the real deal and a damn good copy. You're real. I'll never be the same. Do you know Lt. Commander Data looks human and acts human, but will never be human. He's an android, not a human. It's kind of the same."

Very much related I asked the first transgender inmate I interviewed for this study if appearing more feminine gets you respect in prison: "they [men in prison] think of us as the worst thing. What gets them mad is that we're not real women. The more you can be a real woman, the more they might not get mad." Then she asked me "are you a real woman"? After telling her "yes," she continued with her explanation: "they [other transgender inmates in prison observing the interviewee] see me get attention from men. There's competition. All the girls want to be real girls. But we aren't." Another transgender inmate asked me if I was a "real girl" and when I said "yes" she smiled and said "Oh, that must be nice."

Fortunately for me, sociology, especially the work on "doing gender" and "gender performativity" as well as a body of work on "authenticity and the self" helps me make sense of these and contrasting comments. But, the academic work just doesn't quite get me there—it doesn't quite assuage my curiosity by answering my questions. I say "fortunately" because figuring out the puzzle is the best part of research. For me, once I have satisfying answers, boredom inevitably sets in. I'm not at all bored. I am a biologic and I might be a "real woman." Regardless, I'm not bored when it comes to thinking about what either means—for them, for me, and for us.

6. *How did you manage face-to-face interviews with those whom you knew were likely under threat of sexual assault? Did you ever wish deliberate research weren't so deliberate, and you could just somehow stop the violence?*

My sense is that for transgender inmates, like most inmates, much of prison life is experienced as mundane and routine. As inmates reported to me in a matter-of-fact tone when asked about managing prison life: "It's called doing time instead of letting time do you." As an empirical matter, it is clear that they are more likely to be constantly verbally harassed by officers and other inmates. By their report, verbal harassment in the form of derogatory comments is the most common form of interactional discrimination. This commonly includes being called a "faggot" or being told to "act like a man." Transgender inmates also reported harassment by officers in the following way: "[it occurs] all the time. Today they said my lover is getting dicked down by a black officer"; "my building officer walked up and said 'If I had a grenade, I'd throw it in here' [a housing unit for transgender inmates]"; and "most of the time. Just today an officer said 'your jaw is wired shut, you're out of service.' C'mon, how rude is that? They also call me 'sissy boy.' That gets old." By mentioning this, I do not, in any way, mean to downplay the seriousness or severity of sexual assault, rather, I mean to point to a more common empirical reality.

Transgender inmates are targets for verbal harassment and sexual assault, and hearing about both in vivid terms is certainly disturbing. Doing research on and teaching about hate crime for over 15 years did not leave me prepared to hear the way in which their victimization is manifest and experienced. It's upsetting to hear about human degradation, and, in my experience it doesn't get any easier just because you've heard about quite a few incidents under the rubric of research.

On some occasions, after a long day of interviewing, I was unable to shake off the accumulated reports and images of the day; they left me too sad and too outraged to simply go back to my routine without interruption. On those days, I'm sure I ate more than I should and watched more television in the evening than is healthy. To fully disclose, however, I should acknowledge that I was also moved in positive ways when transgender inmates I interviewed displayed a sense of humor that resonated with mine or told an endearing story. And, I was left shocked and appalled when they reported their own predatory violent behavior. Both the horror and the hope embedded in their reports of victimization, predation, and shenanigans frequently "stuck" with me.

In addition to what I heard from the transgender inmates, some of the most disturbing commentary I heard in the field came from non-transgender inmates with whom I chatted while waiting for an interview. According to my field notes:

> I sat down to interview an inmate, a large, African American, bald, muscular man who kept calling me "Miss Val." He explained to me that he was not gay, that he is "100% real man. The real deal." I asked him about the transgender inmates. He said: "They are what they are. Some of them are taboo. You don't mess with them. Some of them are okay." I asked him who is taboo? He replied, "The ones with AIDS. The ones who sleep around and spread diseases. Those are the ones you need to stay away from. They are dirty." I then asked him how tgs were thought of by other inmates and he said: "Some guys are weak. They can't hold their own in here. There's no women and it gets old using your hand to get off. Oh, I'm sorry; sorry about my language." "No," I said, "please, explain it to me in whatever language makes sense to you and will help me understand." "OK, you're locked up, you have no women, you get tired of using your hand, so you dump in them. They are like a dumping ground. You just dump your load in them. But, we know they are men. You have to act like they are women, but we know they are men. C'mon, man, they have what men have. Still, you can dump your stuff in her." I asked, "Why would she let you do that?" "Hey, I didn't say I do it! I'm not weak. But, they want what women want: security, protection, comfort, companionship, someone to be nice to them and take care of them. But, also, some just want the sex. Some really like it. Others just do it to get what women want. They are not all the same. Ask *them* why they do it." I asked him if they were good for anything other than sex. "Yeah, some guys like to talk with them and use them to, you know, keep the cell clean, wash their clothes, iron, sew, cook, you know, all the shit women do. I've done that too. I mean, I don't want to do that shit. And like I said, some of them do it because they like it—it makes them feel like women. But, others do it just to get what women want: men protection, comfort, companionship, someone to talk to, you know. I guess,

really, it's like on the outside. But like I said, we know they are men. We don't get fooled in that way. But we've got to talk to her like a woman because that's what she wants."

As I was escorting him out of the office and down the hall, he said "Miss Val, don't think I'm not a gentleman. I treat women well. I know women like you don't get treated the way these girls in here get treated. I bet you get treated real nice. I know the difference. My momma raised me to respect women and I do. I hope I didn't show you any disrespect, did I?"

This account was upsetting to me on so many levels. This comment speaks volumes about what is, from my point of view, the worst part of modern U.S. society. It's depressing. I'd like to stop mass incarceration. I'd like to stop racism. I'd like to stop sexism and homophobia. I'd like a lot of things to be different. But, in the moment, my focus is on encouraging him to keep explaining things to me *from his point of view*, trying to write as fast as he speaks, and managing all three of these tasks at once is about my limit.

This study is proof positive that retrospective/self-report data can paint vivid pictures. The vividness of their reports of victimization did not prompt me to desire "less deliberate research" or motivate me to "just somehow stop the violence." Rather, it prompted me to recommit to engaging in the interview experience specifically and the data collection more generally in a way that enabled me to "get it"—really "get it"—beyond the numbers and the counts and beyond the particulars of any given incident report.

In more lofty terms, the goal in the field is to develop a greater capacity to engage in what Gloria Anzaldúa (quoted in O'Brien 2009) calls "open-hearted listening," which is not mentioned in methods textbooks but is nonetheless crucial to "good" data collection as well as to the honorable treatment of human subjects in research. This kind of listening requires resisting the immediate and sometimes overwhelming urge to "fix it" so the pain associated with hearing disturbing details of the less desirable side of the human condition goes away.

The challenge now, as we analyze the "data," is to interpret the reports of transgender inmates' lives in the form of "findings" that reveal patterns and trends as well as novelty, uniqueness, and oddity. For me, presenting the forest as well as a bunch of trees is no easy task. It is a task made all the more difficult by my own reaction to hearing about their suffering, their struggle, and their survival juxtaposed against hearing about their reported flirtations, frivolity, and fucking. My ability to interpret the data and disseminate the findings is as good as my ability to engage in open-hearted listening.

In this context, I want to describe and honor—but resist the seduction of simplifying and glorifying—lives in order to tell an interesting sociological story about the underdog and how she does gender, violence, victimization, and predation in prison.

> 7. *Can you talk about the ways—we assume there are lots of them—that*
>   *your respondents avoided victimization?*

Unfortunately, we did not design a study that enabled us to systematically examine strategies for avoiding violence and victimization. I wish we had. However, Jennifer Sumner, who served as a Project Manager for the research and completed more interviews than anyone else on the research team, wrote a dissertation on transgender inmates code of conduct. Her work provides an empirical window through which we can see the guidelines for action that inform how transgender inmates navigate prison life, including trying to stay safe in an institutional environment that is organized around the threat of violence and in which transgender inmates are much too frequently on the receiving end of prison violence. Tellingly, a previous tentative title of her dissertation was *Fighting, Fucking, and Keeping House: An Understanding of the Transgender Inmate Code of Conduct in Prison* (Sumner 2009). I'm not sure if Jenn would agree, but from my point of view, fighting (with other inmates), fucking (other inmates), and keeping house (for another inmate) are primary activities that transgender inmates ostensibly engage in—sometimes preemptively and sometimes reactively—to minimize threats to safety. As the first person I interviewed, an African American transgender inmate who worked as a prostitute for over 20 years and in the process experienced considerable violence on the streets of LA, explained: "Abide by the prison laws. It's the way you carry yourself. Not being a slut and whoring around. Be a lady. If you're a lady you might not get hurt."

Interestingly, comments by the transgender inmates I interviewed lead me to believe that the pursuit of safety was not, at the end of the day, *the* top priority for many transgender inmates. Instead, they routinely made clear that the desire to be around male inmates as potential suitors or partners in a marriage-like relationship was of paramount concern. Indeed, when we asked transgender inmates if they would prefer to be housed in a women's prison, the majority of the time the answer was an emphatic "no." As a middle-aged Mexican American inmate in a maximum security prison, who has a very active sex life with other inmates, explained to me when I asked if she would rather be in a women's prison: "I don't want to be with women. I don't want to be a lesbian. I don't have a "lick-her" license. Others are into that, but not me. No, no way." In agreement, a transgender inmate who has been serving a life sentence for over 30 years in what I would describe as one of California's older and rougher prisons exclaimed: "No, not a women's prison! I would die. I want to be around men. I like that song 'It's raining men.' It would be safer [to be in a women's prison], but…."

8. *Did your study of COYOTE help prepare you for the transgender study? How? (We're asking because you studied a group of self-con-scious prostitutes; those who had at least some analysis of their own marginalization.)*

My study of the prostitutes' rights movement (Jenness 1993) taught me no fewer than six lessons that have served me well during my career, including this study of transgender inmates. First, it taught me that perseverance is a virtue, especially for a researcher interested in topics that, at first glance, are not viable.

Second, it taught me that interviewing people who live lives that you don't understand and can't relate to, at least at first, is a heck of a lot of fun, results in lots of personal growth, and, if done well, can generate professional recognition.

Third, being upfront with "human subjects" is the best way to get people who are suspicious of social science research to find a reason to participate in research when an academic approaches them with their "little project."

Fourth, being too preoccupied with whether or not you're being hustled is a barrier to meaningful data collection. (This, unfortunately, is a lesson I have to keep learning.)

Fifth, most folks, however marginalized and suspicious, want to tell their story and want to have their story understood. The key is to provide a viable forum for them to do so, which includes feeling safe in doing so and feeling heard when doing so. With regard to the former, for as much as I like to com-plain about IRB (and I do!), it does serve to ensure layers of protections for prisoners are in place. As for the latter, one of the most important pieces of feedback I received on a preliminary draft of the interview instrument came from a very experienced interviewer who had conducted many interviews with transgender inmates. Her most valuable comment came in the form of expressing concern that the interview would not be engaging or enjoyable for the transgender inmates. Specifically, she feared it would leave them feeling subjected to a battery of social science tests rather than provided with an opportunity to tell about their lives. I agreed with her assessment and, fear-ing that the mere chance that this would occur would be disastrous, I revised the instrument with a more consistent eye toward how *they* would experi-ence it and a less consistent eye toward what data *we* would get.

Sixth, it's been my experience that social science researchers face a barrier along these lines as a result of our inability to explain, in simple terms, who we are, what our research is about, why it matters, and how we are committed to maintaining confidentiality and getting the story "right." This continues to be a struggle for me. Lapsing into academic exposition comes too easily.

9. *How has the "up close and personal" aspect of this research changed you? And what difference do you think it will make to the research you do from now on?*

I often joke with a few close friends, most of whom are middle-class fellow academics, that we live in a bubble and routinely run the risk of making the mistake of thinking that life as we know it is representative of life in general. As so many studies have demonstrated incontrovertibly, status and value-based homophily is a powerful force in structuring our lives. Commonly organized around age, gender, class, organizational role, and so forth, homophily plays to psychological comfort and resists diversification of experience and interaction. Conducting this study has worked against homophily in my life. It's helped get me out of my bubble. And, that's a good thing. A very good thing. When I venture out of my bubble—my comfortable routines, predictable interactions, and familiar social milieu—I am often confronted with my own hubris and ignorance. When confronted, I am appalled. This makes me want to do more fieldwork with another group of people whose lives are very different from my own. The learning curve is predictably steep.

At the same time, conducting this research has been nothing short of exhausting. More than once during fieldwork I have said "I'm too old for this." While sitting in a confidential room interviewing a transgender inmate is invigorating, all that surrounds getting to that point—securing all the necessary approvals, getting gate clearance to enter prisons, physically getting in and out of prisons, being "on" with CDCR officials on whom you depend for access to prisons and the inmates who reside in them, and the seemingly endless travel up and down a very large state—has left me apprehensive about taking on another project that requires this magnitude of fieldwork. It has left me with a newfound appreciation for easier ways to collect data, the many reasons senior scholars cease to engage in original data collection that requires what I call "trench work," and why essay writing—like what I'm doing now—seems like a more attractive way to spend my professional time.

At the end of the interviews, we asked: "If there was one thing you'd want people to understand about being transgender in prison, what would it be?"

The most common answer was some version of "We're people, too" or "We're human like everyone else." An inmate I interviewed succinctly elaborated: "I'm a person, too. Not a street walker, not a crack whore, not a criminal. A person. At least a person first."

The Tenth Question
What was the worst (or most difficult or most embarrassing) interview/ encounter in the field you ever had?

The most embarrassing moments came when I was confronted with my own self-centeredness coupled with my inability to read the environment. For example, at the beginning of a long day of interviewing transgender inmates, two other interviewers and I were escorted by an officer into a visiting room that had been reserved for our interviews. As we approached the visiting room, we saw what appeared to be all the transgender inmates—I'd estimate about 30 inmates—standing in a very unorganized single file line waiting for us. They were more than waiting, actually, they were talking, giggling, calling out to us, and otherwise enjoying being out of "lockdown" (the officer informed me that they had been on "lockdown" status for months).

The sociability among them reminded me of teenage slumber parties I had with girlfriends in junior high school. This was a daunting situation for a number of reasons: it violated protocol, which assumes we see one inmate per hour per interviewer in order to conduct interviews in an orderly fashion and minimize how much inmates can "mingle" while waiting to be interviewed; it concerned me that with only three interviewers it would take all day to see all of them, and the inmates we couldn't get to soon might not wait that long to see us; and they were calling out to us in a way that signaled to me that we had already lost control of the situation or, more accurately, never had control of the situation! Most notably, an inmate toward the end of the line yelled, "We've got lesbians." I assumed this was a comment about me or us— the interviewers—directed to the other transgender inmates in the make-shift single file line. The two interviewers who were with me receded into the background as I ignored the comment and I stepped forward to introduce myself to the entire group, explain who we were, why we were there, and ask for their cooperation. Slightly altered, the comment—"The lesbians are here"—was delivered again. And, again I ignored it.

Fast forward: we worked all day, doggedly interviewing all of the inmates presented to us, and at the end of the day the person I was interviewing responded to a question by recalling her earlier comments—"We've got lesbians." At that moment I was asking her if she'd been in any marriage-like relationships in prison and she said yes. I then asked her about her most recent marriage-like relationship in prison and whether the most recent person with whom she was in a marriage-like relationship is transgender. She, like so many transgender inmates I interviewed, was aghast at the thought of being involved with another transgender/girl. She answered "no" and explained "But we do have some lesbians here. I thought you'd want to talk with them. I tried to get them to the front of the line." At that moment, I learned she was not referencing me or any other member of the research team when she yelled "We've got lesbians." Later, during debriefing, another interviewer confirmed that she had interviewed two transgender inmates, each of whom confirmed they were part of a couple with another transgender inmate. Cringe. What I really learned is that it's not always about me. But the lesson needed to be relearned.

One final memorable moment: in the middle of a very easy-going interview, a transgender inmate asked me: "Do you like animals." I said "sure" and went back to my line of questioning. She said: "Do you want to see my snake?" I thought it was a reference to a part of her anatomy and thought "Okay, here we go." I said "No, that's okay" and she responded, "But I really want to show it to you," and immediately proceeded to pull out of her shirt pocket a snake—an elongate reptile of the suborder *Serpentes*. I laughed and she asked, "What's so funny." I said "nothing" and then proceeded to admire what appeared to be a small garden snake. As I was petting the snake, she explained that she found the snake on the yard, has been taking care of it in her cell, and now feels very responsible for the snake. I suggested that the snake might be happier back out in the yard and perhaps in the fields beyond the walls. She said she'd never thought about that. She seemed chagrined when she said: "I can't set her free now, she won't survive." I didn't know if this was a reference to just the snake or to herself as well. I regretted pointing out that she imprisoned the snake just as others had imprisoned her.

What did you really want to do for a living? What were you afraid you would end up doing?

Oh, this one is easy, but life-course sensitive. During my youth I wanted to be a world-class athlete. Women were gaining visibility in collegiate athletics and Billie Jean King set an example of how to make a good living being an athlete, and I wanted to do the same. Only later did I learn she, like so many women, was compensated less for her labor than her male counterparts. In my 20s and 30s I wanted to be a political consultant. I wanted to be the one whispering in the Senator's ear during intense congressional hearings. I wanted to be the one who knew the issue inside and out, was close to power, but not out front. Now, in my 40s, I mostly want to be a famous blues or rock and roll singer who has a loyal following who pay lots of money to her tell her stories, even when she's well past her prime. Etta James, Cher, Tina Turner, and Bette Midler come to mind.

I don't recall ever being afraid I would end up doing anything in particular for a living. But, my grandmother worked for decades at a turkey processing plant in Central California and I remember thinking it was hard, undesirable, deadening work. She came home exhausted and smelling like boiled turkey. Years later, when my mother retired after 52 years of paid employment, including in some pretty demanding jobs, I asked her if she'd ever quit a job because she couldn't hack it. She told me yes, it was the job she had at the turkey plant—the very turkey plant her mother worked in.

What's the study you never did but really wanted to do?

In graduate school, I wanted to study the National Association for the Advancement of Fat Acceptance as a social movement contesting cultural standards around acceptable body forms. It struck me as a good site to study the workings of stigma. Access proved to be problematic when I was greeted with suspicion by members and leaders of the organization, many of whom made it clear that I wasn't fat enough to be an insider and assumed my personal interest in the issue must be connected to my attraction to fat people, my involvement with a fat person, etc. None of the imputed motivations were acceptable motivations. I couldn't secure interviews or get access to meetings. I abandoned the project. But, I've retained an interest in the topic, most recently fueled by reading *Fat Rights: Dilemmas of Difference and Personhood*, by Anna Kirkland (2008). Chapters in this book, "The Challenge of Difference," "Imagining Legal Protections for Fatness," "Shifting the Blame," "Balancing Functional Individuals and Embedded Selves," "Governing Risk," and "Accommodating Fatness," remind me I have not strayed that far from what originally interested me about the NAAFA. Now, over 20 years later, I laughed out loud when Sarah responded as follows after hearing about my interest in NAAFA and why I didn't study it: "Well, you could study them now."

SECTION IV

THE RESEARCHER AS...

13.
KARYN LACY

1. *One of the distinctive aspects of your study of the "new" Black middle class (Blue-Chip Black 2007) is your disabuse of the notion that Black racial identities are relatively static and even homogeneous. Was this powerful notion that identities are crafted and deployed depending upon the situation that you experienced and then confirmed more broadly, or did this insight emerge later through the evidence you found?*

No, I didn't go into the field already aware that Blacks' identities vary according to identifiable patterns or even among different groups of middle-class Blacks, although it seems obvious now that the book is done. I set out to understand how middle-class Black suburbanites made their housing decisions. How do Blacks who presumably earn enough money to live wherever they want end up in either majority Black Prince George's County or predominately white Fairfax County? I had read a lot of literature on residential segregation, most of which points to the coercive aspects of Blacks' housing decisions. So, I went into the field expecting to hear heartbreaking stories from infuriated Blacks about how their housing options were constrained by racial discrimination. But the Blacks in my sample didn't think about their options the way I had anticipated they would. They saw buying a home as relatively uncomplicated: choose a realtor, find a house, buy it, and move in. What they really wanted to talk about was each other. Blacks in PG County drew clear distinctions between themselves and Blacks who live across the river in Fairfax County. And Blacks in Fairfax County believed the PG County Blacks were different from them. There was really nothing in the existing literature about this kind of internal differentiation *within* the Black middle class. That's how a study that began as a story about spatial patterns turned into a book about identity, a new theoretical model for thinking about Black identity. In that sense, *Blue-Chip Black* is truly an example of grounded theory.

2. *Surely one of the most fraught moments in qualitative research—especially for graduate students—is the pursuit of a sample of people to interview. Very few researchers talk much about how they did it, how it felt, and what stumbling blocks were put in their way. In the fascinating methodological appendix in* Blue-Chip Black *you do talk about the difficulties gaining access to Black middle-class respondents (and their white neighbors). You didn't exactly make it sound easy, but our hunch is you rightly left out some of the emotional ups and downs. Would you share some examples with us and offer any advice to those graduate students just entering the field in search of respondents?*

Hmm, emotional ups and downs. Well, no matter how many books I write from here on out, *Blue-Chip Black* will always be my favorite. Collecting data for a dissertation and then turning the data into an actual book is so magical. Take Eli Anderson's *A Place on the Corner* (1978) or Mitch Duneier's *Slim's Table* (1994): amazing first books, in part because you can almost feel how eager Eli and Mitch are to really understand the social worlds of their subjects and to get the story right. There is a novice's authenticity in their approach to ethnographic observation that is packaged very differently in their subsequent books and the second and third books of other expert ethnographers as well. Why do I say this? I don't mean that second and third books aren't as good as a scholar's first effort. Rather, what I mean is the first book is probably the only time that an ethnographer will have that much free time on her or his hands. Most graduate students don't have kids, so they don't have to think about parenting. You don't have committee assignments, a teaching load, or any of the obligations that distract you from your research once you become a professor. It's your time—to investigate the target group's world, to bring all the skills that you've learned in graduate school to bear on a project, and to spend as much time hanging out at your site as you like. And you'll never have an experience like that one again. It's very special. That was a *major* emotional high for me. I loved being in the field, and I loved the idea that I was possibly doing something that could matter for how people think about the Black middle class.

Of course, that doesn't mean that I didn't face any difficulties in the field. I wrote about most of the problems with gaining access in the appendix to *Blue-Chip Black*. It's really important for ethnographers to write about obstacles. When we don't, we mislead graduate students into thinking that ethnographic observation is a lot easier than it really is. My biggest hurdle was getting started in Fairfax County, where I didn't have any established contacts. It all worked out in the end, but I remember feeling devastated when none of the strategies I tried were working. I would tell graduate students to be persistent in your pursuit of respondents, don't give up, even when you think you've exhausted every option, there's likely still something that you haven't tried. I would also advise them to play up their graduate student status. People are very kind to graduate students. You're young and cute, and people want to accommodate you. In my case, respondents were sympathetic to the fact that I was bugging them because I was attempting to graduate from Harvard with a PhD, a pursuit they perceived as extraordinarily productive, not only for me, but for the Black community. It also helps to talk to a lot of people about your research, not just residents of your target community. You never know who will point you in the right direction. Perhaps most importantly, to convince people to talk to you, *you* have to be comfortable meeting new people and talking to *them*. It is very difficult to do this work well if you are a painfully shy person.

We're sure readers would be fascinated by any ideas you have to reclaim or sustain those satisfying "novice" feelings in subsequent research. Have you found a way?

It's a real challenge. When you're engaging in ethnographic observation for a dissertation, you're trying to prove to everyone that you can do it—your advisor and dissertation committee members, the people in your sample, established scholars in your subfield, and, of course, yourself. You don't know yet if you have what it takes to pull off a project of this magnitude.

That's part of what makes you so eager to get the story right. But, once you've done it successfully, then the question is, how do you maintain that passion? I don't think it is possible to recapture the novice's perspective in subsequent studies. That isn't necessarily a bad thing. I interviewed a woman for my first book who had two children, a 7-year-old and an infant. The baby started to cry while I was meeting with her. I said, "Do you want to take a break so you can see about him?" She said, "No, he'll be all right. When we had our first son, we would check on him all the time. We'd get up in the middle of the night to make sure he was still breathing. But once you have a second child, you think, 'oh, he's okay' and you keep sleeping." Conducting a second ethnographic project is a lot like raising a second baby. You worry less about what could go wrong because you've gained confidence in yourself as an ethnographer simply by doing the ethnography. You've learned something about how to interview successfully, how to take comprehensive field notes, how to deal with difficult people and situations. And now you know which strategies work best for you. There's something very satisfying about getting to that point in your intellectual development.

3. *We know you didn't study poor or working-class Black communities. However, we wonder how a new understanding of middle-class Blacks and their negotiation of their worlds should change our understanding of the lives of poor or working-class Blacks and the identities they construct? And shouldn't it change some of the conclusions we draw from research on them?*

That's a really good question. We should think differently about how we define the Black middle class. When surveyed, most people claim to be middle class, social scientists employ a variety of measures, and yet there is no consensus about what we mean when we use the term. We need clarity about who we are referring to when we say "Black middle class." Most ethnographic studies of the Black middle class are actually about working-class Blacks, sometimes referred to as lower middle-class Blacks. The data presented in *Blue-Chip Black* show that the experiences of lower middle-class Blacks are not generalizable to the Black middle class as a whole. We needed a model of Black identity that considers the identity work of middle-class Blacks apart from that of working-class/lower middle-class Blacks. That's the model that I present in the book. So, it's true that *Blue-Chip Black* is not about poor Blacks or working-class Blacks, but the conclusions that I draw could be relevant to them. For example, we need to know more about what prevents poor and lower middle-class children from moving up. Studying the upward trajectories of middle-class kids could provide those missing links.

4. *This question is similar to one we posed to Mary Pattillo and to Mitch Duneier, both of whom have done studies of Black communities. One of the most interesting insights you offer from your experiences interviewing Black middle-class respondents centered on your surprise that almost all of your respondents were comfortable and forthcoming with you. You allude to the possibility that in the case of your white respondents, class (evidenced by your Harvard credentials) "trumped" race, and allowed them to open up. With Black respondents, how did your status position(s) shape your engagement with them, what they weren't telling you, what they were telling you, and how you heard their stories?*

Now that I am working on a second book project on a different population of middle-class Blacks, it's possible to think about how social class impacted my interactions with Black respondents in both research sites. When I was collecting the data for *Blue-Chip Black*, Black respondents read my class position as Harvard student + appearance + family of origin. My respondents knew that I was a graduate student at Harvard, and almost everyone I interviewed was intrigued by the Harvard mystique. Respondents asked me an array of questions about Harvard: what's it like to be a student there, don't most people who attend Harvard have lots of money, what famous people have you met there, and so on. So being a graduate student who needed to collect data in order to obtain my degree was an advantage in this setting. I was able to secure interviews because the middle-class Blacks in my study wanted me to be successful. They saw participating in the interview as contributing to my career trajectory. At the same time, my Harvard affiliation served as a clear marker to respondents that I was middle class, perhaps even upper middle class. Respondents occasionally commented positively on my clothing choices as representative of a middle-class lifestyle, while signifiers incompatible with a middle-class status position were conveniently overlooked. For example, I drove around in my little old blue Volkswagen, in a city where nearly everyone of means drives a luxury car. But respondents saw my old, economy car as a temporary sacrifice, a problem that I would resolve once I graduated. Respondents' questions about my parents and upbringing coupled with these other status markers signaled to them that I must be middle class, and this comfort level was the basis for fruitful interviews. They understood that someone wanted to tell their story and they trusted me to do it. In rare instances, some subjects were off limits for some respondents: one woman refused to tell me how old she was or how much she and her husband had paid for their home.

My current project focuses on how mothers in the elite social organization *Jack and Jill* help their children to develop racial and class-based identities. There, respondents read my class position as University of Michigan + college professor + childless. Harvard is not a factor; most respondents don't know that I am a Harvard PhD. Family of origin is not a factor. Unlike for my first book, at the new site I am a professor, a "real" adult, not a student. My status as professional adult generates a different pattern of interaction with Black respondents than the one that dominated my interactions with respondents in *Blue-Chip Black*. The *Jack and Jill* respondents discuss intimate details of their lives with me as if I were one of their girlfriends. An example: I was sitting around one evening with a handful of *Jack and Jill* mothers. We were talking about relationships, and someone said, "has anyone been to a sex store?" followed by a chorus of "um-hmms" and "oh, yeahs." A different woman asked, "What did you go there to buy?" I can't tell you how uncomfortable I was. I'm there with a group of Christian women, all married (except one divorcee), and this is a discussion that I don't want to have. And that has happened so many times with my work on *Jack and Jill*. I'm constantly thinking about how much of my personal life should be revealed in these interactions. I really appreciate you posing this question because it's forced me to think about how people's perception of an individual's class position changes over the life course.

> *We imagine this comes up for researchers quite frequently, but is seldom discussed. What do you think the nature of the discomfort really is? What is at stake for the researcher and the research?*

For me, the source of the discomfort is that while I am a nimble interviewer, I don't really want to reciprocate. I would prefer not to talk much at all about my personal life in my interactions with respondents. The problem, of course, is you can't make any headway with respondents when you are guarded about your own life. You can't convince people to discuss intimate details of their lives unless you're also willing to talk about your own life. But, it's also possible to over-share, to dominate the interaction with too much information about yourself. The trick for ethnographers is to find the balance, to reveal just enough so that people feel comfortable opening up, but not so much that you lose sight of your research agenda. This is especially important when your population is middle class. You won't entice them to participate by offering money, but the fact that you share a professional status could make potential subjects curious enough about who you are to meet with you.

5. *Over the last 30 years, the academy has become a more diverse place, which makes us wonder how the dynamics you describe in your book*

might play out for scholars of color in sociology and other related disciplines. Given your research and professional experience, does life in academe modify or intensify the pull to construct private spaces and identities. Why?

There was an article in the *New York Times* about Black men who hold MBAs and other professional degrees. They were facing an uphill battle in their job searches. We're a meritocratic society, so the rules say acquiring the right credentials puts you in the running. But these Black men had played by the rules and they were not finding jobs, in part because white employers in the article expressed a preference for people who look like them, people who they implied would fit into the corporate culture as it exists today. Back when I was in graduate school, I was talking with my dissertation advisor about my career trajectory and we drifted into a discussion about why there were so few Black women in the top 10 sociology departments. I have to give him credit because even though my former dissertation advisor is white and male, he didn't try to avoid talking about this. He said something like maybe there are too few Black women PhDs, or maybe they choose not to seek employment at top programs. This was 1996. Northwestern didn't have Mary Pattillo yet, Penn didn't have Camille Charles, Berkeley didn't have Sandra Smith, the University of North Carolina didn't have Karolyn Tyson. They were some of the first Black women to be tenured at top sociology programs and that didn't happen until the 21st century. I'm the first Black woman to be tenured in sociology at Michigan. I started ticking off some of the Black women sociologists a generation ahead of us who are household names. I don't think any of them were employed in the top 10 departments. Perhaps they were hesitant to take their chances in the top 10. But I think a more likely explanation is the top programs don't necessarily think of Black women as people like them. Some top sociology departments still don't have any Black women.

What this means for Black women is that negotiating academia is a lot of work. For Blacks in corporate America, it's a lot of work. It's *additional* work that dominant group members don't have to do. And that is why Black professionals today are as protective of Black spaces as the previous generation of middle-class Blacks was under segregation. Just as neighborhoods can be integrated without much interaction across the color line, workplaces can become more diverse without the shift in the racial balance meaning very much. If we were really an inclusive society, there would be no *Jack and Jill*, there would be no AKAs, there would be no Links. Blacks—middle-class Blacks in particular—might not feel the need to seek out Black social spaces.

6. *In* Blue-Chip Black, *you make it crystal clear that race is not always the most salient identity, and one story you tell is about the identity work that is required of middle-class Blacks, constituting what you call "strategic assimilation." What are the implications of your research for how we think about identity more generally?*

What is the relationship between the rising socio-economic status of a group and its identity options? If we're talking about white immigrants, ethnic markers fade from view. Being middle class and Italian or Irish or Polish doesn't determine where you work, live, who you can marry, or what social clubs you can join. If we're talking about Blacks, the prevailing view is that race does *not* recede. Instead, race is a master status, meaning Blacks don't have any choice but to identify as Black in all times and places. But blue-chip Blacks don't conform neatly to the prevailing view, so strategic assimilation is a new theoretical model which captures the kind of identity work that the middle-class Blacks in my study are doing.

To begin with, complete assimilation is not a desired goal. There are limitations to the kinds of things the middle-class Blacks in *Blue-Chip Black* are willing to give up in order to fit in, in America. These Blacks work in predominately white environments and (some) live in white neighborhoods, so they are integrated into the American mainstream, yet they prioritize maintaining social connections to other Black people.

It turns out that these Blacks believe that a connection to other Black people is critical to the construction of a Black identity. Parents worry that their kids will not be Black enough, or that they could forget where they had come from. It is important to them that their kids possess a Black racial identity, and being properly socialized into that identity requires spending time with other Blacks.

So, I coined the term *strategic assimilation* to capture the work that is involved in balancing becoming a successful member of the American mainstream with maintaining a connection to Black people. The goal is to travel back and forth across the Black–white color line while maintaining a foot on either side. The classic model of assimilation doesn't capture this process.

7. *You don't talk a great deal about colorism among the Black middle-class. What is its role in the dynamic interplay of race and class among the groups you studied? Is colorism used in what you describe as "exclusionary boundary-work" to distinguish middle-class Blacks from poor Blacks?*

Yes, that's right, I don't address colorism in the book. You will also notice that I don't include skin color in my descriptions of the respondents. I decided not to include these data in the book because skin color was not among the criteria respondents used to carry out their boundary work. Respondents in *Blue-Chip Black* did use *my* skin color as a benchmark for their descriptions of people secondary to the study. One of the women mentioned a close friend (not involved in the study) who had married inter-racially. She said, "Her kids are *light*, they are lighter than you!" Those kinds of comparisons came up again and again. Respondents used my skin color as a basis for comparison to help me understand how light or dark someone was. But, there was no evidence that respondents were using skin color to either exclude individuals or to include them. This doesn't mean skin color was irrelevant. It simply means that skin color was not a basis for boundary-work.

Colorism is more salient in *Jack and Jill* than in the suburban communities featured in *Blue-Chip Black,* in part because of the way that the Black middle class emerged. Historically, Blacks at the top of the class structure were mulattoes who tended to marry one another. Their world was a closed circle and it was very difficult for mono-racial Blacks to gain acceptance among this group. The founders of *Jack and Jill* came from this inner circle of elite Blacks. They were very light-skinned, educated women who were married to Black professional men. And the way *Jack and Jill* expanded then is the way members are selected now: you have to be invited to join. In other words, to penetrate *Jack and Jill*'s inner circle, you would have to already have a relationship with the women in that network. As a result, there are a lot of very light-skinned women in *Jack and Jill*. Skin color is not an explicit component of the selection process, and not everyone who is invited to join has light skin, but a disproportionate percentage of the women do.

8. *You discuss both Black neighborhoods and* Jack and Jill *as "construction sites," where each can provide a place to develop and confirm a Black identity as Black people respond to the conditions they face in their communities. What is the future of the Black middle class, as such conditions continue to change, and identity strategies shift?*

I think of strategic assimilation as an intermediate step on the road to a symbolic racial identity for middle-class Blacks. I do realize that the experiences of blue-chip Blacks are not typical by any stretch of the imagination. They earn very high incomes, especially in comparison to the "average" Black. They live in communities that are not typical for Blacks—a predominately white suburb and a heavily Black, distinctly middle-class suburb. The notion that race could one day become symbolic for blue chip Blacks just as ethnicity is now symbolic for whites is not so far-fetched. But we would need to see a shift in the way Americans conceive of the middle class. When most people hear the term *middle class*, they envision a white face, not a Black one. The public face of the middle class is white. That would have to change.

9. *What related questions will you pose in later work—or more speculatively, what questions will your students pose as scholars in 10 or 20 years? What is the research agenda implied by your work?*

I suspect my students will devote greater attention to investigating what it means to have some diversity *within* the Black middle class. The Black middle class has changed dramatically in the last 40 years, and, as a result, polarization between the Black middle class and the Black poor—the fault line that has long held the attention of social scientists—will not be the most important distinction among Blacks in the 21st century. We will need to know more about how being lower middle class vs. middle class or upper middle class affects the life chances of individuals. I think graduate students will commit themselves to this research agenda.

Then too, there is renewed interest in understanding how Blacks think about their incorporation into American society. I coined strategic assimilation theory as one way of understanding how middle-class Blacks in DC move back and forth across the racial divide. Graduate students are already beginning to test this theory among other racial and ethnic groups. I'd like to see students test the theory among other groups of middle-class Blacks in different regions of the country. How different are the assimilation trajectories of middle-class Blacks in the South from those in the Northeast or on the West Coast? We don't know the answer to that question yet.

The Tenth Question
> *What was the worst (or most difficult, or most embarrassing) interview/ field encounter you've had?*

My most embarrassing moment was the one I discussed in response to Question 4.

> *What did you really want to do for a living? What were you afraid you might end up doing?*

I'm doing what I wanted to be doing. I don't find administrative work interesting, so I have no aspirations to be a dean or the president of a university. My greatest fear pre-tenure was that I might end up having to work my way up to manager at The Gap—although the employee discount would be some consolation!

What's the study you never pursued, but always wanted to?

I'm fascinated by random assignment. My middle-class respondents live where they live because they chose that community. But what if middle-class people were randomly assigned to their neighborhoods the way poor people are in Moving to Opportunity (MTO) studies and the Gautreaux Assisted Housing Program? What effect would these residential assignments have on people's willingness to cross the color line? Clearly, we can't impose this model, for all sorts of reasons, but it would be really interesting.

14.

FRANCE WINDDANCE TWINE

1. *Your first book,* Racism in a Racial Democracy: The Maintenance of White Supremacy in Brazil *(1997), is based on extensive field research in Brazil. What led you to this study of racism and anti-racism? Looking back, what story or stories might you tell now as a sociologist that you did not tell as an anthropologist? Or, are those distinctions bearing on disciplinary socialization even pertinent to your work?*

I grew up in Chicago during the 1970s. Chicago is a very racially segregated city. White supremacy flourished—though challenged and mediated by a visible Black middle class. When I was 6 years old, with insurance money from an accident on her day job, Frances, my maternal grandmother bought a home in a working-class Irish American neighborhood that was in transition. As a child attending a Catholic school, I stood out as one of the few U.S. Black students among a population of predominantly Irish and Polish second generation immigrants. It was a challenging experience at times and exposed me to both white racism and white anti-racism at a young age. Within a few years white flight radically changed the demographics of the neighborhood and it became a Black neighborhood. On occasion, I accompanied my grandmother, who was then in her 70s, to her part-time job as a domestic servant for an upper middle-class Jewish family who had moved to Highland Park. We would drive to their white suburban enclave, also a product of white flight. This family had two daughters, one who was my age. They invited me to their daughters' birthday parties. I was the token Black girl but I was treated kindly and I learned a lot of important lessons about what conventional sociology calls "stratification" from these experiences. I was a good girl, which meant that I was quiet and kept my opinions to myself. I learned to quietly monitor the differences in the quality of my life, which I had thought was adequate. We lived on a quiet street among U.S. Blacks and the occasional West Indian—all two parent and employed families. My mother was the only divorced woman on the block which was a stigma at that time. I quietly recorded the differences between their lives and mine. The produce in the Highland Park grocery stores was more diverse and appeared to be fresher and of a better quality. I began to desire foods that were not available in the local store so my grandmother would drive further away to buy foods that were deemed "exotic" like mangoes and kiwi and asparagus. I had never seen artichokes until we went to the suburban stores. When I went shopping with Ms. Z. there was produce from places like Chile, Mexico, and other countries I had no familiarity with at that time—foods that I never saw in the stores we shopped in on the South Side. I slowly began to become aware of the gap between my life and their life in material terms.

I had what might be called a nervous breakdown in primary school. Although I earned straight As I began to question the nuns about slavery, and about the role of the Catholic Church in the slave trade. I began to see myself as "different." I didn't like being different. I wanted to blend in like the immigrant children from Eastern Europe who seemed to be accepted more easily. When I was 10 years old my mother decided that it was emotionally damaging for me to attend a predominantly white school and that I needed to be around more Black children. (We did not use the term *African American* and I still prefer the term *Black* to self-identify and reserve this term for first generation immigrants from Africa to the United States.) My mother transferred me to Holy Angels, a Black Catholic school that was run by U.S. Black priests, rather than the Irish Catholic priests who ran my previous school. Holy Angels was known for its radical curriculum. It was the same school that my father and aunt had attended. I commuted more than 1 hour each way by bus to go to this school. This was a very healing experience for me or what might be called a "corrective emotional experience." I was no longer a minority. The children I went to school with looked like me—or at least some of them did. We read Black poetry; we learned about our legal rights, we read history that did not denigrate Black people, and the Irish, African, and U.S. Black nuns treated me with respect. At some point I became aware that I was the descendant of slaves and I had a hard time accepting this because I had acquired an idealized view of the United States. During this period, I began to feel pride in my heritage and I also gained a sense of confidence that carried me through college. At the age of 12 I entered St. Thomas Aquinas Dominican High School and graduated at 16. I then went to Northwestern where I graduated at the age of 20. My paternal grandfather, Paul Twine, Sr., a Civil Rights Activist, who co-founded the Catholic Interracial Council, brought together Catholics of diverse racial backgrounds to fight for equality. These experiences of growing up around racism and also having white teachers (primarily nuns and Jesuit priests) who were both racist and anti-racist had a profound impact upon my consciousness.

Almost two decades later I ended up going to Brazil to study racism. It was not my first choice. My initial research project was to examine how Black communities in the Southwest negotiated their relationships with Native Americans and Latinos. My aim was to conduct an urban ethnography of Black–Native American relations—a study that would illuminate how these two groups negotiated and sustained racial and ethnic boundaries—without necessarily disrupting white supremacy. Black–Native relations has been neglected except in historical studies so I was interested in examining a group that has been virtually invisible in contemporary studies of racial and ethnic relations: Native Americans who live off-reservation. My proposal for this study was rejected and I had to come up with an alternative. Brazil was my backup because, like the United States, it began as a European colony whose economy was based upon plantation slavery. Brazil, the largest country in this hemisphere, also has the largest population of people of African descent in the Americas. Yet there were crucial differences in the national ideology and in the composition of the country. I decided that Brazil would be a compelling comparative case study of race and racism because, like the United States, they had a history of white supremacy yet the Brazilian state never had state sanctioned racial segregation and never criminalized interracial marriages. Nevertheless the descendants of Europeans held and continue to hold the bulk of economic, social, and government power. My dissertation committee at UC Berkeley consisted of three sociologists (Troy Duster,

Kristin Luker, Pedro Noguera) and two anthropologists, so I was trained by two departments. The stories that I told were shaped by my being trained by feminists, anti-racists, and neo-Marxists (in Anthropology). I was shaped by the debates occurring when I was in graduate school and to a large extent by my own history and experiences as a brown skinned woman of mixed ancestry who self-identified as Black, and as a feminist scholar who had learned very little about the African Diaspora outside of the United States. As someone trained by Marxists and feminists I wanted to understand how racism, class inequalities, gender, presumed ancestry, and nationalism structured an individual's understanding of oppression.

> *There is, perhaps now more than ever, a push toward hybridity in the academy.* Mixed methods *and* interdisciplinary *are terms that are used with increasing regularity. What distinct benefits did interdisciplinary approaches hold for you?*

As I mentioned, I am a disciplinary hybrid in terms of my training. Being trained by sociologists and anthropologists was a wonderful experience because in Anthropology, I was trained by theorists who wrote beautifully. My first theory teachers were the Foucault scholar Paul Rabinow and the feminist Nancy Scheper-Hughes. In the Sociology Department I enrolled in courses in classical theory (Marxism) taught by Michael Burawoy and in qualitative research methods taught by Kristin Luker.

The anthropologists taught me how to listen and how to write a compelling narrative. Like historians and novelists, in Anthropology how one tells the story is just as important as the facts, so I learned to appreciate beautiful writing and struggled to do this as a social scientist. As a discipline anthropologists place more emphasis than sociologists upon the importance of crafting a beautiful and compelling narrative that presents research findings but in a way that seduces the reader. The sociologists, who were more theoretically driven, taught me how to conduct an analytically rigorous and careful methodological study that would enable me to synthesize theory with established research standards. I learned how to travel between disciplines and to be multi-lingual. I learned how to translate my research so that I could speak across disciplines. In the process I became a certain sort of sociologist who integrated theory, narrative, and empirical rigor.

2. *Your current work continues to explore the intersections and dynamic boundaries of race and racism, gender, and class in settings outside of the United States. For about a decade now you have conducted research on the everyday anti-racist parenting practices of white mothers of Black*

children in the UK. You have just published a book based on this field research. What did you find?

My book titled *A White Side of Black Britain: Interracial Intimacy and Racial Literacy* (Twine, 2010) is a longitudinal ethnography based upon 12 years of field research and participant observation. This ethnography of racial consciousness builds upon my earlier research in Brazil to another national context. In my first ethnographic study *Racism in a Racial Democracy* (Twine, 1997) I examined the meanings of race and racism among upwardly mobile Brazilians of visible African ancestry. Like Brazil, the UK never criminalized interracial marriage, nor did they legally define Blackness. For the UK project, I conducted interviews and participant observation with 108 members of Black–white interracial families. This research is a strategic and instructive case study of the crucial role that white parents of children who may be socially classified or come to self-identify as Black or mixed race play in negotiating race and racism. Under what conditions did some of these white parents become anti-racists? What struggles occurred within these families over the meanings of race? One of my most surprising findings is the degree to which the white members, typically the mothers, were expected to do the race-training in the family. Black fathers were not expected to provide the training and were not punished for not providing it but white mothers were expected to learn how to negotiate racism with very little guidance.

What unique challenges are associated with conducting a decade long ethnographic study in another country?

A longitudinal ethnography offers challenges as well as theoretical advantages. By returning nearly every year to the field, I was able to develop long term relationships with family members that allowed me to re-visit the same themes and to track movements between positions. For example, some family members who were initially opposed to interracial relationships, nevertheless were able to develop emotionally close and supportive relationships with their sisters-in-law. Following participants over time allowed me to identify and track the dynamic nature of the changes in their racial grammar, racial logics, racial discourses, and strategies for countering racism, instead of presenting a snapshot portrait that reflected one particular moment in the life cycle of a marriage.

Among the subset of 42 families that I followed over a decade, I witnessed shifts in their racial logics and their use of racial terminology to describe their children. These changes reflected changes in their children's experiences and in their networks. During the course of my longitudinal ethnography, I found some members of working-class families typically changed the terminology they used in response to school forms. The British government and local school authorities employ "ethnic monitoring" forms to track the number of racial and ethnic minorities. The terms on these forms often do not match the terms used by family members themselves. In 1997 the term *half-caste* was commonly used. By 2000 this term was replaced by the terms *mixed-race* or *dual heritage*. I would have missed these changes and their impact on the racial logics circulating in these families if I had not conducted a longitudinal ethnography.

One of the most challenging aspects of conducting such a study is maintaining relationships across time and geographic region. Longitudinal studies can be emotionally taxing because the individuals who participated ceased being simply research subjects and became people for whom one cares deeply. Traveling to another country each year also requires an investment of substantial resources including time, money, and emotions in sustaining relationships. I became embedded in family dramas. People began to have expectations of me. They wanted to visit me in the United States and see how I lived. Three of the women who participated in this study visited me in the United States, sent me updates via e-mail, phone, and letters describing births, divorces, conflicts, pregnancies, mental illness, job losses, and deaths. It became more challenging to maintain boundaries that positioned me simply as the researcher. My first husband accompanied me on my pilot research so some of the families who participated met him. When I filed for divorce— one that was very public and unpleasant—some of the participants in my research study demanded answers to what I viewed as personal questions about my marriage. How could I not answer them when they had shared so much with me? I struggled with this issue. I reluctantly relinquished some of my privacy because the people who gave me access to their homes and their lives wanted to know about me.

3. *In 2002, you co-edited a special volume of* Signs *on feminisms and youth culture. At UC Santa Barbara, you also regularly teach courses on girlhood. In what ways, if any, is your research influenced by your own childhood or adolescence? Are there distinct ways in which your experience as a girl helped to shape your sociological imagination?*

My childhood shaped my research in many ways. First, after my parents divorced when I was 5 years old, I was raised by a single mother and a grandmother in a multi-generational household. We moved several times during my childhood and I lived in four different urban neighborhoods including the Ida B. Wells housing project—a poor and exclusively Black residential community. Then we moved to a working-class Irish and Eastern European neighborhood, and later a middle-class area of predominantly unhyphenated white professionals. These experiences heightened my awareness of racial and class segregation. As a girl I also became aware of the potential violence always present when one crossed over into different racial and class zones. My movements were constantly and carefully monitored by my mother who was always concerned about my safety, particularly sexual assault. I learned not to talk, to observe, and not to call attention to myself. In college I unlearned these lessons.

When my mother married an Irish American police officer and we then lived in a middle-class neighborhood on the Lake Front, I was constantly reminded of how my experiences diverged from those of many of my Black peers at my high school. I commuted 3 hours per day round trip from the Northside back to the Southside to attend an all girls Catholic high school. So as a teenager (13–16) I lived in a white neighborhood on the Lake Front, while I went to school in a Black middle-class neighborhood. My experiences were not typical for girls of my racial and class background. I also grew up in a multi-generational household and was told stories by my maternal grandmother about her life growing up in Baton Rouge, Louisiana. My maternal relatives were part of the Great Migration and thus I was very self-conscious of being a member of the first generation to grow up in the North. Yet, they constantly reminded me that I had to work harder than non-Blacks to achieve. The biggest influence on me was the degree of violence that affected my friends and relatives. I was raised under strict surveillance and not allowed to spend overnights at friends. I was also not allowed to remain on the basketball team that I loved because I would get home too late. I grew up being taught that there was no safety net and that I could not make a mistake (such as being sexually active and becoming pregnant). I lived a somewhat cloistered life and had a few friends and basically I was very shy.

4. *In this volume, Meda Chesney-Lind describes the many advances made by feminists in the academy over the last several decades. She also comments on the backlash against feminism. What power does feminism continue to hold for you? What role does an anti-racist feminism play in a world that is believed by many to be "post-racial" and "post-feminist"?*

I have self-identified as a feminist and embraced feminism since I was 8 years old. My feminist identity has been central to my identity, idealism, scholarship, and teaching. It is impossible for me to separate my feminism from my anti-racism because as a child, I became aware of sexism and racism simultaneously. Feminism saved my life. It gave me a trans-racial and ethnically diverse community of women with whom I identified at an early age. Feminists gave me dreams. The first feminist in my life was my grandmother and later the Irish Catholic nuns who taught me in elementary school. Several of my elementary school teachers left the convent and became feminists. They had a profound influence on me as educated women who seemed to live exciting lives. I identified with them as a child.

I have never accepted the notion that we live in a post-feminist world. In my view, the circulation of the myth that we are living in a post-feminist world is a direct product of the backlash against feminism. Feminism is the reason I have a teaching position and it is the reason that I enjoy teaching. I have always identified as a feminist even though my first book focuses heavily upon Brazilian race relations. Being a feminist scholar is evident in my teaching and research. Gender is always present in my analyses of race, class, and nationalism. My interest in intimacy and how women and men negotiate race, racism, and class inequality in their lives reflects my feminist training.

A feminist lens has kept me from losing my sanity. It is one of the reasons that I am emotionally stable despite the racism, sexism, and elitism that I have encountered in my life. Feminist and anti-racists have taught me how to see the institutional structures that impact upon me and therefore help me to identify those spaces of constrained agency. I am very grateful to the generations of feminists who have preceded me and created institutional space for me in the academy.

5. *This question is somewhat related to the previous question. In a recent publication (Twine and Gallagher, 2007) you and your co-author, Charles Gallagher, consider the future of whiteness and introduce the concept of "third wave whiteness." As Mary Pattillo writes in this volume, much of urban sociology and urban ethnography has been focused on the study of low-income African Americans and Latinos, especially men. Why should sociologists study whiteness? How is field research well suited to the study of whiteness?*

Why is whiteness important? In the words of Ruth Frankenberg, whiteness "is a complexly constructed product of local, regional, national and global relations, past and present" (1993: 236). Critical studies of race and racism must include stories of whiteness. White supremacy is sustained and reproduced, in part, through the power of its invisibility. For the vast majority of whites, their racial privileges are invisible to them. White people appear to be unaware of all of the areas in which their whiteness is a form of capital. Whiteness studies, whose origins can be located in the scholarship of W.E.B. DuBois, is an important sub-field of critical race studies because it is impossible to understand how race is both a fiction and a brutal reality without understanding how the boundaries between "whites" and those not physically qualified for whiteness are produced.

The question of how white people become white and how they learn not to see themselves as racialized or as racially privileged is central to the dismantling of racism. The sociology of racism and anti-racism demands an analysis of members of racially dominant groups. Studying up—that is, studying members of the racially dominant group presents its own set of challenges, but it is important to understand and to teach students how age, gender, class, and sexuality inflect the experience of white people and the resulting consequences. The study of whiteness provides sociologists with an opportunity to analyze how power operates among racially dominant groups. Until recently there was an interdisciplinary imbalance within the field now known as whiteness studies. With the exception of DuBois, much of the groundbreaking research in this field was done by labor historians such as David Roediger, George Frederickson, as well as literary scholars including Toni Morrison. It is my view that sociologists have a lot to offer to this interdisciplinary conversation. The methodological arsenal that sociologists possess, combined with theoretical rigor can illuminate the ways that race and racial meanings are produced before our eyes. Racial meanings are always under contestation. Thus, if we are to understand the meaning and lived experience of "race," white people and their diverse experiences of racialization as inflected by age, class, gender, region and political histories, must be carefully studied. The theoretical and moral stakes are too high to narrowly restrict the focus of racial studies to the experiences of racial and ethnic minorities.

6. Researching Race, Racing Research: Methodological Dilemmas in Critical Race Studies (Twine and Warren 2001) *features chapters on the many challenges of negotiating race and racism in the field. In this volume we have asked several scholars to consider how race and, more generally, the intersection of our various identities shape the stories we tell, how we tell them, and how they are received. Nearly a decade after publishing* Researching Race, *what methodological dilemmas persist when it comes to representing race in field research?*

The issue of "race" continues to present challenges because racial identities are complicated; they are the outcome of material inequalities, the legacy of slavery, ancestry, and they are, like gender, performances. First, the boundaries between racial and ethnic groups are not always clear-cut or visible and thus race, like gender, must be performed and embodied through practices.

Of course, race is also an ascribed status and a position that has material consequences. One reason that it is so challenging to represent race is that it is a fugitive. It is a proxy for class, culture, citizenship, or religion. To the extent that class, culture, and other aspects of identity are intertwined with what comes to be thought of as "race," it is challenging to adequately represent the complexities of race as it is "read," perceived, and performed in everyday life.

The idea that race is "natural" challenges the realities of racial identities and the ways that they are activated and can shift through migration to another country, through marriage, though class mobility, and political mobilization. The term *Hispanic* was added to the U.S. Census in 1970. Hispanics did not officially exist prior to this time. There were Mexican Americans, Puerto Ricans, Cubans, Dominicans, and others, but the national Hispanic community that exists today is different from the pre-1970s community. The ways that the Census categories lack any historical integrity across time and the numbers of categories that have been added and removed, suggest that "race" is a product of power relations and this will always present particular methodological dilemmas for sociologists. Harris and Sim (2002) discovered that students of multi-racial heritage tended to self-identify as one race at home and a different one at school. How can sociologists adequately address this issue in survey research?

7. *You have used visual sociology and visual ethnography throughout your career. For example, your documentary,* Just Black? *(1991) used family photos to elicit interviews during your longitudinal research in the UK. What does visual sociology tell us about society that text-based sociology cannot do alone?*

As a graduate student in 1991 I enrolled in the first course on visual ethnography taught at the University of California, Berkeley, I conducted video interviews to complement the taped interviews that I had already conducted for a qualitative research methods course taught by Kristin Luker. This was a transformative experience. The video-taped interviews provided me with a direct comparison to the audio-taped ones. These interviews resulted in a documentary that I co-produced with Jonathan Warren titled *Just Black?* The year after I completed it—it earned two awards including one from the National Educational Film Festival. This film was immediately picked up for distribution by Filmmakers Library, a New York educational film distributor and became their top selling documentary and the first to explicitly address multi-racial youth. Young people who were not physically qualified for whiteness and were likely to be socially classified as Black, nevertheless, embraced their European American mothers' heritage. They struggled with how to make sense out of their ascribed identity as "just Black." It was powerful but also directly confronted the viewer with their own folk logics about race.

What became clear is that the gap between ancestry, social experiences, and how individuals were positioned by those outside their families can be more vividly captured on film than in written descriptions alone. Viewers were challenged by their own assumptions about what a body reveals about an individual's ancestry, socio-racial identity, and social experiences. The fiction that race is natural and thus always obvious was contradicted in a way that is more compelling than simply describing how an individual self-identifies. Visual ethnographies also capture and reveal the intensity of the emotions of an individual in a way that words fail to capture.

In my research I have found that photographs and film can economically and effectively illustrate and communicate how racial identities are created, contested, translated, and written on the body in a context of competing and contradictory racial logics. The viewer of a photograph or a film is able to more clearly see their ideological investment in classifying an individual as a member of a particular racial group and how that is learned. They become more conscious of the fact that we are taught how to look, how to see, how to racially classify and how to erase and deny any information that contradicts or complicates binary categories. It is much easier to discuss and illustrate the ways that race is both a fiction and a reality. Visual images are pedagogically powerful because they force the viewer to confront her or his own assumptions about the meanings that they attach to the body. But these meanings rarely, if ever, reflect the complexity of an individual's ancestry, identity, and social history. Thus in my own research and teaching I use photographs and documentary film as another form of evidence that is used in dialogue with the written word.

8. *In this volume, we ask Christine Williams to reflect on the challenges of conducting field research as one becomes more senior. This seems to be a special challenge for women, who are often sought after to take on much of the administrative work in academic settings. How do you prepare your students to take on a research life that is often in conflict (or at least some tension) in what we are expected to do as in-resident teachers, colleagues, and mentors?*

Sustaining a research agenda for several decades, particularly for ethnographers, is very challenging. One of the challenges is not only the demands placed upon women to mentor, do administrative service, and teach but to balance their lives as parents or domestic partners. I am not sure that I have adequately prepared my students for this challenge because it is really something that varies by institution. Some institutions provide more support and internal research funding than others. There is a lot of inequality across institutions. I encourage my students to carefully think about what type of institutions (community college, liberal arts college, Public, Private or Research I university) they think they would ideally like to work in. I strongly encourage them to do research on the labor conditions, the demographics, and the social life at these institutions because they vary in terms of their demands. I mentor students who are not necessarily based at the university where I teach. One of the things that I tell them is to invest energy early in their career in networking with people who share their interests and develop collaborative relationships so that they can lay the groundwork to perhaps share the field research on joint projects. This is particularly crucial for students who want to have children while completing their degree or begin their family while in graduate school.

9. *You have spent much of your career in the University of California system, where you are now a professor in the Department of Sociology at UC Santa Barbara. In the past, you have written about how attacks on affirmative action and the criminalization of poverty threatened public education. The public education system in California is currently in crisis—what type of analysis or activism is necessary now? What is at stake?*

I am a first generation college student. I believe in public education because it is the public universities that educate the vast majority of people such as myself who are from working-class backgrounds and who are not racially privileged. We are witnessing one of the great public university systems begin to be dismantled and reconfigured in ways that constitute a betrayal of the goals established five decades ago. The current crisis is a product of policy decisions made and legislation passed which, in my view, was a backlash against affirmative action and the expansion of the university system. What is at stake is the ability of individuals from lower middle-class, middle-class, and minority backgrounds to access an affordable education. The stakes are so high because this is not only about future generations of educated citizens, but it is also about our funding priorities as a nation. Legislators and voters have essentially defunded public education which will restrict it to elites and the very special over-achievers from the working classes.

The Tenth Question
   What was the worst (or most difficult, or most embarrassing) interview/
   field encounter you've had?

In the summer of 1995 I went to England to conduct pilot research in London
and Leicester for my project on transracial mothers. I had few contacts and
initially relied on faculty members at Leicester University to announce my
research to their classes and to give me referrals to students who had white
mothers of multi-racial children in their friendship or familial networks.
One of the first people I contacted was a single mother who agreed to be
interviewed at her place of employment. I did not inquire where she worked.
I was simply told that she received some government support and worked
"off the books." I took a taxi to what appeared to be a respectable, middle-
class neighborhood of detached and semi-detached homes. I rang the bell. A
tall, statuesque white woman dressed in a Black leather outfit—a professional
dominatrix—answered the door. She introduced herself as the employer of
the woman I was scheduled to interview. She was a professional sex worker
and provided services out of her home. She welcomed me in and I immediately saw dildos of various colors, sex toys, and videos. I heard a voice in the
other room answering the phone and providing contract prices for various
services. "50 pounds for urination," "100 pounds for 2 hours of domination."
I was shocked but tried to conceal my anxiety and maintained a fixed smile
on my face. It occurred to me that I was conducting my first interview in
an independently operated brothel. I was told by Allesandra, the woman I
interviewed, that it was not against the law to provide sexual services in one's
home if you didn't advertise and didn't hire anyone else. I sat in the living
room and was served tea as I waited for my interviewee to get off the phone.
    During my interview, D. (the dominatrix) was upstairs providing ser-
vices to a man in one of her three bedrooms. I tried to focus on my interview
schedule but I kept being overwhelmed by the fear that somehow the woman
being interviewed would detect my anxiety and interpret it as judgment of
her. I was embarrassed by my level of discomfort and ashamed because I
thought of myself as progressive, as tolerant, as accepting of "alternative lifestyles," but I had never purchased sexual services, had never known anyone
who sold services in their home, and didn't quite know what other roles the
single mother in front of me played in this business. I was ashamed that I had
to consciously "work" at suppressing moral judgment. I felt that the woman
I was interviewing was closely monitoring my facial expressions and looking for any signs that I was not comfortable. I was afraid of being rejected
by her and thus losing potential access to her network of single mothers. I

feared being seen as provincial, not cosmopolitan, and as sexually inexperienced, but most importantly I did want to be perceived as an experienced researcher who could go into any setting and get the job done. This was one of the most challenging experiences that I had. Several weeks later I was invited to a birthday party for this same woman. I felt that I had to attend the party or she would feel rejected. So as the handcuffs were being passed out, as a joke, one of the women—a feminist—handcuffed me. Once again, I felt that I was being tested to see if I had the metal that it took to do field research in this community. As a control freak I found this quite emotionally challenging. I had never been handcuffed and it is not something that I fantasize about—especially when conducting field research! I spent more than an hour handcuffed to another woman while my husband looked on with amusement. I knew that if I resisted then I might not be seen as someone who could understand her life. I guess I must have passed the test because I was eventually accepted by the women at the party and they gave me access to my first snowball sample of other women who lived a more conventional lifestyle *and* were self-employed as professional dominatrixes.

What did you really want to do for a living? What were you afraid you might end up doing?

When I was a young child I really wanted to be an architect. Growing up in Chicago, the birthplace of American architecture was amazing because it is like living in a modernist architectural textbook. It is a perfectly realized grid city and the place where steel frame buildings and skyscrapers were invented. My father was a steel worker. I fell in love with Frank Lloyd Wright, Mies van der Rohe, among others. I became a fan of mid-century modernism. I thought that it would be great to design buildings. However, I soon learned that there were virtually no women and no Black architects. There were no role models and by the time I was 15 years old I had replaced this dream with new ones. My next dream was to become a gynecologist. I was on a pre-med track when I entered Northwestern University at the age of 16.

My biggest fear was that I would end up in a profession that was a dead end and boring. I wanted to be intellectually stimulated. I have always been an avid reader so I wanted a job that would enable me to keep reading.

What's the study you never pursued, but always wanted to?

The study that I never pursued is one on interracial friendships formed among women in the military and their potential for transforming the consciousness of individuals who grew up in racially and class segregated communities. As someone who has a number of relatives who are currently on active duty in Afghanistan and who grew up in exclusively Black communities, I have always been interested in how people transition from living in mono-racial and racially segregated communities to interracial organizations like the U.S. military.

15.

DENISE SEGURA

Chicana

1. *For many years you were the only Chicana in a UC sociology department. Would you talk about what that has meant in the way you have understood your UC career?*

Until the 2006–2007 academic year, I was the only Chicana/o or Latina/o tenure-track faculty in the sociology department at UC Santa Barbara. Until 2004–2005, I was the only Chicana sociologist in a sociology department in the entire 10-campus UC system. Given the demographics of California, I consider this an outrage! However, this imbalance is not surprising given the historical exclusion of Chicanas/os in higher education.

I got my first glimpse at understanding what it might mean to be a UC professor in 1975 when I was called into the office of the Provost of Oaks College at UC Santa Cruz where I was a junior majoring in sociology. Provost

Blake told me that he wanted to nominate me for a major fellowship because he thought I had "what it takes" to go to graduate school and become a professor. Frankly, I was stunned. I had never thought of becoming a professor and told the Provost that I saw myself as working *for* my community as a teacher given the need for Chicana/o teachers. He smiled broadly and said, "There are many ways to serve the community. Some of us become teachers; others enter other professions to serve. And all of these paths are important." Then he asked, "Do you know how many Chicana professors there are?" "Hardly any," I replied. "Right," he said. "You can contribute to your community in a way that many cannot. Will you do this for your community?" Well, when put that way, how could I refuse? I viewed my application to the sociology graduate program at UC Berkeley as part of a larger social movement to "bore from within" to work for change in the university especially to increase student diversity and undertake much-needed research on Chicanas/os.

In 1986 I became the third Chicana to receive a PhD in sociology from UC Berkeley. I remember clearly the day I "walked" to be hooded by my dissertation chair, Arlie Hochschild, partly because it was such a momentous day, but mostly because my 3-week old baby was screaming in the audience, hungry, and not at all impressed by the solemnity of the occasion. The fact that I could not hold my baby in the sociology graduation but could do so in the Chicano graduation that same week, spoke volumes of the challenges I faced as one of the few Chicana graduate students and mothers in that department and as one of the few Chicana assistant professors/mothers in the UC system. How often was I forced to choose between going to a faculty meeting or committee meeting and being home with my children? How many irretrievable moments of their childhoods did I miss by going to conferences and giving invited lectures to build my career? Wrenching choices all, but the strong community praxis I began to develop as an undergraduate ripened over the years and served as the guiding light that steered me through the tough graduate school years and informed my pathway through the UC professoriate. I believe I am here for my community and have striven to develop research that not only interrogates past and present pejorative assumptions about Chicana/o culture, educational values, or work attachment but provides new knowledge of Chicana/o ways of being grounded in women's voices. The strong, proactive mentorship I had at UC Santa Cruz instilled in me the desire to teach and mentor undergraduate and graduate women and men committed to social change.

I think my presence made a difference even though the cost was heavy when it came to my personal life. At the same time, my kids knew, come hell or high water, I would bake cupcakes for their entire class every single birthday of every single year while each of my three children was in elementary school. I went to every school play, parent conference, and jog-a-thon.

2. *You've devoted a lot of your time to changing your own institution. What value has that brought to your scholarship?*

When I look back and reflect on the work I've done, particularly in numerous committees, to try to make the university more accessible to a diverse student body and a more hospitable place for Chicana/o research, I keep in mind the moment in Luis Valdez's play, *Zoot Suit* when the protagonist, after being brutally beaten up says to the audience (whose members are gasping in horror), "Hey, don't take the *pinche* play so seriously!" These are words to live by. And here is one of the ways that sociology is kinda neat: we learn, write, and teach about the iron cage of bureaucracy wherein social institutions are hard to change but not invulnerable to suggestions to increase efficiency. The key for me has been to figure out how to present ways to increase access to the university by historically marginalized groups that highlights socially desirable outcomes including developing the reservoir of talent and excellence in all of our communities. This is hard work and very time consuming but essential for those of us interested in democratizing the institution. There are days of great despair when the initiatives I thought would pass go nowhere. But before I throw myself out a window (figuratively, of course), I remember Valdez's words and pick myself up and reflect on ways to strengthen my approach, consult with people I trust, and move forward.

I have focused significant attention on researching and teaching about the lives and struggles of Chicanas/os in the United States. This is a group that is growing at a fast rate but whose education and employment profiles are disproportionately among the working poor. Many of the students I teach are Chicanas/os and Latinas/os who are the first in their families to attend the university. I am committed to developing their sociological imaginations, much as mine was challenged long ago by Provost Blake at UC Santa Cruz. I believe that mentoring students promotes retention but also strengthens the educational pipeline to graduate school. I have also observed that Chicana/o and Latina/o students, who form my key interest area, tend to be community-oriented. They engage in significant levels of volunteer work among local Latina/o youth, especially in schools and tutoring programs. So years ago I thought to myself: "Might it be possible to enhance the retention of Chicana/o students and prepare interested students for graduate study by developing a curriculum and mentoring program in sociology that builds on their desire to 'work for' their community while providing them with research skills?"

Intrigued by this possibility while serving as Director of the Center for Chicano Studies, I headed a team that developed a campus proposal for extramural funding from the W.K. Kellogg Foundation titled, *"Enlace y Avance*: Students and Families Empowered for Success," which received a $100,000 planning grant in 2000–2001 and $1.5 million over 4 years (2001–2005) with matching funding from UCSB and the community colleges for $1.7 million. *Enlace* was an extremely complicated program that involved three community colleges, several school districts, and numerous community-based organizations. UCSB *Enlace* was one of only 14 projects nationwide to receive such support and has been mentioned in numerous reports on Latino education. The overarching goal of the *Enlace y Avance* partnership has been to produce more Latino/Hispanic college graduates by increasing their academic preparation across the K-12 pathway leading to greater college enrollment, retention, and graduation rates. Integral to this undertaking is linking the resources of the many partners and coordinating service delivery to enhance family involvement and parent empowerment in each community. In addition, we developed, implemented, and evaluated strategies to address unequal educational access by Latino students in different school settings *Enlace y Avance* sought to effect school-centered, systemic change in order to assist "at promise" students to achieve academic excellence and to realize productive and successful careers.

One core part of *Enlace* was the Undergraduate Research and Mentorship Program which I directed. Over the years I worked with 110 undergraduates, most of whom were Latinas/os and first generation college students. Of the 110 undergraduates who participated in *Enlace*, all have graduated. One-third have pursued graduate study and another third have pursued teaching credentials and are working in the schools. Each month I receive a number of e-mails and letters that speak to the positive impact of *Enlace* on their lives. My correspondence with my former undergraduates is very gratifying to me and allows me the opportunity to maintain a strong mentorship role. I firmly believe that mentorship is a lifelong commitment and I strive to teach my students to practice this as well. I have published one research report on *Enlace* and will submit several articles in the near future on the importance of merging the research priorities of the university with the applied interests of many undergraduates. The *Enlace* experience deepened the range of my scholarship in the area of education and Chicana/o and Latina/o communities.

3. *You have just recently embarked on an ethnographic and interview study of elderly Chicano men who lived and worked in the Los Angeles Watts neighborhood. What do you want to explore with this study? What meaning does it hold for you?*

One thing I rarely discuss with friends or colleagues is my sense of not feeling at "home" in the institution. My commitment to developing borderlands research is one way to explore the ways in which marginalized "others" deal with living "between and betwixt" (Anzaldua 1987)—not feeling legitimate in an institution structured to exclude Chicanas, particularly if they are doing research on Chicanas/os. Negotiating a space for my work has been one of the most time-consuming challenges I have faced, but it is one I do gladly because each inch I gain is one less inch the Chicanas/os that follow will have to fight for. This struggle occurs at so many levels across space and time, which brings me to the Watts study and reclaiming "home." I say this deliberately for ultimately how Chicanos go about re-creating a sense of belonging and "home," is what my study is about.

About 2 years ago, one of my aunts died after a long struggle with leukemia. At her funeral I overheard my uncles talking about something called the "Watts Reunion." I asked them to tell me more whereupon they revealed that each year since the 1960s, about 100 to 200 men and some women who had grown up in the 1940s, had gotten together to celebrate their "home" community, Watts (a section of South Central Los Angeles). The key organizer of the Watts Reunion has been a Chicano barber whose barbershop had been the center of the Chicano male network from the 1930s until the present day. Fascinated, I asked one of my uncles, "Do you go to this Reunion each year." "Oh yes," he replied, "your tia (aunt) and I look forward to it each year. A lot of 'old timers' go. It's a chance for us to get together, catch up with one another and talk about the old days." I started asking other relatives about the Watts Reunion and found out that many of the members of my extended family and their friends had been attending since they had left Watts during the 1960s.

Fascinated by the attachment of a large group of largely Chicano men to organize a reunion to maintain and perhaps re-create "community," I resolved to find out more. Questions emerged in my mind including: Why do the self-identified "Watts Old Timers" get together each year? What do they get out of it? How is it that men are the main organizers? Is this a way to re-create a sense of community or "home"? What were some of the experiences that bring the Old Timers together? Who goes to the Reunion and who does not go?

I feel a strong urgency to do this research since so few Watts Old Timers remain. Many have died and the remaining Old Timers are between the ages of 75 and 85. Thus far I have interviewed 10 Chicano male Watts Old Timers, including the main organizer. I have gone to three reunions including a more recent alternative reunion organized by a man who spent 30 years in prison. So far, I've identified several features about the Watts Reunions that are interesting and potentially significant sociologically. First, the main organizer is a Chicano man whose barbershop was (and is) the "hub" of this male-oriented community reunion. Second, the men appear to be committed to strengthening the networks that originated in their childhoods in Watts. This type of responsibility for nurturing social networks departs from traditional depictions of Mexican masculinity. I see this study as potentially rounding out our understanding of Mexican masculinities. Third, the men self-label as "Watts Old Timers" and they articulate a strong sense of "belonging" to a community even though none of them lives there anymore. Nevertheless their interviews describe myriad shared experiences that bind them together and inform their political consciousness. Fourth, the men are survivors and unpacking the ways Chicano men negotiated survival in pre-Civil Rights era is important. These men escaped gang warfare (although nearly all bear gang tattoos) either through sports or the military (or both). They secured gainful employment that allowed them to buy homes and support families.

This is a story then, of men who navigated across racism and class inequality to assert their right to "belong" in the United States. They exhibit strong patriotism but also a strong sense of ethnic pride. Their eyes brim with tears as they relate instances of racism including police harassment, educational neglect, and seeing older brothers beat up by sailors during the Zoot Suit riots. The community they honor each year is one that is nuanced and critical. Ultimately they honor their "home" and in doing so, have helped me to reconnect with my own roots in this neighborhood where I also was born. All of us have moved beyond the geographic terrain of Watts but the lessons of survival and the strength that emanates from the community is a sociological story I hope will both illuminate and inspire.

4. *The preponderance of your work represents an exemplar of public sociology. How have you understood the relationships among research, teaching, and social change? What research projects have been especially emblematic of what you've wanted to achieve?*

I use a public sociology approach. For me, the union between research, teaching, and social change necessarily centers on the need to develop new paradigms and epistemological tools to tackle pressing societal problems. One of my earliest projects that illustrates both goals is the Isla Vista Research Project, a 1994 to 1996 community study of Chicanas/os, Latinas/os, and their families in the community adjacent to UCSB. This research project was the centerpiece of The Undergraduate Research Internship Program I developed in the UCSB Center for Chicano Studies. A number of undergraduate and graduate students participated in the Isla Vista Research Project developing, administering, and analyzing two surveys on "housing" and the "quality of life," as well as follow-up interviews on these topics. The Isla Vista research project contributed new and essential knowledge on immigrant adaptation and the barriers to socio-economic integration important for analysis and debate by local policy makers, schools (including the university), and community-based organizations. The report, "Latinos in Isla Vista: A Report on the Quality of Life Among Latino Immigrants" (Segura 1999) was widely disseminated throughout the local community and led to the successful funding for a teen center located in Isla Vista where local youth receive a wide array of recreation and educational support services.

From 2000 to 2005, my Graduate School of Education colleague, Richard Duran, a team of graduate students, and I examined the academic challenges, progress, and intervening influences on achievement of a cohort of 35 6th grade students as part of the Kellogg *Enlace* program. Utilizing a case study developmental methodology, I trained and deployed 20 to 25 undergraduate mentors each year to work with these students and their families in Isla Vista/Goleta. In addition, the project worked closely with the community colleges in selected rural sites in Ventura County to work with cohorts of 11th and 12th graders to provide them with additional counseling and academic tutoring. We also met with parents and families under the aegis of local community-based agencies to provide family-based services and informational seminars (on a wide range of issues including education, immigration, health, and financial management).

On a personal note, one of the high school students from the rural community of Oxnard who attended Ventura Community College was accepted into UCSB and took one of my undergraduate classes! In light of the abysmal transfer rate of Latinos to the 4-year universities from the community colleges, it was very gratifying to see her and know that over 60% of the students we've mentored in this area have enrolled at UCSB or other universities! One key accomplishment is that the *Enlace* model (close coordination of academic preparation services with the University, community colleges, community based-organizations, schools, and families) is now institutionalized within the structure of educational preparation programs and outreach at UCSB. It is no longer a "special" program but part of business as usual. I think that may be my greatest accomplishment given that it is one way that research and service have come together to make a difference in people's life chances.

5. *Last year, you and feminist anthropologist Patricia Zavella served as guest editors for the special issue of* Gender & Society, *titled "Gendered Borderlands" [2008]. In the introduction you outline the various complexities implied in what you call "borderlands feminist projects." What are some personal experiences that draw you to an understanding of a "borderlands" existence—where one doesn't claim a conventional home, and must exercise agency as "other"?*

In our co-authored "Introduction" to the special issue of *Gender & Society*, "Gendered Borderlands," Patricia Zavella and I discussed the growth of borderlands-centered research in the humanities and social sciences. Borderlands research explores relations of power and domination, resistance and agency, among women and men typically cast as marginalized "others." We suggest that a feminist borderlands project interrogates the multiple meanings of borders and borderlands. There are four key dimensions of borderlands: structural, discursive, interactional, and agentic, any one of which can be a site of feminist analysis.

Structural dimensions of a feminist borderlands project critique the effects of globalizing economies, neoliberal state practices, and growing regional interdependence. One example of a feminist borderlands project that engages in a structural analysis would focus on the growth in women's immigration and transnational motherhood. Although I am a third-generation Chicana, my children's father was an immigrant and I remember the sadness in my former mother-in-law's eyes as she described the anguish of losing a child to pneumonia that he caught from crossing the Rio Grande River at night and the poverty and fear of deportation that prevented her from seeking health care for him. He died in her arms and was buried in an unmarked grave in South Texas.

Borderlands projects also disentangle the complexities of intersecting discursive power relations and interrogate how discourses of race, class, gender, and sexuality are reified ideologically but undermined in practice. I remember when my son was born with the dark purplish spot on his backside which, according to my ex-husband's family signified indigenous "blood," I received both compliments and comfort. Some of the family noted his dark skin with pride but others hugged me saying, "Don't worry, he will lighten up as he gets older." I accepted both sets of comments as consistent with the contradictions of racial discourse vis-à-vis Mexicans in the United States. Historically, those of us with lighter skin and more classic European pheno-types have enjoyed higher social mobility and greater acceptance from white society. But the internal dynamics of the community also articulate pride in the great Indian civilizations of ancient Mexico. The complexities of these intersecting discourses of race and power are constantly evolving and are intertwined with tensions of sex and sexualities whose nuances are critical borderlands projects.

Feminist borderlands projects can be informed by personal experiences but typically embrace a larger reality. That is, the main questions may begin at home but become broader and more refined as I observe the world, talk with people, and try to make sense of the ongoing dynamics of the inter-face between structure and agency. Ultimately a feminist borderlands project explores how women voice their complex human agency within economic, political, and cultural transformations occurring in the borderlands between the United States and Mexico and beyond. Moreover, given the community praxis embodied within Chicana feminist sociology, developing research and policy initiatives or programs to address the economic marginality of women of all race-ethnicities and their families is essential.

6. *One of the most cited articles in feminist sociology is your article co-authored with Beatriz Pesquera, "Chicanas in White Collar Jobs: 'You Have to Prove Yourself More'" (1992). That line of research on Chicana professionals was formative in many respects. What was your experience as you broke new scholarly ground with this topic?*

One of the joys of doing research on Chicana workers is that after some ini-tial hesitation, women enjoy sharing their stories. Interviews can be one of the few times that they have permission to speak about themselves without guilt or fear of reprisal. I learn so much from other Chicanas! It's a strange feeling to talk to women whose family backgrounds are so similar but have ended up in such different social worlds. One of the things that has always impressed me is the generous spirit with which women share their stories—always checking in with me to ask if what they are telling me is "helpful." Their desire to be helpful reminds me of my own responsibility to be con-structive. I try to be mindful that I am responsible for developing an analysis that builds on women's lived experiences and telling their stories with integ-rity. I am always humbled by women's generosity and their hope that their stories about work, family, and experiences of race/gender discrimination can help others. I don't know if my work has helped other women workers directly but I hope that students and professionals who access this work can develop policy and programs attentive to the dilemmas of gender, race, and class in the workplace and in our society.

> 7. *As a UC "baby" (i.e., someone who is schooled by, and spends one's entire career at UC) you've grown up in a university and a discipline which was often unwelcoming to white women and people of color. Perhaps we are speaking again of "borderlands," but within those conventional categories, feminists of color are left to negotiate uncertain political territory. How did you do it?*

Sometimes I wonder if it has been an advantage or disadvantage to receive all of my higher education in the University of California. For me, it was the only path I could take to access higher education, given the culturally gendered expectations in my family that young women in the 1970s should stay as close to home as possible, or at least in the same state!

Growing up in an environment and time period where Chicanas simply did not leave their families until they got married, I dreamed of leaving my home in Los Angeles. Craftily I figured that the only acceptable way I could break with the tradition of staying home until I married would be to be accepted at an out-of-town university. However, I also knew I couldn't go "too far" otherwise the odds of securing parental consent would diminish. I applied to UC Santa Cruz because a close friend applied who my family knew which gave them a degree of comfort with the process. It was the only college I applied to. I put all of my eggs in one basket reasoning that if it was "meant to be" I would be accepted; otherwise I would do what my uncles said I *should* do—attend the local community college (across the street from my home), and then transfer to Cal State Los Angeles or Cal State Long Beach—*if* I didn't get married, of course. Such were the culturally gendered expectations of a Chicana in 1972. Much to everyone's surprise (especially my high school counselor), I was accepted at UC Santa Cruz.

My mother was advised to keep me at home but influenced by my stepfather, she allowed me to leave. I think she didn't know where Santa Cruz actually was located, and confused it with San Jose where her family had worked in the fields during her childhood. But she and my stepfather silenced my uncles' objections and drove me to UCSC. I don't think she or I have done anything harder in our lives than to say good-bye at the doorstep of the university apartment I was going to live in. I remember she bought me a huge box of Tide detergent and lots of sanitary napkins so I'd be well-prepared for the quarter. I cried all night and wondered why I hadn't even thought to apply to UCLA so I could live at home.

After my homesickness wore off, I became both fascinated and appalled by the differences in privilege and power among the undergrads. One of my roommates was going to college on a trust fund; another was the daughter of a wealthy attorney. They had designer clothes that they eschewed in favor of torn jeans and faded peasant blouses. The guys next door had a killer stereo system but threw out their bed frames as a mark of affinity with the hippie counter-culture popular at that time. In the midst of the privileged classes developing their own space, the Chicanos, overwhelmingly from the rural poor with a smattering of urban working-class representatives, found one another and tried to figure out what the rich white people were doing throwing out bed frames and wearing torn-up jeans! Most of us had saved our money to buy new clothes and had bought new linens for our beds. Some had not had the luxury of even *having* their own beds before, and so quietly collected the discarded bed frames to "relocate" them to their families' homes. These class and race disjunctures were both fascinating and frustrating. Learning how to live with privileged students was a key lesson that has served me well in the university. So perhaps being a "UC baby" has been helpful, after all, in teaching me the skills to survive and thrive in a culture that is fundamentally distinct from mine but essential to negotiate.

8. *In past writings, you have spoken of the challenges of "reclaiming Chicana subjectivity in a post-Chicano movement era" (Segura 2001: 545) What has that meant for you over the years as Chicano Studies has slowly accepted Chicana scholars?*

My research and teaching on Chicana workers, feminism, Latina/o education, and the dilemmas of Latina/o immigrant adaptation and innovation have been important to building a field of inquiry—Latina/o sociology—whose development stems from crucial empirical and theoretical contributions of research on race-ethnicity and gender. My research is unique in that it merges theories and writings from three distinct disciplines (Sociology, Chicano Studies, Feminist Studies) into one coherent area of study and research (Latina/o Sociology). The method of inquiry I utilize brings a race-ethnic, class, and gender analysis into productive feminist dialogue on Chicanas in the labor force, Chicana feminist discourse and theory, and Latina/o education. Finally, my research provides a grounding of Chicana/o and Latina/o experiences within a sociological qualitative analysis that reveals processes of stratification, resistance, and empowerment among this growing population.

In general, my research on Chicanas and on the Chicana/o and Latina/o community as well as my professional service has tended to be validated more often in Chicana/o Studies, Latina/o Sociology and Feminist Studies venues than in mainstream sociology. Most of my publications have been in Chicana/o Studies or Feminist Studies journals or in books on Latinos/as and women of color. I know some of my colleagues consider publishing in specialized outlets as a form of academic ghettoization or perhaps I should say, "barrioization," but I see this as my choice since one of my primary goals in the academy has been to contribute to the development of Chicana scholarship and Latina/o Sociology.

I see my work within the Chicana feminist tradition that validates connections to our communities and centers on women's voices and experiences. Chicana feminist sociology explores how women voice their complex human agency within economic, political, and cultural transformations occurring globally but experienced more directly in the United States and Mexico. Moreover, given the community praxis embodied within Chicana feminist sociology, developing research and policy initiatives or programs to address the economic marginality of women of all race-ethnicities and their families is essential.

9. *What sorts of advice do you give to your Chicana/o graduate students today about the work lives they will face in the academy? Do they, like you, see those clear connections between research, teaching, and community empowerment?*

Currently I chair the MA or PhD committees of 11 Chicana/o or Latina/o graduate students in sociology. I am on numerous other committees as well. I am deeply committed to my graduate students, but before I take on a new student I warn him or her that I will be a little tough but will support the student as best as I can intellectually, spiritually, and politically, if they work hard. Each of them understands my community praxis which means that sometimes they will have to wait for appointments or letters if I need to address concerns or questions from undergraduates or community members. I tell my graduate students that my undergraduates—who are often women, Chicana/o, and Latina/o or first generation college students—often have no one else to talk with. Because most of my graduate students are also first generation college students, they honor the principle of strengthening the pipeline even if it means that they must wait and indeed help the undergrads as well.

One of the more controversial things I do with my graduate students is not chastise them when they ask me for "last minute" letters of recommendation. Rather I tell them, "I will do this for you because someday you will also do this for someone. So, remember…." And then I tell them the story of Maxine Baca Zinn who mentored me while I was at UC Berkeley and she was a visiting faculty member from the University of Michigan, Flint. Because she was not a tenure track UC faculty member, I could not put her on my dissertation committee. Nevertheless she worked with me and gave me critical feedback on the dissertation. I remember one day going into her office, exhausted from caring for three children including a one-month old baby, trying to finish up the final revisions of my dissertation. My chair, Arlie Hochschild had given me some comments that I was too tired to address so I asked Maxine for her advice. She sat down with me and patiently talked me through Arlie's comments and helped me craft the necessary revisions of that chapter. When we were done I remember asking her, "Why are you doing this, Maxine? You can't get credit for this since I can't put you on my committee? And you have so many demands on your time." She smiled at me and said, "I do this because someday you will do this for someone else."

I tell this story to every single one of my graduate students. And each of them tells me, "Denise, I will do this too." And so it continues, the tradition of service and excellence among our small but growing Chicana/o and Latina/o community in the university.

I affirm the service orientation with which my graduate students come to UCSB. I try to set an example whereby they are shown the importance of taking care of their academic "business" in order to be in the position to do the community and university service that advocates greater academic preparation and access to the university for historically disenfranchised groups. I try to show by example, that it is possible to have children, if that is their desire, secure the respect of their colleagues, and engage in meaningful research and significant service. In 2009, my students honored me by supporting my nomination for the Outstanding Latino/a Faculty in Higher Education (Research Institutions) Award given by the American Association of Hispanics in Higher Education (AAHHE). It was both humbling but gratifying to hear of their support. I learn from them every day and feel blessed that I paid attention to Provost Blake in 1975 when he advised me that "There are many ways to serve the community."

The Tenth Question
   *What was the worst (or most difficult, or most embarrassing) interview/
   field encounter you've had?*

When I was conducting interviews for my dissertation in 1984, one of the first ones was with a Mexican immigrant woman who was working in a garment factory. I remember that she had a quiet and dignified demeanor which did not prepare me for the anguish of her story. When I asked her about her family she said in a flat voice that she had one child in Mexico that she'd had to leave behind but had since given birth to another child in the United States. My inexperience led me to ask her how she felt about having a child so far away. Of course she said that she felt as if a part of her had been torn away and could never be recovered and that the greatest sadness was that her child talked to her as if she were a stranger and preferred instead to speak to her grandmother with whom she was living.

While we spoke I noticed that her hands plucked gently at the trimmings of her apron. Her voice did not change but remained flat as she continued her narrative. I asked her why she had come to the United States and she said "to work." I asked her "to make a better life?" "To eat," she replied. "In my small town, there was not enough food. So I came here." Many years have passed since that interview but the simplicity of her words carried a power that has stayed with me. Then, I asked her how she went about finding jobs. "I walk," she replied. She said she would walk and apply at every sewing factory until she found one. And the man in charge asked her if she was okay working with the material. And here is the question that embarrassed me, "Why did he ask you that? Did the material cause allergies?" "No, it causes cancer," she said. Nonplussed I didn't know what to say. So she gently said while getting up to get me a cup of coffee, "I said it would not bother me. We need to eat."

This interview was one of the first interviews I conducted for my dissertation. And I learned more about myself than I did about her. For her story was not unlike that of many Mexican immigrant women who had left families behind to work in hazardous conditions out of dire economic need. But I learned so much about what I did not know and how privileged I was vis-à-vis immigrants in my community. This woman did not live that far from me geographically but socially we were inhabiting completely different worlds. It was difficult to think that a working-class Chicana could be so different from a Mexican immigrant woman—and so ignorant about her life. Cancer indeed! What I learned by asking that question was to listen not just with my sociologically trained mind, but with my cultural heart. At the end of the interview I touched her arm and we shook hands gravely but with respect.

I sometimes wish I could re-write my dissertation now that I am more comfortable with who I am and what I do not know. I guess that's not an unusual thing to feel but writing about my most difficult field situation makes me think about how rich and varied women's experiences are and how important it is to chronicle them.

What did you really want to do for a living? What were you afraid you might end up doing?

I don't remember ever having a strong career goal. I always assumed I would get married, have children, and if I was really lucky, have enough money to stay home. I remember in college reading *The Feminist Mystique* (Friedan, 1963) and being pretty mystified by it. Who would not want to stay home and take care of their children and family? In my community, having the economic means to stay home, have a nice home, and be able to send children to good schools and volunteer for good causes like my school or the church, was a dream. So I guess being an affluent stay-at-home mom would have to be my first "career" dream. But after leaving my childhood behind I started seeing so much injustice directed against Chicanas/os and Blacks that I was determined to do "something" about it. What that "something" might be was never well-defined. My only fear was that I would not be able to follow that path. But in reality, the fear was never strong because I had a feeling I would be an educator, which is what I ended up being!

What's the study you never pursued, but always wanted to?

Once in a while, maybe just once in a lifetime, a person gets the opportunity to do something that is personally meaningful and socially significant. I believe my Watts Old Timers' study will realize my dream to bridge the gulf between the community and the university by exploring a key Chicano borderland "home."

16.
CHRISTINE WILLIAMS

1. *Your earlier work,* Still a Man's World, *on men employed in jobs stereo-
    typed as "female" contributed greatly to our understanding of work and
    gender (Williams 1995). Were you to begin that work today, would you
    do anything differently with respect to such elements as research design
    or theoretical perspective?*

Definitely, yes. Reading that book today reminds me of how little I had incorporated "intersectionality" into my sociology in the early 1990s. Intersectionality is an approach to studying gender that takes race/ethnicity, class, and
sexuality into account. This approach treats gender not as an abstract and
timeless essence, but as an embodied and historical practice. It insists that
claims about gender take into consideration how the *particular* men or women
whose experiences are being analyzed are located in social space. Moreover,
as a geometric metaphor, intersectionality draws attention to how meanings

of social identities are socially constructed through binary oppositions: masculine/feminine, male/female, white/Black, straight/queer, rich/poor.

Intersectionality deepens our understanding of how gender is socially constructed. Without it, research isn't necessarily *wrong*; but it is *partial*. That's what I see when I re-visit my work on men in non-traditional (i.e., predominantly female) occupations, like nursing and teaching. In my work, I argued that these men often benefited from their token status. I labeled this pattern the "glass escalator" (to contrast it with the "glass ceiling" experienced by many women in male-dominated occupations). I showed that men in these jobs were often assumed to be better leaders than women, so many were drawn into administrative positions. Homophobia kept them out of specialties that are closely associated with children, but since these jobs tended to be lower paying, the consequence was to push men up to higher paying and more prestigious specialties.

Although in my work I noted that the glass escalator was not available to all men—in particular gay men and racial/ethnic minority men—I didn't elaborate or theorize the reasons for this difference. This is an example of what Adrienne Rich (1979) would have called "white solipsism," the tendency "to think, imagine, and speak as if whiteness described the world." White solipsism is not the assumption of white superiority; rather, it is the assumption that white experience is the standard, the average, or the starting point for every analysis; whoever doesn't "fit" the white model is "different," and to the extent that they are included in the analysis, the focus is on that particular difference.

Adia Harvey Wingfield (2009), in contrast, has taken an "intersectional" approach in her study of Black men nurses, which reveals the limitations of my research. Adia found that Black men nurses are often seen as *less skilled* than women nurses. While many of the white men I interviewed said that patients confused them with doctors, few Black men encountered this assumption. Comparing our results, it seems that behaviors that denote "leadership" ability in white men are interpreted as "menacing" behavior from Black men. Adia has also found that Black men faced stigma *inside* the profession, and social acceptance on the *outside*—which is exactly the opposite of what the white men I interviewed experienced. And while most of the men I talked to seemed to disavow a "caring" motivation, Adia is finding that Black men embrace this rationale for the work they do, sometimes linking it to their Christianity, which did not show up at all in my data, but resonates with Richard Pitt's work on masculinity and the African American Church (Pitt 2010).

The experience of Black men nurses is not simply "different" from that of white men. The two are flip sides of the same coin. Hegemonic masculinity is based on White privilege; we cannot fully understand the mechanism of the glass escalator without an understanding of racism. The same is also true for homophobia: the exclusion of gay men from the glass escalator is not merely an exception to the rule; it is part of the process of reproducing hegemonic masculinity.

2. *Reading* Inside Toyland *(2006), it is sometimes quite clear that your analysis draws productively from your earlier work. How do you think the work on men in female jobs enhanced your study of stores and shopping?*

My previous books focused on the exceptions: men and women who "cross over" to work in occupations considered appropriate for the "opposite" gender. So I was conditioned to be on the lookout for anyone who was out of place in the toy stores. But I observed very few instances of crossing over. The few people who did work in "non-traditional" jobs stood out and often suffered mistreatment, giving me renewed respect and empathy for the men and women in my earlier studies.

Over the course of my fieldwork, I witnessed only two women who crossed over, and both of them were African Americans who had been hired to work in the backrooms. Their jobs involved unloading and storing the inventory. Both of them claimed to like their jobs, but Chandrika told me that she encountered so much misogyny and racism in the backroom that she requested and received a transfer. Darlene stuck it out, but she was subjected to a great deal of ridicule and joking behind her back.

The few men who crossed over did so to fill in temporarily when there weren't enough women to do the "women's jobs." Thus, Jack was assigned to work the baby register on a day when Patricia didn't show up, which was a clearly humiliating experience for him. Carl had to work with me in the Barbie section on a particularly busy day; he performed the job in a campy way, swishing about and lisping—his idea of parodying the assumed homosexuality of any man interested in Barbies. Deshay flat out refused to work the cash register. My previous work had alerted me to anticipate all of these reactions.

In *Still a Man's World* (1995), I found that men were rewarded with higher status and pay for distancing themselves from women's work and qualities associated with femininity. But the benefits of the glass escalator were not evident in the toy stores I studied. Part of the reason may be that the toy store workers did not identify with their jobs in the same way that professionals often do. In my follow-up interview study, I have found only a handful of workers who aspire to a career in retail; the more typical goal is to escape the industry as soon as possible. One reason is because some stores lack career ladders, which was the case at the big box store I studied. No one—men or women—could work their way from the floor into management. Moreover, none of the associates earned living wages (although men generally earn more than women in retail employment). These were *bad jobs*. With turn-over rates of over 100%, a revolving door may be a better metaphor than an escalator (or ceiling) to describe the experiences of most retail workers.

3. *As you say in* Inside Toyland, *Joan Acker (1992) first alerted us to "gen-dered" institutions. Yet, the experience one has while reading* Inside Toy-land *is that it is chock full of concrete examples—not just that institutions are gendered—but of* how *they are gendered, raced and classed. Were you aware of the dynamic character of this gendering while you were a worker, or did these qualities strike you only later?*

I joke with my students that an occupational hazard of being a sociologist is noticing inequality wherever you go. So as a regular shopper, I was very much aware of the importance of race, gender, and class in structuring the retail environment before I undertook the research. What was surprising to me is how much I became interpellated into these systems of inequality. As a critic on the sidelines, it is relatively easy to identify and denounce the mechanisms of social reproduction. But once I was subjected to these forces of stratification, it became much more difficult to resist them. Over time, I found myself giving in.

For instance, shoppers in the upscale toy store often asked me for advice on what to buy. They always specified gender and age: "What should I get for a 7-year-old girl?" The managers urged us workers to resist gender stereotyping and inquire about the child's interests. But customers would act confused and rankled if I did this. They'd follow up my question about her interests with, "You know, she's interested in things that interest a typical 7-year-old girl." So after a few half-hearted attempts at suggesting trucks for girls and dolls for boys, I gave in to the culture and promoted gender socialization. One time I helped a shopper pick out a gift for a young girl. We happily decided on a Bar-bie accessorized with an infant in a pink crib. Only later, when writing up my field notes, did I realize how far I had come from my feminist critique. What was I *thinking?* I realized that it's one thing to criticize gendered organizations from afar, quite another to disrupt interactions in the moment.

4. *For a number of qualitative researchers in our discipline there seems to be an inverse relationship between the age of the researcher and the initiation of new field projects. As lives get complicated, investments in field research seem too labor intensive, too demanding, and too*

disruptive. You went "Inside Toyland" at 41. Was it much more difficult than it would have been at 31?

I also have noticed that qualitative researchers stop doing fieldwork at a certain age, and it strikes me as curious. I think it was easier undertaking a field study in my 40s compared to when I was younger. My first book, which was my dissertation, took me to the Pentagon, and also to Parris Island, South Carolina, where I spent 2 weeks interviewing, observing, and participating in Marine Corps basic training. Those ventures were the hardest things I had ever done to that point. I was insecure, I missed my friends, and I had very little money. It was an era before the Internet, credit cards, and cell phones, all of which make ethnographic work much easier today.

The hardest part of qualitative research for me is the emotional work involved in contacting gatekeepers and potential respondents. As a graduate student and later as an assistant professor, much was at stake in my successful access, which heightened the emotional stress. What if people refused to be interviewed? What if I couldn't get in? Today the stress is still there, but my self-concept is not severely impacted if people turn me down (which rarely happens, anyway). Because I am more confident and self-reliant today, fieldwork seems less daunting than before.

Those first "high risk" emotionally fraught moments in the field are universally reported as the most difficult. How do you talk to your students first facing this sort of challenge?

I punted this question to my current and former students, as I cannot recall saying anything specifically about this. My former student Patricia Richards remembered that I told her to "suck it up and do it." Kirsten Dellinger said that I told her to quit worrying about access because "some things are just too important to worry about" (which became our personal koan). Gretchen Webber always knew that she had to be entrepreneurial in finding respondents—it is a requirement of the job—so she never questioned it, and we never talked about it. Cati Connell, one of my current students, wrote this:

> First, you always remind me that worrying about access is a waste of energy and a potential limitation to research. You tell me to approach any project with the ideal study in mind—what kind of sample makes sense? What kind of sample would I like to have? Samples and sites can always be altered down the line if access issues arise, but you can't get access at all to the perfect sample if you don't try. (And, as in your experience, I have yet to have any major access problems, despite my initial worries!) Second, you remind me that, in general, people enjoy talking about their experiences. Requesting an interview is much

easier when you go in confident that this conversation might be enjoyable and beneficial to both parties. (At the same time, you remind me to be humble about the fact that this is a great favor they are doing for you—sociologists expect total access to people's lives, with little to give back in return.) Going in with a balance of confidence and humility has made it much easier to approach people as time goes on.

5. *Of your fieldwork at the two toy stores, you mentioned how important it is to have actually been employed as a worker. Can you describe some of the insights that you gained, which might have been lost had you only interviewed workers and managers?*

Most of my previous studies used in-depth interviews. I undertook fieldwork for this project to learn more about the methodology. As others argue, participant observation (or observant participation) generates an appreciation for the embodied dimension of social life. These jobs really beat me down. I don't think I would have fully appreciated the physical and emotional intensity of the work if I hadn't put myself through it.

Putting my body on the line also enhanced my understanding of the skills needed to be a successful worker. Many people believe that retail work is unskilled—even many of those who work in these. But I'm convinced that the jobs are labeled "unskilled" because they are low wage jobs, not the other way around. It's just that the skills are undervalued and invisible. For example, I was stunned at how hard it is to work a cash register. Each store uses a different system, so learning to be a cashier is not unlike learning a new software program. From the customer's perspective, it looks insanely easy— beep, beep, beep—but they don't see the huge book of instructions on what to do when the system breaks down. How do you manually insert credit card numbers, search the inventory, call the manager? And how do you do all this when you have a line of angry and impatient customers staring at you and making huffing noises? Retail workers learn a whole informal system of rules from their peers about coping with the stress. The learning period is intense, but after a few weeks of very public and often humiliating trial and error, the work becomes second nature. That process of acquiring this bodily knowledge would elude the researcher who uses only interview methods.

Another problem with in-depth interviews has to do with access. I have been working on a follow-up interview study of retail workers to fill in some of the gaps that remained after *Inside Toyland*. Recruiting participants for this study has been surprisingly difficult. Some of my former undergraduate students volunteered for interviews, and I snowballed out from them, but since I wanted a more inclusive sample, these networks were clearly inadequate. My research assistant, Cati Connell, and I struggled with this. We posted ads on Craigslist, wrote invitations to employee list-serves, tried snowballing from personal contacts, and even confronted workers directly in stores to ask them to participate (although the latter approach was forbidden by our IRB). Even with the offer of a $15 grocery gift card, it was difficult to generate enthusiasm from potential respondents. We suspect that this reluctance stems, in part, from the low social status that attaches to retail work. Virtually all of our respondents insisted that they had nothing important to say about their jobs. I also believe that workers are wary of participating because they fear losing their jobs. In one case, a worker at Office Max was reprimanded for talking to me, even though our conversations occurred while she was on break and off-the-clock. This was a much different experience than I have encountered when interviewing workers in professional careers, who in retrospect seemed eager and even proud to share their work histories with me. How this occupational difference may have impacted the sociology of work is worthy of an independent investigation.

> At the same time, you imply that you didn't think of this work as a *"proper ethnography."* What do you think was sacrificed?

Inside Toyland isn't a "proper ethnography" because it is based on 3 months of fieldwork (6 weeks at each of the two stores). Anthropologists usually spend at least a year in the field. The goal in such extended stays is to develop more intimate understandings of people and their relationships to each other, both in the field setting and beyond. Because I didn't have a year to devote to the fieldwork, I sacrificed this more intimate knowledge. I would have loved to hang out with my co-workers after work, meet their friends and families, and develop a better sense of what their jobs meant to them and how they balanced their work and home lives. For example, many of my co-workers at the Toy Warehouse were single parents. I often wondered how they coped with work schedules that shifted from week to week. I heard a lot of complaints about scheduling, and I noted that some brought their kids into the store with them, no doubt because they were unable to make other care arrangements. It would have enhanced my discussion of how the social organization of retail work impacts employees to observe more of their personal lives first-hand.

6. *Throughout your career, you have often been a critic of institutional racism. Most recently, you were a vocal critic of the behavior of Austin businesses that closed down in anticipation of the arrival of African American spectators to the Texas Relays. [The Texas Relays are a 4-day track and field event that draws nearly 50,000 visitors to town.] Could*

you elaborate on what it is like to engage in anti-racism work in your institution?

It is really cool that you know about this. Texas Relays is an awesome event, bringing Olympic-level athletes as well as high school students to compete in track and field events in a stunning venue on the University of Texas campus. Tens of thousands of African Americans descend upon Austin from all over the country to watch the Relays and to enjoy a party scene that has come to be known as the Black Mardi Gras. It's probably the biggest social gathering in Texas of African Americans.

In 2009, several local businesses and a large indoor mall shut down explicitly in order to avoid the patronage of those attending the Relays. My research in *Inside Toyland* revealed mostly hidden and indirect instances of racism, but this was blatant and galling. I protested in an editorial written for the local paper, I plastered the campus (including the Relays) with fliers, and I participated in an NAACP rally at the mall.

Several of my colleagues throughout the University supported my efforts. Robert Jensen in the Journalism Department is a wellspring of advice and information on how to wage successful protests. He is the first person I call when I want to generate publicity for some cause. Another resource is the Warfield Center for African and African American Studies, which is led by politically astute scholars who sponsor and support anti-racist research and activism on campus. Two affiliates of the program, Professors Jerome Williams and Geraldine Henderson, conduct research on consumer racial profiling. They offered immediate encouragement to me personally, and then wrote a follow-up article for the newspaper that explained their research findings on racism in stores. Their article also addressed the flood of racist responses generated by my editorial.

Paradoxically, the historical legacy of racism at my University may make it acceptable to engage in anti-racism protests on campus. Few people at the University of Texas dispute its racist past. Administrators constantly struggle to overcome our racist reputation in both material and symbolic ways. This year, for instance, a statue of former U.S. legislator and UT faculty member, Barbara Jordan was erected on campus, a measure aimed to counterbalance the ubiquitous statues of "Confederate Heroes" that ring the campus. Because of this political context, I knew that I would not be pilloried for my anti-racism; on the contrary, I expected to be at worst ignored, and at best appreciated for my efforts.

I suspect that schools with more enlightened histories may be more blinded to contemporary manifestations of racism and more dismissive of activists. (The same probably holds true for sexism—more enlightened institutions may be less willing to embrace feminism and confront ongoing gender discrimination.) At Texas, we have a lot of work to do and we know it. An excellent overview of the history and controversy associated with the Relays was published in the Texas alumni magazine: http://www.texasexes. org/alcalde/feature.asp?p=4422

> *But this consideration of the historical context of an institution's culture and past is seldom (if ever) discussed when sociologists compare the ease or difficulty in making change within them. Care to comment?*

I am troubled by your observation. In my opinion, sociology without historical context is bad sociology. Last week I attended an anniversary celebration of Women's Studies at the University of Texas. Gathered together were a group of our "foremothers," who are now professors emeriti, provosts, and deans. They reflected on the barriers they confronted 30 years ago, including anti-nepotism policies, blatantly sexist administrators, and a normalized culture of sexual harassment. Nothing that I do today would be possible without their earlier struggles.

On the other hand, I don't want to exaggerate the effectiveness of any protest activity at my University compared to other places. Social change is tricky, and "progress" on any issue is very hard to detect, especially when the fight is still being waged. Moreover, even successful social movements can have unintended consequences, including the fueling of backlash.

> 7. *You say it is a "middle-class conceit" (Williams, 2006: 19) to imagine that where one works is necessarily a reflection of a person's interests, values, and aptitudes. What other such "conceits" did you collide with as a worker?*

As a professor, I expect people to treat me with respect, at least in face-to-face interactions. I am also used to people asking my opinion, like you are doing with this project. When I went to work at the toy stores, I was completely unprepared to be treated like an idiot by customers. At first I fought back, using words like *ideological* and *hegemony* when shoppers acted out. (Then I realized that I was being a jerk instead of taking in the social environment, like a good researcher is supposed to do.) I also was unprepared to suffer the abuses of despotic managers. It had been a very long time since I had a boss telling me what to do and publicly criticizing me when I failed. Dorothy, my manager at Diamond Toys, would stand behind me when the store was busy, saying "faster, faster, faster" as I furiously checked out customers. She was openly contemptuous of all of us, and complained with dripping sarcasm whenever we didn't anticipate her needs. Just thinking about her gives me a knot in my stomach. And that was in the *unionized* store!

My experiences made me see how conceited I had become as a middle-class professional. Just as my current job promotes an unrealistic sense of my self-importance, the way that low wage retail jobs are structured undermines the self-esteem of workers. Experiencing constant ridicule and disrespect from managers and customers inevitably diminishes one's sense of efficacy and self-worth, and probably helps to explain why so few protest their working conditions.

8. *This returns us to the very important question you raised in your answer to question 5: the middle-class lens through which much of the Sociology of Work has peered at jobs may have made a huge difference to our understanding of those jobs. It shouldn't surprise us, we suppose, but it seems as if while we are more aware of gender and race, we are myopic when it comes to class. What sort of "corrective lenses" would you prescribe?*

Isn't it strange? "Race, class, and gender" has become a sociological mantra. But "class" nowadays refers to an individual's identity, or style, or consumer practices—not to a person's relationship to the means of production. Weirdly, some writers even celebrate class "diversity" in their work. So what to do about it? I think it is important to link individual practices and dispositions to corporate interests. Sociologists can ask, "Who benefits?" from particular configurations of practice. I don't think we need to revive the concept of false consciousness to analyze the ways that our culture justifies economic exploitation. We just need to include global capitalism as the master context in understanding how local group differences unfold.

9. *In one way or another you have been examining the impact of segregation of various sorts (race, gender, class, physical ability) for over 20 years. What do you think is the future of such inequality?*

Like many of my cohort, I started out in graduate school allying myself with "socialist feminism." Sometime in the 1990s, with the rise of identity politics, the critique of capitalism became submerged in feminist sociology. My own work contributed to this, insofar as I focused on documenting and explaining inequality in the workplace instead of criticizing worker exploitation.

Working in the toy stores brought me back down to earth. I realized that concerns for wage equity are class-biased. What is the point of arguing for gender or race equality in low wage jobs? These jobs do not pay living wages and they offer no opportunities for advancement. My biggest fear is that workers will achieve equality (which I still strongly support), but lose the battle for economic justice and worker rights.

The Tenth Question
What was the worst (or most difficult, or most embarrassing) interview/ encounter you have had in the field?

As I've been pondering this question, it occurred to me that this is a boilerplate question asked today of many job seekers. I was asked a version of this question when I attended a job fair at a toy store. The recruiter asked the five or six of us gathered to describe our most embarrassing moment and explain how it made us a better person. We were all stumped. Then one woman bravely admitted that she often has trouble controlling her children in stores when she takes them shopping—they are so disruptive that it embarrasses her—so now she tries to leave them at home. The interviewer looked a little perturbed by the answer. After all, this was a toy store that catered to child customers. To help my potential co-worker, I wracked my brain for an embarrassing moment. I blurted out a story about a drill instructor at Parris Island who mistook me for a Marine Corps recruit when I was doing interviews for my dissertation. (I was yelled at for crossing my legs.) I wasn't exactly embarrassed by this moment, but I was startled. And I'm not sure it made me a better person.

Blank stares all around. I did not get that job.

What did you really want to do for a living? What were you afraid you would end up doing?

Even though I'm happy where I am, I might have let other people down. My advisor and mentor Neil Smelser encouraged me to obtain psychoanalytic training. He is a professional psychoanalyst, as is Nancy Chodorow, another important influence on me. In my opinion, psychoanalytic theory offers the most compelling explanation for gender differentiation, but I have resisted taking the step to go through professional training. I prefer to keep my attention focused on organizational patterns and social inequality, and leave the study of internal dynamics to others. I'm more forest, less trees.

What's the study you never pursued, but always wanted to?

I always tell my students the same advice that a professor once gave me: "never turn down a research opportunity."

17.

VERTA TAYLOR AND LEILA J. RUPP

1. *The two of you are from quite different disciplines, but your interests have obviously converged: Leila's "historical" path from an interest in European and American women's movements, and Verta's sociological interests in largely American social movement-making: but always with a feminist sensibility. Can you talk about your collaborations a bit for us to get a sense of how you capitalize on those differences in training and perspective? Do the differences ever get in the way?*

Our first collaboration, which blossomed along with our relationship in the late 1970s, came about because Leila was starting a study of the U.S. women's movement in the 1950s and, when she met Verta, she learned that Verta was an experienced interviewer from her days as director of the Disaster Research Center at Ohio State. Leila was an avid archival researcher but had never done any interviewing (or "oral history" as historians call it), and she knew that it would be important to combine interview data with archival research for this project because she set out to examine the persistence of women's movements in a period when scholars and the general public assumed there was no organized women's movement. Other than the differences in methods, and the different approach to theory in history and sociology (history not having to employ theory in any systematic way), we find that our approaches are very compatible. Verta brings social movement theory to our collaborative projects, and Leila has even used Verta's collective identity framework to organize her sole-authored analysis of the transnational women's movement, *Worlds of Women* (Rupp 1997). Perhaps the only ways in which our differences ever get in the way is in choice of language: sociologists have to be very precise (e.g., *transnational* vs. *international*), while historians have the flexibility both to avoid jargon and sometimes to use terms such as *transnational* and *international* interchangeably in the interest of avoiding numbing repetition. But mostly we find that we think along the same lines and write very compatibly. In fact, Verta likes to say that throughout our 30 years together if we have hit a patch when we are not getting along as well as usual, writing something together makes everything better.

2. *What assumptions about sex, gender, and transgender did you bring to your study of drag queens? How were these assumptions shaped by your previous work?*

It is very difficult to think about what assumptions about sex, gender, and transgender we brought to the drag queen study because our ideas have been so shaped by knowing the drag queens. We certainly went into the study familiar with the notion of "performing" or "doing gender," as conceptualized by Butler (1990, 1993), West and Zimmerman (1987), West and Fenstermaker (1995), and Fenstermaker and West (2002). What the study did was really put flesh (or drag queen finery) on the theoretical bones of those arguments. We did not have any particular assumptions about transgender or whether the drag queens should be considered transgendered. Based on our knowledge of the transgender movement, we assumed that the drag queens would use female names and pronouns in accordance with their gender of presentation at any particular moment, but that proved not to be the case at all. We became very accustomed to calling them by their drag names and female pronouns, and even switching mid-sentence from male to female pronouns, as they do themselves.

We found that some of them fit in the category of transgender and some did not. And we were surprised to find that they had very little knowledge of transgender—for example, some of them had real issues when a "tittie queen" (a drag queen with a penis and breast implants) joined the show because she was not really, in their minds, a drag queen. And during the course of the research, Sushi, the house queen, had an epiphany one day while watching a television show about transgendered people and announced that she was not really an out and proud drag queen; she was really a closeted transgendered person. As we quoted her in *Drag Queens at the 801 Cabaret* (Rupp and Taylor 2003), Sushi described the difference between being a drag queen and transgendered in this way: "A drag queen is someone like Kylie who never has ever thought about cutting her dick off. Ever. I think about it once a day, sometimes more." At a panel discussion at UC Santa Barbara—the first time the drag queens came to perform on campus—they had real trouble with a drag king, calling him "she." When we interviewed them after the book came out, one of the things they commented on was that they had come to learn a lot more about transgender from some of the younger girls who had joined the 801 troupe. As a result of all this, we certainly came to understand gender and transgender in a less theoretical and more embodied way.

What do you think your (and their) shifting understanding of gender means for the evolution of their performances and the impact of their performances on the public?

We think that our and their understandings shifted together in a lot of ways, since we regularly talked about what we were seeing in the shows and what we were finding out about what audience members thought about their performances. This was probably most clear in conceptualizing their troubling of gender and sexuality as political. It's not that our talk about the political aspects of their performance made them more political—from the beginning we could see from audience reactions and from talking with focus group members that a political message was getting across. Instead, it was that they began to talk in a more explicitly political way about what they were doing. For example, when we were well into the research, the Key West newspaper interviewed Sushi for a story about drag queens in Key West, quoting her as saying, "We're not just lip-synching up here; we're changing lives by showing people what we're all about." And another time, Sushi insisted, "I'm not just doing a number. Anybody can do a number.... I'm trying to make more of an experience, a learning thing.... And I have a platform now to teach the world." Although we think Sushi always was trying to teach the world, earlier she probably would not have articulated her role as a consciousness-raiser in quite the same way.

When the book came out, the girls were proud of it in a very personal way. Sushi commented in an interview we conducted and that was published in *Sexualities (2005)* that "people are amazed that the drunken drag queens at the 801 actually have a book out" and Scabby added, "After they read it, I think they realize there was more to us than just being a bunch of drunks." Kylie told us that, although they had always intended to challenge the way people think, our research had made them realize that they *did* have an impact on people, that they *did* make audience members think in a more complex way about gender and sexual categories and about the oppression that queer people experience in their daily lives.

It was clear from our focus groups that audience members heard the message. Almost 90% of our focus group members said that the shows made them realize the labels of "gay" and "straight" and "female" and "male" don't always fit. As a straight male tourist put it, "One of the beauties of attending a show like this is that you do realize that you…shouldn't walk out and say, 'I only like men,' and you shouldn't say, 'I only like women.'" Or as a young gay man expressed it, "They're challenging the whole idea of gender and so forth and they're breaking that down."

A heated debate in the Key West gay newspaper shortly after our book appeared is interesting in this light. One night we went to the show with a friend, Connie Gilbert, a self-identified queer feminist. That night Colby Kincaid, the "tittie queen" whose addition to the troupe caused some controversy, was performing, and her new implants were a main attraction. We were all rather put off by the fact that the crowd, especially the straight couples, were going wild and behaving as if they were at a straight stripper bar. Connie wrote a piece for the paper comparing the reaction to Colby's topless performance and Kylie's stripping at the end of the show, commenting that "the only way Colby might have made a gender-bending political statement would be to bare presumably still-male genitalia," because the straight men and women seemed not to realize that Colby "wasn't just another sex kitten," and that, this was not "as Sushi was quoted in the book, 'changing lives.'"

Two friends of Colby's—one of whom, according to the other girls, had paid for her implants—responded with letters to the editor. After accusing Connie of being jealous, bitter, or eager to see a penis, one noted that "Colby is a professional entertainer, not a politician or activist…she is not there to promote any political agenda"; the other insisted that the 801 Cabaret should be an entertainment venue, not a political action committee. Despite our disgust with the personal attacks on Connie (our reply was published under the headline "Authors Saddened by Misogynic Remarks"), we were heartened by the fact that our analysis of the political nature of drag shows had indeed begun to challenge the way people in the community thought about the show.

3. *Did you find a distinct difference between the "girls" of the 801 Cabaret as performers and as people? How did that inform your work?*

The difference between the drag queens' personalities in and out of drag are generally very striking, and that was a very important part of understanding why performers do drag and how it functions for them as people and as performers. R.V. Beaumont, for example, is one of the best hosts for the show because she is such a great talker. We thought her interview would be easy, but when we met with Timothy, he was shy and not very forthcoming. We realized at the time that we should have interviewed her in drag. Gugi Gomez told us she feels like herself only when she is in drag. Sushi, who never really looks entirely out of drag, says she is, sexually, a top in drag and a bottom out of drag. Many of the girls told us that, ironically, drag was a way of hiding themselves while flaunting (a different part of) themselves and getting a lot of attention.

Toward the end of the research, Sushi said that we had really come to understand drag but that the last thing we needed to do was to be put into drag as men performing as women. She wanted us to do the lesbian number from *Rent*. When we said we couldn't perform, she exclaimed, "You're professors, aren't you?" We begged off but agreed to go out on the street to hustle up business and walk around the bar with the tip bucket. We had entirely different reactions to this: Verta was afraid wearing such hyper-feminine dress, especially when a straight man wearing a large gold cross kept eyeing her, while Leila felt powerful and enjoyed the in-your-face nature of the performance in front of straight tourists. But even Verta behaved in ways she never would ordinarily—squeezing a male friend's butt, for example. It helped us to see how it is possible to hide in plain sight and how drag, or at least the style of drag that the 801 Girls affect, is not about impersonating women, but rather is more aggressive and sexual than what is generally considered feminine behavior. Thus, while the girls may have adopted a drag queen identity as a way of resisting hegemonic masculinity, their gender performances nevertheless reflect elements of conventional masculinity.

4. *Carol Stack, the author of the classic* All Our Kin *(1976), can tell stories of her respondents that she purposely left out of the book, but which clearly made a difference to her understanding of them. Are there some aspects of your research with the drag queens that you didn't share with your readers, but which were nevertheless important to your experience?*

We told almost everything we learned about the 801 girls in the book, because Sushi in particular urged us to "tell the truth" about them. One thing we had to be careful about was their use of illegal drugs. When we first gave them the prospectus for the book at a weekly drag queen meeting, they objected to a line about them sipping cocktails and snorting coke in the dressing room before the show. They knew that people in Key West are aware of their drug use, but they did not want us to describe any particular place or time they used drugs out of fear of being arrested. R.V. gave us the perfect line, so we wrote that they "sipped cocktails and powdered their noses" before the show. We tried to be careful throughout not to get them in any danger, but their use of drugs is important in understanding them. After the book came out, Kylie at first accused us of "betraying" them in our discussion of drug use, but then decided that we had handled it well. A tourist sitting in the bar the night Kylie confronted us as she was passing around the tip bucket spoke up, reminding Kylie that the 801 Girls perform numbers about drug use in their show and that it is clearly no secret to anyone who has seen the show. R.V., for example, performs Mary Poppins' "A Spoonful of Sugar" with flour that she cuts with a giant razor blade and snorts through a straw made out of pvc piping.

The other thing we did not include in the book was the fact that one of the girls—Scabby—was HIV-positive. She told us about her status pretty late in our research but asked us not to reveal this in the book. In the *Sexualities* interview (2005) we did with them later about the impact of the book on their lives, Scabby said at first she was glad that we didn't put her HIV status in the book, then reversed herself and said she was sorry she had made that decision, that everyone she cared about already knew and "it's not a big deal anymore." We were pretty sure that her former lover had died of AIDS, although Scabby claimed at the time that we interviewed her that it was liver cancer. In the book, we reported what Scabby had told us about his death and also quoted another of the girls telling us it was a different disease, in that way hinting that it might in fact have been AIDS. The impact of HIV/AIDS on the drag community is an important story, and we did report the crucial role that the 801 Girls played in doing benefits for the local AIDS Help organization.

In some ways, it was pretty amazing that we could describe things such as some of them accusing others of stealing tips, tension around Milla sleeping with Sushi's boyfriend, and other acts of betrayal while still remaining on good terms with all of them. In fact, it was coming to understand how they could do such things to each other and still remain close that helped us to understand what they call the "801 family" or the "drag mafia."

5. *For a long while, Verta, and later Leila, served as editors of the wildly successful textbook* Feminist Frontiers *(1983), which is now in its eighth edition! There are obvious upsides and downsides to doing a text, but have there been some unexpected pleasures in editing the textbook over such a long period of time?*

For a book that seemed doomed from the start, it is ironic that we are about to undertake a ninth edition. The story of how the book came about reveals how risky a venture it was to edit a textbook in Women's Studies when Laurel Richardson and Verta first began the project. At the time, Verta held a joint appointment in Women's Studies and there were no texts for use in social science-oriented introductory courses. Laurel initially had a contract with D.C. Heath, but she invited Verta, an untenured assistant professor, to join her as co-editor. When Laurel and Verta delivered the manuscript to the publisher, the editor indicated that D.C. Heath had decided to drop their sociology list. Verta was up for her fourth year tenure review that year and had devoted a great deal of time to the book. Shortly afterwards, the Addison-Wesley editor visited the Sociology Department at Ohio State looking for new authors. Verta proposed the project to him, and he reluctantly offered them a contract, expressing concern that there would never be a significant market for textbooks in Women's Studies. After the first edition was published in 1983, Random House acquired Addison-Wesley's list. A young pro-feminist sociology editor, Phil Butcher (who was later promoted to publisher at McGraw-Hill), was enthusiastic about the book, and it was only on this, the third edition, that Verta and Laurel collected any royalties. When McGraw-Hill assumed Random House, Phil Butcher made the book the centerpiece of what eventually became a respected and successful list in Women's Studies. Leila came on for the seventh and eighth editions and is now part of the team, along with Nancy Whittier, Verta's former graduate student. So the perspective over the long haul is Verta's.

Probably the greatest pleasure is seeing how much the field of Women's Studies has changed over the years. If one were to compare the first to the eighth edition, what would be immediately striking is the extent and nature of coverage beyond the United States, the attention and centrality of diversity, and the sophistication of theory. At the same time, the basic structure of the text has remained pretty much the same, and there are some feminist classics that are still there through all of the editions. But all of the ways that the field has developed can be tracked by the inclusion of different kinds of articles.

Working on the text over so many years has meant staying up on new questions, new topics, and new ways of looking at gender and its intersections with race, ethnicity, class, sexuality, nation, ability. When not actually teaching women's studies, or the sociology of gender, which Verta has not for a while because of her administrative responsibilities, it is a way of keeping up with developments in the field. Bringing Leila on to the seventh edition reinvigorated Verta's and Nancy's enthusiasm for the project because Leila had moved back into Women's Studies when we came to UCSB, and she brought a fresh new (to her) West Coast perspective to *Feminist Frontiers*.

6. *What has it meant to your careers—both politically and intellectually—to be the "professors of lesbian love"? Or, perhaps it's what Verta deemed "high risk activism." The context for this question comes from our interest in discussing what it means to take risks in our research, or to assert that something is worth scholarly attention when others might forcefully disagree.*

We came to be called the "professors of lesbian love" while working with the drag queens. The very first time we went to see Sushi, the house queen of the 801 Cabaret, perform, she was hosting a night at Bourbon Street, the "boy bar" across the street from what became the 801 Cabaret, the "girl bar." We showed up at Bourbon Street because some visitors wanted to see a drag show. Sushi came on stage and, in a political statement about gay marriage, asked for the couples that had been together the longest to raise their hands. When it turned out that we had been together for the most years, Sushi called us up on stage and announced, "Of course it's the lesbians." After that, we were forever announced as the "professors of lesbian love." In fact, when the drag queens first visited UC Santa Barbara to perform to 1,000 students in Verta's introductory sociology class, Verta realized that she had to come out in the class session before the show. She was certain that the drag queens would refer to Leila and Verta as "the professors of lesbian love," and in fact they did.

So that title has meant a lot to us as a label bestowed on us by the drag queens, but it has also reminded us of what it has meant to be out in academia. Working on lesbian topics and being out in our departments has been wonderfully rewarding in some ways and challenging in others. We have both experienced discrimination of various forms for being out as lesbians and working on queer topics. For one thing, being out and a couple made it very hard to pursue opportunities to move to other universities. At one job interview, Verta was told outright that there would never be a position for Leila. Verta was contacted about applying for an endowed chair at another university, but when the search committee recommended that she be brought in for an interview, the powers that be dropped her from the list because her research on lesbians and drag queens would be too controversial for the donor of the chair. Leila dropped out of one search when the best the university could suggest was that Verta might teach at a local community college. UC Santa Barbara was unique in creating positions for the two of us together.

In a variety of ways, we have experienced the kinds of negative consequences Verta and her student Nicole Raeburn wrote about as "high-risk activism" for gay, lesbian, and bisexual sociologists (Taylor and Raeburn 1995). One of our favorite comments—from a colleague of Verta's at Ohio State—overheard by a student in the hallway, was that "the graduate students all come with long hair and boyfriends, then cut their hair and get girlfriends." When Leila was up for tenure, one of the gay men in the department told her that there had been a discussion at the College tenure and promotion committee of whether she taught "from a lesbian perspective." Later, when she proposed to write a section on the gay and lesbian movement for a text her department was producing, one of her colleagues commented that it was "silly, but if Leila wants to do it, she can go ahead." More seriously, when Verta was teaching a very large section of the introductory sociology class at Ohio State one term, she came home to find a note on the door of her house reading "I'll kill you, you dyke."

At the same time, working with lesbian graduate students has been incredibly rewarding, and teaching and researching topics about gay and lesbian history and the lesbian, gay, bisexual, transgender, and queer movement feels like an important contribution to bringing about change in the world. Verta has been dubbed the "lesbian den mother of sociology" because of the large number of lesbian graduate students she has trained and mentored at Ohio State and at UC Santa Barbara. When Verta received the Simon and Gagnon Award from the Sexualities Section of the American Sociological Association in 2008, Joan Huber (her former dean and provost at Ohio State) wrote: "Good for you. I can remember years ago when some of the people in the department thought you were making a mistake to focus on sexuality, but you had the pluck and courage to continue anyway. It was always the right thing to do." At the reception where Verta received the award, the most meaningful thing the president of the section said about her was that there was not a person in the room whose career Verta had not helped.

Leila, too, is very proud of the lesbian and gay undergraduate and graduate students with whom she has worked. She sees her synthetic books on queer history—*A Desired Past* (1999), which was named in *The Advocate* as one of the best books on gay and lesbian studies, and her most recent book, *Sapphistries: A Global History of Love Between Women* (2009)—as important in their ability to reach a wider audience beyond academia.

7. *Some will view this question as irrelevant to what sociologists do, but we disagree. Both of you have now had fairly extensive academic administrative experience. How have the trials of administration changed, improved, or altered your ways of working as scholars?*

The obvious answer to how administrative work affects scholarship is that it takes a lot of time away from research and writing. That said, it has made us have to figure out how to fit research and writing into small chunks of time. It's been a very long time since either of us had the luxury of a sabbatical or even a quarter off for research. Leila grew up loving to write and is a very fast writer and, over the years, Leila's passion for writing rubbed off on Verta. For both of us, our research and writing can be a lovely respite from the sometimes-tedium and challenges of academic administration.

Our experience doing administrative work undoubtedly made us better and more sensitive field researchers. As performers, drag queens take pride in their "bitchiness," in doing, as one drag queen put it, "exactly the opposite of what people expect." Desiray once told us, and the other 801 Girls agreed, that the only reason we were able to conduct this research is because we "weren't bitchy queens." We can't count the number of times that the drag queens failed to show up for an interview, attempted to embroil us in some dispute or drama, made fun of our lesbian haircuts and shoes, or complained about the food we cooked for them. The thing about being an academic administrator is that in order to survive one simply has to learn to take difficult people in stride, not to make snap judgments, and to avoid any inclination to hold deep and bitter grudges.

There were times that it would have been easy to walk away from the drag queen project because, in the end, the drag queens are men and, as we wrote in "When the Girls are Men" (Taylor and Rupp 2005), they frequently used male advantage to level the playing field with us as researchers, just as our colleagues sometimes do. It was patently clear that at first the drag queens did not trust us, which is something every department chair has felt in dealing with particular faculty members. It was only through keeping our word by finishing the book, something so many others promised but failed to do, that we earned their trust, respect, and eventually love.

8. *In* Drag Queens at the 801 Cabaret *you discuss the "politics of vulgarity" engaged in by the drag queens as they perform, engage in a lot of bawdy sex talk, and even fondle and strip the customers. You argue that in some important respect this is shocking enough to blur the boundaries between marginal and normal. When both performer and audience*

are transgressive, change can happen. Have you used this "shock and destabilize" method in any other work or in your teaching?

It was one of the reviewers of our manuscript—historian Joanne Meyerowitz—who pushed us to think about the impact of the vulgarity of the drag queens in their shows. That was when we realized that they forge solidarity with audience members and level the playing field by challenging the boundaries of respectability. Perhaps nothing illustrates that better than one night when we came into the bar. It turned out that the daughter of the secretary to the dean of social sciences at Ohio State was there, and she had been told by her mother to be very respectful of us because we were "very powerful women." When Sushi saw us, he called out, "the pussy lickers are here!" The same process was at work when three of the drag queens came to our campus to perform. Sushi called for "pussy lickers" to come up on one side of the stage and "cock-suckers" to gather on the other. So there were lesbians and heterosexual men in one category, straight women and gay men in another, with some bisexuals in between. As Sushi was quoted in the campus paper, "You suck cocks or you lick pussy. Who cares? We're all the same."

As all of that suggests, it's impossible to talk about our research—in our teaching or at the many different universities where we have been asked to speak—without shocking our audiences. Just exposing students or academic colleagues to that kind of talk in a way implicates them in the vulgarity of the drag queens. When Verta presented on our research at the University of Milan, her Italian translator asked her nervously, "Do I have to translate all these words?" Likewise, Leila found that when she talked about her project on a global history of desire, love, and sex between women, it involved straight talk (pardon the expression) about women engaged in tribadism, cunnilingus, and all sorts of other sexual acts that shock audiences and, hopefully, normalize female same-sex sexuality.

Are you saying that to shock is to normalize? Is that the dynamic when the drag queens come to Sociology 1?

Hmm, that's a good question. Maybe what we really mean to say is that to shock is to de-stigmatize or familiarize certain words and acts. In the examples we used above, the very idea of putting people into categories as "cock-suckers," "pussy-lickers," or "both" is at first sight so strange and vulgar that it forces people to confront the fact that the ordinary way they think about categories is on the basis of sexual object choice—which really makes no more sense than creating categories based on sexual acts. And when the drag queens came to Sociology 1, it was the fact that men dressed as women were dancing on the stage where professors usually lecture and venturing out into the audience to sit on laps and fondle willing students that made a classroom both more than a classroom and also precisely a classroom.

Here's an interesting example of this complicated process. After the drag queens performed in Verta's Soc 1 class, some staff members at the Women's Center called us in because they were worried that the audience-fondling sent the message that sexual harassment was acceptable. We tried to explain that the drag queens are very good at reading audience members for their willingness to engage in such interactions—so that the message of consent got conveyed. One of Verta's teaching assistants had just had someone come to her sections to talk about sexual harassment, and she reported that the students both understood the difference between consensual and non-consensual touching and that the drag queen performance had made them understand that preventing sexual harassment does not mean being anti-sexual.

9. *What has Phoebe's role been in your research? We are thinking primarily of her (presumably) constant presence in the Key West study, but also more generally, how has Phoebe (and your other canine companions over the years) made a difference to your research, and to you as researchers?*

If Phoebe had come into our lives earlier, we might have had to cut short the drag queen study, because as a puppy the loud music in the bar made her shake uncontrollably, and Leila worried that she was going to lose her hearing. Emma, her predecessor, was older when she first went to the bar and never seemed to be bothered by either the noise or the smoke. Emma had an important role in our research because some of the drag queens—Milla and Gugi especially—really liked her and would take her up on the stage when they were performing. Gugi told us recently that she was worried when Emma died and we got Phoebe that she wouldn't like her as much, but she does. Eventually Phoebe got used to the noise, and now she performs on stage with Gugi, Sushi, and Samantha, who joined the show after our research ended.

We should mention that both Jessie (the dog Leila had when she met Verta and who quickly worked her charm on Verta, who was a little afraid of dogs), and Emma, our first Maltese, were published authors. Jessie's essay, "Specism: The Dialectics of Doghood," appeared in the women's studies newsletter at Ohio State and was reprinted in the first edition of *Feminist Frontiers* (Celiasister 1983). Emma's "Maltese and Women: Some Historical

Reflections," appeared in the Maltese column of the American Kennel Club magazine (Rupp-Taylor 1992). Phoebe is a kind of "girls just want to have fun" dog and so has refused to publish a thing.

To be honest, the biggest impact that Phoebe, and Emma and Jessie before her, have had on our research is that they have made it difficult for Leila, who is the main dog caretaker, to pursue the kind of travel that her historical research has required. They all would mope when Leila left for long periods, and there's nothing like a grieving dog to depress the one left at home. So Leila pursued her research in England, France, Germany, and the Netherlands for her book on the transnational women's movement in small spurts, not one extended visit. It has made her very fast and efficient in archives. And of course having Phoebe or her predecessors under our desks while writing has been a joy. It's hard to think of writing as a lonely endeavor when a sweet little dog is snoring or having doggy dreams at your feet.

The Tenth Question:
   What was the worst (or most difficult or most embarrassing) interview/ encounter in the field you ever had?

The worst encounter in the field—that's an easy one. After *Drag Queens at the 801 Cabaret* came out, Sushi told us that her mother wanted to meet with us. Sushi claimed not to know why (which was a lie, but she hoped we could change her mother's mind). Sushi's mother was visiting Key West at the time, so we went to Sushi's house, met a chilly reception from her mother, and went across the street to a café, where Sushi's mother started to cry and proceeded to demand to know why we had written a book that shamed her family. She was really angry, and at first we felt horrible, although we did wonder why she wasn't blaming Sushi for telling us the thing—that Sushi had sold sex in drag on the streets of Los Angeles—that so upset her. This went on for almost 2 hours, and after feeling guilty and sorry, we began to understand why Sushi has no shame. Her mother, who was born in Japan and married an American GI, maintains the kind of sense of honor and shame that is so important in Japanese culture. In response, presumably, Sushi is not ashamed of anything she has done. We later found out that, in fact, Sushi's mother had shamed her family by refusing to marry the man chosen for her and running away to marry an American.

Seven years later, Sushi's mother still hates us. She refuses to speak to us (she now lives in Key West about a block from us in the house that Sushi and several other drag queens rent) and makes it very difficult for us when Sushi invites us over on holidays. It is some consolation that she hates almost everyone else, too—including Sushi's boyfriend and Sushi's best friend Kylie, who lives in the house as well. It was this incident that made Leila declare that she really wanted to go back to studying dead people.

What did you really want to do for a living? What were you afraid you would end up doing?

Verta: I really wanted to be a politician. My father was a politician and I think I really would have enjoyed being a part of the Clinton team, but Leila reminds me that, as a lesbian, I wouldn't have gotten very far, especially in Arkansas, where I was born and grew up. I also would have liked to have been a doctor, but that was not a possibility that ever occurred to me, being the first in my family to go to college and, even then, I practically had to run away from home to go to college.

Leila: I hate to say it, but what I'm doing is really *really* what I wanted to do for a living. I used to say that I wanted to be a downhill bicycle racer (I came in second in the Chapel Hill, North Carolina, "Wheels of Fire" bicycle race, women's division, in 1972) or that I would love to forge the kind of historical documents we all wish we had—an 8th century Byzantine peasant woman's diary, for example. When I was finishing graduate school and contemplating the lack of jobs in the field of history, I was afraid that I would end up a waitress, since that was the bulk of my job experience at that point.

What's the study you never did, but always wanted to?

Verta: The study I never published, although I started writing it up, was on the coming out process. I gave a paper on it at the ASA and even had an article drafted, but one of my colleagues at Ohio State told me that I would never get tenure if I wrote it. So much for good advice.

Leila: The only study I wanted to do but haven't is, I think, an impossible one: I wanted to study "maiden aunts," women like my Aunt Leila and her friend Diantha who made a life together for more than 50 years but, as respectable ladies and school teachers, did not seem to claim a lesbian identity in a context where such an identity existed. But mostly I've studied all the things I ever wanted to study.

EDITORS' AFTERWORD

Sarah Fenstermaker

*What was the worst (or most difficult, or most embarrassing) interview/
field encounter you've had.*

One of the nice things about getting older is you forget a lot of those moments
where you wish you could turn back time, drop into the floor, or simply evap-
orate from whatever difficult moment is unfolding. Perhaps because it was so
long ago, I do remember my first survey interview—a "cold" call, randomly
selected from the Evanston, Illinois phone book—as we were piloting the
survey instrument for our study of household labor (for discussion see Fenstermaker Berk et al. 1976 and Fenstermaker Berk and Berheide 1977). Even
when I'm not calling strangers, I have a dash of phonophobia, so this was
particularly difficult for me. But, I had my little speech in front of me ("Good

morning! May I speak to the head of the household?"), which explained the
survey and that we wanted to know "everything" about the work people do
in their homes. On the first call—the *first*—I gave my spiel and the respondent on the other end of the line said, "I don't do any housework." I was ready
for this. This is what we *knew* they would say, so I had practiced this very
moment. I said, "Well, I understand that you may not do very *much* housework, and it may not feel as if it would count, but we are *really interested* in
whatever you do." Again, she said, "I really don't do any." I went one more
round with her, trying to convince (read: browbeat) her that even if she didn't
think it was important, or difficult, she really, really needed to tell me what
she did. Finally, exasperated, and not a little annoyed, she said, "I've been
completely paralyzed for 10 years. I just don't DO any housework!" With
that, she hung up. And quite right too. Moral: Sometimes survey respondents really are just telling you the truth.

> *What did you really want to do for a living? What were you afraid you
> would end up doing?*

For most of my childhood I was pretty much unaware that girls really weren't
supposed to have occupational goals, and I told everyone I wanted to be a
pediatrician (for elaboration, see Fenstermaker 1997). After I began to figure
out the world of women (and heard about something called organic chemis-
try), I abandoned the idea of being a doctor. After that, I was pretty much in a
daze with respect to what I would do, until I sort of fell into graduate school.
All my life people told me I should be a stand-up comedian, but I somehow
knew that making people laugh in informal settings was very, very different
from the hard reality of doing it for a living. Besides, at that time, except for
Moms Mabley and Phyllis Diller, all the stand-up comedians were men. As
a very young feminist in the early 1970s, I thought the worst thing would
be to be a housewife, like my sister, and my mother before her. I saw that it
made smart women crazy, and often very, very unhappy. Now I know there
are even worse existences for women in the labor market, too numerous to
name.

> *What is the study you never pursued, but always wanted to?*

Sometime during the late 1980s, I woke up in the middle of the night and
designed a study of token women presidents in higher education. At that
time, my own chancellor was a woman—much maligned by the faculty—and
I thought it would be a great way to look at the workings of gender in organizations. I can't remember why I didn't pursue it. I don't really remember

much of anything during the period in which I was a single mother of a small child; it's kind of a blur. I do still have a short list of research projects I'd like to undertake, and I'm happily making my way through it.

Nikki Jones

What was the worst (or most difficult, or most embarrassing) interview/ field encounter you've had?

Over the last 10 years, I've interviewed respondents in a number of settings: a city jail, a youth detention facility, homes, and coffee shops. Often, it is the setting that makes these interviews difficult: waiting for women to be released from their cells to conduct, in light of their current circumstances, a relatively unimportant research task. People tend to feel more comfortable in their homes, and I found that adolescent girls and boys and some of their family members tended to drop their tough fronts more easily in this setting, at times showing emotions would be seen as a liability in a more public setting. Coffee shops come with their own challenges, mostly maintaining some semblance of privacy and making sure that the background noise doesn't drown out the recorded voice of my respondents. My most difficult interview (so far) occurred in a coffee shop. Not because of concerns about privacy or background noise. Actually, I'm not sure *what* it was that made it so difficult. It is something I am still figuring out.

I was interviewing a man who was, by his account, trying to change his life. This is the topic of my current research project: how people with criminal or incarceration histories shed their criminalized identities, and, more importantly, how members of their community, in this case residents of the San Francisco's Fillmore neighborhood, either help or hinder their efforts to do so. I first met this resoponent when I was walking to one of the federally subsidized housing projects in the neighborhood (I lived in the neighborhood for 2.5 years) on a weekday afternoon in December. I was dressed in what was at the time my field research uniform: dark blue jeans, black loafers, a black cotton turtleneck and a brown corduroy jacket. As I approached the housing complex, I noticed a short, dark skinned man dressed in a blue security uniform. A white badge on his right arm read "Private Security." He was talking to a thin, middle-aged man seated on a red motorized scooter. The security guard sat on a folding chair while the two men chatted. As I walked by the men, I looked to the security guard and asked, "whatchya-guardin'?" "You," he replied quickly. I laughed, smiled, and waited for his answer. "Just kidding'" he said and explained that he was watching over the building behind us, The Buchanan Lane Homes, a new housing development of two- and three-bedroom, single family townhomes. The homes went on the market in 2007 in the upper six-figures.

I ran into him again the next day. "You gonna ask me what I'm guarding?" he yelled from across the street. "No," I laughed. I crossed the street and decided to conduct something of a preliminary interview. I'd been interested in the role of private security in the neighborhood—I knew that some men trying to find legit work hoped to get a "security card" as a way to secure part-time employment. I asked if he was a resident of the Fillmore. "Born and raised," he said, as those born in the Fillmore often do. I hand him a project brochure and tell him that I'd like to interview him. I write my cell phone number on the brochure and tell him to read it over. Let me know if you're up for it, I say.

We met for our interview about two months later. The interview lasts about an hour and a half. The conversation covered ground that was now familiar to me after 6 months of living in the neighborhood. Like other men I met, his family migrated to the Fillmore from Texas. The Fillmore was united then, he tells me, as others have, not divided into warring fiefdoms as it is today. He echoes stories shared by others about how crack damaged the personal networks that sustained the mostly poor and working-class Fillmore before its arrival. As we talk, I gather that he has struggled with addiction. He punctuates his sentences with a series of quick rubs down the front of his face much like what I observed when interviewing women in the city jail who were going through withdrawal. He begins to share stories about his life as a pimp. He explains why he beat his pregnant girlfriend. He talks about the violence he used against others too and how that led him to prison. He makes at least two references to not being gay, a preoccupation that I've observed among some men who have spent time in prison.

After the interview, he says that he feels like a load has been lifted, moving his arms in a lifting motion away from his chest. I feel unsettled. I am only beginning to understand why. It is not the level of violence he shared in his stories. I have heard difficult stories before. It is, I think, that as my respondent, as a man whom I recruited into my study, I knew I owed him the same level of empathy that I extended to others. As a field researcher, empathy is unconditional. It is necessary in order to engage in the type of "open-hearted" listening that Valerie Jenness describes in this volume. However, as his story unfolded, I felt less and less empathetic. I was raised to be a feminist. Yet, there I was, listening to his story, at times, sharing a laugh with a man, a former pimp, who has used extreme forms of violence against other men and women. I never imagined that I would be laughing with a former pimp.

After I turned off the recorder, we sat and talked for a few more minutes. He admitted that he was still using but that he was stopping. He tells me that somehow my project was an inspiration for him, an epiphany moment of some sort. This, I think, may have also contributed to the complicated set of feelings that washed over me as I walked back to my apartment. Eventually, I would have to develop a theory about what change looks like for men like him. An honest account of my field research will have to account for his experience too and that was going to be even more difficult than I anticipated. He left the interview feeling liberated. I left feeling a heavy weight.

What did you really want to do for a living? What were you afraid you would end up doing?

As a young girl I never imagined that I would become a university professor. My father worked for AT&T for 30 years, beginning as a technician and ending his career in management. When I was a child, he would bring home a large bright-orange plastic phone receiver that he used to test phone lines in other people's homes. I thought then that I'd like to be a telephone man too. I imagined myself climbing up telephone poles to test the lines. The way I imagined my future changed after I began playing basketball (at the behest of a middle-school teacher who, I think, worried about my potential to drift into delinquency). I didn't dream then of becoming a professional basketball player, which still wasn't a real possibility for girls. As my skills improved over the years, I began to think that basketball could get me to college and, more importantly, a college out-of-state. Basketball was how I would leave the town I grew up in. If there was anything I was afraid of it was living in the town I grew up in for the rest of my life. I was heavily recruited out of high school and eventually settled on a small, Jesuit college in Philadelphia with a rich basketball tradition. I began as a business major, but was quickly recruited by a young, energetic professor, David Kauzlarich, to study sociology and criminal justice. It was in his class that I began to think that I'd like to become a professor. When I shared my idea about becoming a professor with another faculty member as graduation neared, he encouraged me to do something else for a couple of years. If I still wanted to return to get a Ph.D. after being out in the real world, then I should. I did, and I did.

What is the study you never pursued, but always wanted to?

I'm finishing up the study that I really wanted to do and hope to be as productive and creative over the course of my career as many of the scholars in this book. I recently moved to Oakland, just blocks away from the historic

Paramount Theater. The Art Deco building was completed in 1931. It had its "movie palace glory" for about a decade before it fell victim to decades of decline and neglect. It was restored in the 1970s and is now on the National Register of Historic Places. Today, it is home to the Oakland East Bay Symphony (http://www.paramounttheatre.com/history.html). The theater also hosts a number of popular African American entertainers including comedians and actors like Mike Epps and Mo'Nique (who recently won an Oscar for her role in *Precious* but has generated much of her support from Black audiences). It has shown popular plays by Tyler Perry like *Madea Goes to Jail*. Next month, the Paramount will host the Bay Area Black Comedy Competition Finals. It seems to be a key stop on the Black entertainment schedule and I think an interesting ethnographic study could be based on these performances. Who goes to these performances? What's funny? What does what people laugh at tell us about the lives of African Americans today?

REFERENCES

Acker, Joan. 1992. From sex roles to gendered institutions. *Contemporary Sociology* 21: 565–569.

Anderson, Benedict. 1991. *Imagined communities: Reflections on the origin and spread of nationalism*. New York: Verso.

Anderson, Elijah. 1978. *A place on the corner*. Chicago: University of Chicago Press.Anzaldua, Gloria. 1987. *Borderlands La Frontera: The new mestiza*. San Francisco: Spinsters/Aunt Lute.

Baus, Janet, and Hunt, Dan (Directors and Producers), *Cruel and unusual* [video]. http://www.cruelandunusualfilm.com/

Becker, Howard S. 1963. *Outsiders: Studies in the sociology of deviance*. New York: Free Press.

——— 1998. *Tricks of the trade*. Chicago: University of Chicago Press.

——— 2008. *Art worlds*. Berkeley: University of California Press.

Belknap, Joanne. 2004. Meda Chesney-Lind: The mother of feminist criminology. *Women & Criminal Justice* 15: 1–23.

Billingsley, Andrew. 1972. *Children of the storm: Black children and the American child welfare*. New York: Harcourt College.

Bowker, L. (1988). On the relationship between wife beating and child abuse. In K. Yllo and M. Bograd (Eds.), *Feminist perspectives on wife abuse* (pp. 158–175). Thousand Oaks, CA: Sage.

Brooks, Scott. 2009. *Black men can't shoot*. Chicago: University of Chicago Press.

Burawoy, Michael. 1998. The extended case method. *Sociological Theory* 161: 1–30.

Butler, Judith. 1990. *Gender trouble: Feminism and the subversion of identity*. New York: Routledge.

——— 1993. *Bodies that matter: On the discursive limits of sex*. New York: Routledge.

Celia, Sister, Jessica. 1983. Specism: The dialectics of doghood. In Laurel Richardson and Verta Taylor (Eds.), *Feminist frontiers: Rethinking sex, gender, and society* (pp. 354–355). Reading, MA: Addison-Wesley.

Cesaire, Aimé. 1972. *Discourse on colonialism*. New York: Monthly Review Press.

Chesney-Lind, Meda, and Katherine Irwine. 2007. *Beyond bad girls: Gender, violence and hype*. New York: Routledge.

Cloward, Richard A., and Lloyd E. Ohlin. 1960. *Delinquency and opportunity: A theory of delinquent gangs*. Glencoe, IL: Free Press.

Cohen, Cathy. 1999. *The boundaries of Blackness: AIDS and the breakdown of Black politics*. Chicago: University of Chicago Press.

Daniels, Marian. 1996. *Prevention and parity: Girls in juvenile justice report*. Indianapolis, IN: Girls Incorporated National Resource Center & Office of Juvenile Justice and Delinquency Prevention.

DeVault, Marjorie. 1999. *Liberating method: Feminism and social research*. Philadelphia: Temple University Press.

DuBois, W.E.B. 1899. *The Philadelphia Negro* (Public Economy and Public Law, University of Pennsylvania series). Boston: Ginn.

Duneier, Mitchell. 1994. *Slim's table*. Chicago: University of Chicago Press.

——— 2000. *Sidewalk*. Chicago: University of Chicago Press.

Edin, Kathy, and Maria Kefalas. 2005. *Promises I can keep: Why poor women put motherhood before marriage*. Berkeley: University of California Press.

Fenstermaker, Sarah, and C. West. 2002. *Doing gender, doing difference: Inequality, power, and institutional change*. New York: Routledge.

Fenstermaker Berk, Sarah, and C. Berheide. 1977. Going backstage: Gaining access to observe household work. *Sociology of Work and Occupations* 4(1): 27–48.

——— C. Berheide, and R. A. Berk. 1976. Household work in the suburbs: The job and its participants. *Pacific Sociological Review* 19(4): 491–518.

Frankenberg, Ruth. 1993. *White women, race matters: The social construction of Whiteness*. New York: Routledge.

Friedan, Betty. 1963. *The feminine mystique*. New York: W. W. Norton.

Garland, David. 2001. *The culture of control: Crime and social order in contemporary society*. Chicago: University of Chicago Press.

Geertz, Clifford. 1973. *The interpretation of cultures*. New York: Basic Books.

Gilroy, Paul. 1993. *Against race: Imagining political culture beyond the colorline*. Cambridge, MA: Harvard University Press.

Goetting, A. and Sarah Fenstermaker. 1995. *Individual voices, collective visions: Fifty years of women in sociology*. Philadelphia: Temple University Press.

Goffman, Erving I. 1959. *The presentation of self in everyday life*. Garden City, NY: Anchor Books.

Gouldner, Alvin. W. 1954. *Patterns of industrial bureaucracy*. New York: Free Press.

Harraway, Donna. 1988. Situated knowledges: The science question in feminism and the privilege of partial perspective. *Feminist Studies* 14: 575–599.

Harris, David, and Jeremiah Joseph Sim. 2002. Who is multiracial? Assessing the complexity of lived race. *American Sociological Review* 67: 614–627.

Harvey Wingfield, Adia. 2009. Racializing the glass escalator: Reconsidering men's experiences with women's work. *Gender & Society* 23: 5–26.

Hays, Sharon. 2004. *Flat broke with children: Women in the age of welfare reform*. New York: Oxford University Press.

Hochschild, Arlie Russell. 1990. *The time bind: When work becomes home and home becomes work*. New York: Henry Holt.

——— 2003. *The managed heart*. Berkeley: The University of California Press.

hooks, bell 1994. *Teaching to transgress*. New York: Routledge.

——— 2000. Feminism: A movement to end sexist oppression. In *Feminist theory: from margin to center* (pp. 18–33). Cambridge, MA: South End Press.

Huff, Darryl. 1954. *How to lie with statistics*. New York: Norton.

Hurston, Zora Neal. 1937. *Their eyes were watching god*. Philadelphia: J. B. Lippincott.

Ianni, Francis A. J. 1974. *Black mafia; Ethnic succession in organized crime*. New York: Simon & Schuster.

Jenness, Valerie. 1993. *Making it work: The prostitutes' rights movement in perspective*. New York: Aldine de Gruyter.

——— In press. From policy to prisoners to people: A 'soft-mixed methods' approach to studying transgender prisoners. *Journal of Contemporary Ethnography*.

——— Ryken Grattet. 2001. *Making hate a crime: From social movement to law enforcement*. New York: Russell Sage Foundation.

——— Cheryl L. Maxson, Kristy N. Matsuda, and Jennifer Macy Sumner. 2007. *Violence in California correctional facilities: An empirical examination of sexual assault*. Report to the California Department of Corrections and Rehabilitation, Sacramento.

Kang, Miliann. 2010. *The managed hand: Race, gender and body in beauty service work*. Berkeley: University of California Press.

——— Katherine Jones. 2007. Why do people get tattoos? *Contexts* 6(1): 42–47.

Kibria, Nazli (1995) *Family tightrope: The changing lives of Vietnamese Americans*. Princeton, NJ: Princeton University Press.

Kirkland, Anna. 2008. *Fat rights: Dilemmas of difference and personhood.* New York: New York University Press.

Lacy, Karyn (2007). *Blue-chip Black: Class, race, and status in the new Black middle class.* Berkeley: University of California Press.

Ladner, Joyce. 1971. *Tomorrow's tomorrow.* Garden City, NY: Doubleday.

Landry, Bart. 1988. *The new middle class.* Berkeley: University of California Press.

Laslett, Barbara, and Barrie Thorne. 1997. *Feminist sociology: Life histories of a movement.* New Brunswick, NJ: Rutgers University Press.

Lemann, Nicholas. 1992. *Promised land: The great black migration and how it changed America.* New York: Random House.

Levitt, Steven D. 2005. *Freakonomics: A rogue economist explores the hidden side of everything.* New York: Harper Collins.

Liebow, Elliot. 1968. *Tally's Corner.* New York: Back Bay Books.

MacDonald, John A., and Meda Chesney-Lind. 2001. Gender bias and juvenile justice revisited. *Crime and Delinquency* 47: 173–195.

Mbembe, Achille. 2001. *On the postcolony.* Berkeley: University of California Press.

Menjivar, Cecilia. 2006. Family reorganization in a context of legal uncertainty: Guatemalan and Salvadoran immigrants in the United States. *International Journal of Sociology of the Family* (special issue on globalization and the family) 32: 223–245.

Moynihan, Daniel. 1965. *The Negro family: The case for national action.* Office of Planning and Research, United States Department of Labor. http://www.dol.gov/oasam/programs/history/webid-meynihan.htm

O'Brien, Jodi. 2008. Sociology as an epistemology of contradiction. *Sociological Perspectives* 52: 5–22.

Parrenas, Rhacel. 2001. *Servants of globalization: Women, migration, and domestic work.* Stanford, CA: Stanford University Press.

—— 2005. *Children of global migration: Transnational families and gendered woes.* Stanford, CA: Stanford University Press.

—— 2008a. *The force of domesticity: Filipina migrants and globalization.* New York: New York University Press.

—— 2008b. Transnational fathering: Gendered conflicts, distant disciplining and emotional gaps. *Journal of Ethnic and Migration Studies* 34: 1057–1072.

Patillo, Mary. 1999. *Black picket fences: Privilege and peril among the Black middle class.* Chicago: University of Chicago Press.

—— 2007. *Black on the block: The politics of race and class in the city.* Chicago: University of Chicago Press.

—— D. Weiman, and B. Western (Eds.). 2004. *Imprisoning America: The social effects of mass incarceration.* New York: Russell Sage Foundation.

Pew Center on the States. (2009). *One in a hundred: Behind bars in America 2008..* Washington, DC: Author.

Pitt, Richard N. (forthcoming). Still looking for my jonathan: Gay black men's management of religious and sexual identity conflicts. *Journal of Homosexuality,* 57.

Reinhartz, S. 1992. *Feminist methods in social research.* New York: Oxford University Press.

Rich, Adrienne. 1979. Disloyal to civilization: Feminism, racism, gynephobia. In *On lies, secrets, and silence: Selected prose 1966–1978.* New York: W. W. Norton.

—— 2003. *What is found there: Notebooks on poetry and politics.* New York: W.W. Norton.

Richardson, Laurel, and Taylor Verta, Eds. 2007. *Feminist frontiers: rethinking sex, gender, and society.* Reading, MA: Addison-Wesley. (Original work published 1983)

Rios, Victor. forthcoming. *Punished: Criminalization of inner city youth.* New York: New York University Press.

Robinson, Cedric. 1983. *Black Marxism: The making of the Black radical tradition.* London: Zed Books.

Rupp, Leila J. 1997. *Worlds of women: The making of an international women's movement.* Princeton, NJ: Princeton University Press.

—— 1999. *A desired past: A short history of same-sex sexuality in America.* Chicago: University of Chicago Press.

—— 2010. *Sapphistries: A global history of love between women.* New York: New York University Press.

—— Verta Taylor. 2003. *Drag queens at the 801 cabaret.* Chicago: University of Chicago Press.

—— Verta Taylor. 2005. The 801 girls talk about drag queens at the 801 Cabaret, July 5, 2004. *Sexualities* 8: 99–112.

Rupp-Taylor, Emma Lou. 1992. Maltese and women: Reflections. *American Kennel Gazette* 109(8): 95–96.

Segura, Denise. 1999. Chicana political consciousness: Re-negotiating culture, class, and gender with oppositional… *Aztlan* 24: 7–33.

—— 2001. Challenging the Chicano text: Toward a more inclusive contemporary causa. *Signs* 26: 541–551.

—— Beatriz Pesquera. 1992. Chicanas in white-collar jobs: You have to prove yourself more. *Sociological Perspectives* 35: 163–182.

—— Patricia Zavella. 2008. Introduction: Gendered borderlands. *Gender & Society* 22: 537–544.

Simon, Jonthan. 2000. The 'society of captives' in the era of hyper-incarceration. *Theoretical Criminology* 4(3): 285–308.

Smith, Dorothy. 1987. *The everyday world as problematic: A feminist sociology.* Boston: Northeastern University Press.

Spergel, Irving. 1966. *Street gang work: Theory and practice.* Reading, MA: Addison-Wesley.

Spradley, James. 1979. *The ethnographic interview.* New York: Harcourt, Brace, Jovanovich.

Sprague, Joey. 1997. Holy men and big guns: The can[n]on in social theory. *Gender & Society* 11: 88–107.

—— 2005. *Feminist methodologies for critical researchers: Bridging differences.* New York: Altamira/Rowan and Littlefield.

Stacey, Jusith. 1997. *In the name of family: Rethninking family values in the postmodern age.* Boston: Beacon Press.

Stack, Carol. 1976. *All our kin: Strategies for survival in a Black community.* New York: Harper Colophon.

STEM Trends. 2009, July 22. Sociology attracts a higher percentage of underrepresented minorities in some states. Accessed March 25, 2010, http://www.asanet.org

Staples, Robert. 1971. *The Black family: Essays and studies.* Belmont, CA: Wadsworth.

Steele, J. Michael. 2005. Darrell Huff and fifty years of how to lie with statistics. *Statistical Science* 20: 205–209.

Sullivan, Mercer. 1989. *Getting paid: Youth, crime and work in the inner city.* Ithaca, NY: Cornell University Press.

Sumner, Jennifer M. 2009. *Keeping house: Understanding the transgender inmate code of conduct through prison policies, environments, and culture.* PhD Dissertation, University of California, Irvine.

Suttles, Gerald D. 1968. *The social order of the slum: Ethnicity and the inner city.* Chicago: University of Chicago Press.

Taylor, Verta, and Nicole C. Raeburn. 1995. Identity politics as high-risk activism: Career consequences for lesbian, gay, and bisexual sociologists. *Social Problems* 42: 252–273.

—— Leila J. Rupp. 2005. When the girls are men: Negotiating gender and sexual dynamics in a study of drag queens. *Signs: Journal of Women in Culture and Society* 30: 2115–2139.

Thai, Hung Cam. 2008. *For better or for worse: Vietnamese international marriages in the new global economy.* New Brunswick, NJ: Rutgers University Press.

Thorne, Barrie. 1993. *Gender play: Girls and boys in school.* New Brunswick, NJ: Rutgers University Press.

Thorne, B., and B. Laslett (Eds.). 1997. *Feminist sociology: Life histories of a movement.* New York: Routledge,.

Twine, Frances Winddance. (Writer and Director) 1991. *Just Black?* USA: Filmaker's Library.

—— 1997. *Racism in a racial democracy: The maintainance of White supremacy in Brazil*. New Brunswick, NJ: Rutgers University Press.

—— 2010. *A White side of Black Britain: Interracial intimacy and racial literacy*. Durham, NC: Duke University Press.

—— Warren, Jonathan. 2001. *Racial revolutions: Antiracism and Indian resurgence in Brazil*. Durham, NC: Duke University Press.

—— Charles Gallagher. 2007. The future of whiteness: A map of the "third wave." *Ethnic and Racial Studies* 31: 4–24.

Van Velen, Jaap. 1967. The extended case method and situational analysis. In A. I. Epstein (Ed.), *The craft of urban anthropology* (pp. 29–53). London: Tavistock.

Venkatesh, Sudhir. 2002. 'Doin the hustle': Constructing the ethnographer in the American ghetto. *Ethnography* 3(1), 91–111.

—— 2007. Urban puzzle. *The Boston Globe*, March 31. Ideas section. Available at http://www. boston.com/news/globe/ideas/articles/2007/04/01/urban_puzzle/

—— 2009. *Off the books: The underground economy of the urban poor*. Cambridge, MA: Harvard University Press. (Original work published 2008 as *Gang leader for a day: A rogue sociologist takes to the streets*)

Wacquant, Loic. 2002a. Scrutinizing the street: Poverty, morality, and the pitfalls of urban ethnography. *American Journal of Sociology* (Review Symposium) 107: 1468–1532.

—— 2002b. The curious eclipse of prison ethnography in the age of mass incarceration. *Ethnography* 3(4): 371–397.

Walby, Sylvia. 1989. Theorising patriarchy. *Sociology* 23: 213–234.

Wenneras, Christine, and Agnes Wold. 1997. Nepotism and sexism in peer-review. *Nature* 387: 341–344.

West, Candace, and Sarah Fenstermaker. 1995. Doing difference. *Gender & Society* 9: 8–37.

—— Don H. Zimmerman. 1987. Doing gender. *Gender & Society* 1: 125–151.

West, Gordon, W. R. Morris, and G. West. 2000. *The case for penal abolition*. Montreal: Canadian Scholars Press.

Western, Bruce. 2006. *Punishment and inequality In America*. New York: Russell Sage Foundation.

Williams, Christine. 1991. *Gender differences at work: Women and men in nontraditional occupations*. Berkeley: University of California Press.

—— 1995. *Still a man's world: Men who do women's work*. Berkeley: University of California Press.

—— 2006. *Inside toyland: Working, shopping and social inequality*. Berkeley: University of California Press.

Wilson, William Julius, and Anmol Chaddha. 2009, December. The role of theory in ethnographic research. *Ethnography* 10: 549–564.

Whyte, William Foote. 1965. *Street corner society: The social structure of an Italian slum*. Chicago: University of Chicago Press.

Williams, Christine. 1995. *Still a man's world: Men who do women's work*. Berkeley: University of California Press.

Wilson, William Julius. 1993. The *truly disadvantaged: The inner city, the underclass, and public policy*. Chicago: University of Chicago Press.

Wood, James. 2008. *How fiction works*. New York: Farrar, Straus and Giroux.

Wright Mills, C. (1959) *The sociological imagination*. New York: Oxford University Press.

Yin, Robert Y. 2002. *Case study research: Design and methods*, 3rd ed.(Applied Social Research Methods Series, Vol. 5). Thousand Oaks, CA: Sage.

Young, Alford. 2004. *The minds of marginalized Black men: Making sense of mobility, opportunity, and future life chances*. Princeton, NJ: Princeton University Press.

—— 2008. Trying to go home again: A personal and scholarly perspective on the tenants of East Harlem [Review of *The tenants of East Harlem*, by Russell Leigh Sharman]. *Sociological Forum* 23(1): 192–198.

CONTRIBUTORS

Scott Brooks is an Associate Professor of sociology at the University of California Riverside. His book, *Black Men Can't Shoot* (University of Chicago Press 2009), is based on 4 years of coaching summer league basketball in Philadelphia. What he saw, heard, and felt working with the young Black men on his team is captured to show how career mobility occurs, and how good players make the transition to great ones. He is currently engaged in qualitative research regarding campus dating and is working on a second manuscript that looks at coaching youth basketball and the repetitive situations, encounters, and personalities that coaches face.

Meda Chesney-Lind is Professor of Women's Studies at the University of Hawaii at Manoa. Nationally recognized for her work on women and crime, her books include *Girls, Delinquency and Juvenile Justice, The Female Offender: Girls, Women and Crime, Female Gangs in America, Invisible Punishment, Girls, Women and Crime,* and *Beyond Bad Girls: Gender Violence and Hype.* She has just finished an edited collection on trends in girls' violence, entitled *Fighting for Girls: Critical Perspectives on Gender and Violence* that will be published by SUNY Press.

Mitchell Duneier is Professor of Sociology at Princeton and a regular Distinguished Visiting Professor at the City University of New York Graduate Center. For 10 years he was jointly on the faculties of the University of California, Santa Barbara and the University of Wisconsin Madison. Among his books are *Sidewalk, Slim's Table,* and, with Alice Goffman, a forthcoming monograph on the history of the idea of the ghetto from classical antiquity to the present. He received the 2003 William Kiekhofer Award for Excellence in Teaching at Wisconsin and the 2009 President's Award for Distinguished Teaching at Princeton.

Valerie Jenness is a Professor in the Department of Criminology, Law and Society and the Department of Sociology and is Dean of the School of Social Ecology at the University of California, Irvine. Her research focuses on the links between deviance and social control; the politics of crime control; social movements and social change; and corrections and public policy. She is the author of three books and many articles published in sociology, law, and criminology journals. Her work has been honored with awards from the American Sociological Association, Society for the Study of Social Problems, the Pacific Sociological Association, and the University of California; most recently, she received the Public Understanding of Sociology Award from the American Sociological Association. She is a Past President of the Society for the Study of Social Problems and Past Editor of *Contemporary Sociology.*

Miliann Kang is Associate Professor in Women, Gender, and Sexuality Studies at the University of Massachusetts, Amherst, and is also affiliated with Sociology and Asian/Asian American Studies. Her book, *The Managed Hand: Race, Gender and the Body in Beauty Service Work* (University of California Press 2010) addresses immigrant women's work in Asian-owned nail salons. It won the Sara Whaley bookprize from the National Women's Studies Association. She is currently researching work–family issues for Asian American women, particularly the intersections of gender and race in shaping motherhood and careerpaths.

Nazli Kibria is Associate Professor of Sociology and Director of Graduate Programs in Sociology at Boston University where she teaches courses on immigration, contemporary South Asia, and the sociology of family and childhood. She was born in Bangladesh and received her undergraduate degree from Wellesley College and her PhD from the University of Pennsylvania. Her books include *Family Tightrope: The Changing Lives of Vietnamese Americans* and *Becoming Asian American.* She is currently at work on a book on the lives of Bangladeshi migrants around the world.

Karyn Lacy is Associate Professor in the Department of Sociology and the Center for Afro-American and African Studies at the University of Michigan. Her book *Blue-Chip Black: Race, Class, and Status in the New Black Middle Class* (University of California Press) is the 2008 co-winner of the Oliver Cromwell Cox book award, conferred by the American Sociological Association's section on Racial and Ethnic Minorities. Her current work examines the construction of racial and class-based identities among members of an elite children's organization.

Rhacel Parrenas is Professor of American Civilization and Sociology at Brown University. She is the author of three books: *Servants of Globalization: Women, Migration, and Domestic Work*; *Children of Global Migration: Transnational Families and Gendered Woes*; and *The Force of Domesticity: Filipina Migrants and Globalization* and the co-editor of two anthologies: *Asian Diasporas: New Conceptions, New Formations*, with Lok Siu, and *Intimate Labors: Technologies, Cultures, and the Politics of Care*, with Eileen Boris. She is currently writing a book on the labor and migration of Filipina hostesses in Tokyo's nightlife industry. Photo courtesy of Jill Posener.

Mary Pattillo is the Harold Washington Professor of Sociology and African American Studies at Northwestern University. Her areas of interest include race and ethnicity, urban sociology, and qualitative methods. She is the author of two award-winning books, *Black Picket Fences: Privilege and Peril among the Black Middle Class*, and *Black on the Block: The Politics of Race and Class in the City*. She is the co-editor of *Imprisoning America: The Social Effects of Mass Incarceration*, and has published numerous journal articles. She is a founding board member of Urban Prep Charter Academies, Inc., a network of all-boys public high schools in Chicago.

Victor Rios is Assistant Professor of Sociology at the University of California, Santa Barbara. He is a former gang member and juvenile ward. He conducts research on urban youth culture, the criminalization of youth, and masculinity with these experiences in perspective. Victor is currently completing a book titled *Punished: The Criminalization of Inner City Boys* with NYU Press. His other publications include, "The Hyper-Criminalization of Black and Latino Male Youth in the Era of Mass Incarceration" in *Souls* (2006), "The Racial Politics of Youth Crime" in *Latino Studies* (2008), and "The Consequences of the Criminal Justice Pipeline on Black and Latino Masculinity" published in *The Annals of the American Academy of Political and Social Sciences* (2009).

Leila J. Rupp is Professor of Feminist Studies and Associate Dean of Social Sciences at the University of California, Santa Barbara. She holds affiliated faculty appointments in the Departments of History and Sociology. Rupp's books include *Sapphistries: A Global History of Love Between Women* (2009); *Drag Queens at the 801 Cabaret* (2003), coauthored with Verta Taylor; *A Desired Past: A Short History of Same-Sex Sexuality in America* (1999); *Worlds of Women: The Making of an International Women's Movement* (1997); *Survival in the Doldrums: The American Women's Rights Movement, 1945 to the 1960s* (1987), also coauthored with Verta Taylor; and *Mobilizing Women for*

War: German and American Propaganda, 1939–1945 (1978). She is a coeditor of the seventh and eighth editions of *Feminist Frontiers*.

Denise Segura is Professor of Sociology and Affiliated Professor in the Departments of Chicana/o Studies and Feminist Studies at the University of California, Santa Barbara. She publishes on Chicana feminisms, education, and employment. With Patricia Zavella, she co-edited *Women and Migration in the U.S.-Mexico Borderlands: An Anthology* (Duke University Press 2007). She is the recipient of 2008 American Association of Hispanics in Higher Education (AAHHE) Outstanding Latino/a Faculty in Higher Education (Research Institutions) award and the 2007 Lifetime Distinguished Contributions to Research, Teaching and Service by the American Sociological Association, Latina/o Sociology Section. Currently she serves as the President of The Sociologists for Women in Society and is Vice President Elect of the Pacific Sociological Association.

Mercer Sullivan is an Associate Professor of Criminal Justice at Rutgers University. He received his scholarly training in cultural anthropology and is widely known for his ethnographic research on youth crime and other urban social problems. His book *Getting Paid: Youth Crime and Work in the Inner City* (Cornell University Press 1989) is frequently cited as a seminal study of ecological influences on youth development. His other research has examined the male role in teenage pregnancy and parenting, the roles of community development corporations in promoting public safety, multiple-victim school shootings, patterns of ordinary school violence, the relation of public perceptions of youth gang activity to actual patterns of youth violence, and the social processes of reentry from juvenile incarrcerations. He has been editor of the *Journal in Crime and Delinquency* and is currently editor of the book series *Qualitative Studies in Crime and Justice*.

Verta Taylor is Professor and Chair of the Sociology Department and member of the Affiliated Faculty in Feminist Studies at the University of California, Santa Barbara. She is co-author of *Drag Queens at the 801 Cabaret* (2003) and *Survival in the Doldrums: The American Women's Rights Movement, 1945 to the 1960s* (1987); author of *Rock-a-by Baby: Feminism, Self-Help and Postpartum Depression* (1996), and co-editor of eight editions of *Feminist Frontiers*. Her articles on women's movements, the gay and lesbian movement, and social movement theory have appeared in *American Sociological Review, Signs, Social Problems, Mobilization, Gender & Society, Contexts, Qualitative Sociology, Journal of Women's History, Journal of Homosexuality,* and *Journal of Lesbian Studies*. She received the John McCarthy Lifetime

Achievement Award in Social Movements and the Simon and Gagnon Award for a Lifetime of Scholarly Contributions to the Study of Sexuality.

Hung Cam Thai is Associate Professor of Sociology and Asian American Studies at Pomona College of the Claremont University Consortium, where he is chair of Sociology and President of the Pacific Basin Institute. His scholarship focuses on gender, family, and international migration across the Vietnamese Diaspora. His first book is *For Better or for Worse: Vietnamese International Marriages in the New Global Economy* (Rutgers University Press 2008). He is currently writing a book on consumption and return migration in Vietnam.

France Winddance Twine is a Professor of Sociology at the University of California in Santa Barbara. She is a consulting editor for *Ethnic and Racial Studies*. She teaches courses on race/class/gender, critical race theory, and qualitative research methods. Her publications include *A White Side of Black Britain: Interracial Intimacy and Racial Literacy* (Duke University Press 2010), *Feminism and Antiracism: International Struggles for Justice,* with Kathleen Blee (NYU Press 2001), *Racing Research, Researching Race: Methodological Dilemmas in Critical Race Studies* (NYU Press 2000), *Ideologies and Technologies of Motherhood: Race, Class, Sexuality and Nationalism* (Routledge 1999) and *Racism in a Racial Democracy* (Rutgers 1998). She is currently writing a book with Celine-Marie Pascale on the changing politics of race and ethnicity.

Christine Williams is a Professor of Sociology at the University of Texas at Austin where she teaches courses on gender, sexuality, labor and labor movements, and qualitative research methods. She is the author of several books and articles on gender discrimination, sexual harassment, and homophobia in the workplace. Her most recent book, *Inside Toyland: Working, Shopping, and Social Inequality* (California 2006), is based on fieldwork she conducted in two toy stores. She is currently editing a volume on gender and sexuality in the workplace, and conducting research (with Chandra Muller) on women scientists in the petroleum industry. Photo courtesy of Marsha Miller.

Alford A. Young, Jr. is Arthur F. Thurnau Professor and Associate Professor in the Department of Sociology and the Center for Afroamerican and African Studies at the University of Michigan. His research explores the experiences of low-income African Americans in urban communities, with particular attention given to how they make sense of work opportunities and the world of work in the municipal regions in which they live. A second line of research explores the views of African American scholars and intellectuals on the social utility of racial scholarship. He has published *The Minds of Marginalized Black Men: Making Sense of Mobility, Opportunity, and Future Life Chances* (Princeton University Press 2004), co-authored *The Souls of W. E. B Du Bois* (Paradigm Publishers 2006), and has published articles in *Sociological Theory, The Annual Review of Sociology, Symbolic Interaction, Ethnic and Racial Studies,* and other journals. He is completing a book titled *From the Edge of the Ghetto: African Americans and the World of Work.*

INDEX

A

Academics
    academic administrative experience, 226
    lives of privilege, 76
Access, 210–211
Accountability, African American scholars,
    21–23
Activism, 26
Adolescents, most difficult interview, 26
African American, *see also* Black
African American clients, Korean merchants,
    relations, 64–65, 67
African American experience, non-African
    American scholars, 48
African American men
    low-income
        fatherhood, 44–45
        gender, 47, 44–45
        meaning construction, 41–43
        situated knowledge, 45
African American scholars, accountability, 21–23
African American sociological thought, early
    tradition, 47
African American Studies, 24–25
African American women
    low-income, 47
African American youth, 111
    girls in housing projects, 80
    indigenous ethnographers, 112–113
        intersecting identities, 113–114
    punitive social control, 111–113
American Dream, 42–43
Anthropology, 179
Anti-racism work, institutional racism, 212–214
Architecture, 189
Arensberg, Conrad, 122–123
Art, ethnography, compared, 37–38
Asian American faculty, student expectations,
    70–71

Asian American survivors of atrocities, 72
Asian American women, 63–72
    competing demands, 69
    model minority stereotype mythology, 68–69
    mothering standards, 69–70
    normative discourses, 68–69
    "opt-out" debate, 69–70
Asian immigrant women, 63–68
Athletics, 160
Audience, 56–57
Auto mechanic, 118

B

Bangladesh, return migration
    constraints of context, 83–84
    policy implications, 84
    transnational status dynamics, 83
Bangladeshi Diaspora, 81
    race, 85
    researcher connections, 81–83
Bangladeshi national identity, post-9/11 climate,
    84
Basketball, 28–40, 235
Becker, Howard S., 135–137
Beliefs, 41–43
Bisexual sociologists
    graduate students, 225
    high-risk activism, 224–225
Black, *see also* African American
Black children, white mothers, 179–181
Black communities, characterized, 21
Black entertainment performances, 235–236
Black faculty
    black middle-class scholars changing
        sociology, 18–20
    black women faculty negotiating academia,
        170–171
    class backgrounds, 22–23
    competing pressures, 31–32

mentoring, 36–37
  outside mentors, 37
  as middlemen, 23
Black gender ideology, 47
Black middle class, 15–16, 165–175
  colorism, 172–173
  data collection, 166–168
  ethnography, 17–18
  exclusionary boundary work, 172–173
  future, 173–174
  identity, 165–166, 172
  methodology, 166–168
  most difficult interview, 170
  normative discourses, 68–69
  out-migration, 16
  researcher status position, 169–170
  study implications for poor or working class
    Blacks, 168
Blackness, boundaries, 23
Blackness project, 21–22
Black urban poverty, 16
Body forms, stigma, 161
Body labor
  different forms, 66–68
  different from other forms of labor, 66
  tattoo artists, 66
Bondage of masculinity
  "father-away" families, 94
  transnational fathers, 94
Borderlands feminist projects, 198–199
  gender, 198–199
Borderlands research, elderly Chicano men,
  195–196, 205
Boundary work, 94–95
Brain drain
  labor migration, 91–92
  Nakakabobo, 91–92
Brazil, racism, 178–179
Brooks, Scott, 28–40

C
California, public education system, 187
Canine companions, 228–229
Career aspirations, 26–27, 40, 48, 59–60, 72,
  80, 97, 106, 110, 118, 120–124, 138,
  160–161, 170, 189, 204–205, 216, 230,
  232, 235
  feminist criminology, 101–102
  trajectory, 128
Change, 196–198, 212–214
  inner city, 124–126
  research/teaching/social change relationship,
    196–198
Chesney-Lind, Meda, 101–110

Chicana/o faculty, 191–193
  institutional change, 193–194
  post-Chicano movement era, 201–202
  service orientation, 202–203
Chicana/o graduate students, advice for,
  202–203
Chicana professionals, feminist sociology,
  199–200
Civil Rights Movement, 16
Class, 215
  Black professors, 22–23
  lines of difference, 79
  mobility, 42–43
  researcher status position, 128–130
Coach, ethnographer, combined, 28–40
Collaboration, 217–230
Collective identity framework, 218
Colorism, Black middle class, 172–173
Coming out process, 230
Community-based research, 2
Contradictory class mobility, labor migration,
  93
Cost, mass incarceration, 106–107
Covert aggression, feminist criminology,
  104–105
Crack epidemic, gender, 125
Crime decline, 125
Criminal justice
  gender, 101–110, 102–103
    intellectual inspirations, 105
    vs. feminist criminology, 103
  policy changes, 133–135
  researcher status position, 128–130
Cross-gender friendships, 78–79
Cross-racial friendships, 78–79

D
Diaspora, 73–76, 81
  contingent meanings, 89–90
  global diasporic movements, 73
  marriage migration, 78
  permanently displaced population, 89–90
  race, 85
  researcher connections, 73–76, 81–83
  researcher personal sharing, 82–83
  return migration, 77, 83–84
Dissertation, turning dissertation into book, 74
Double consciousness, sociological imagination,
  34–35
Drag queen study
  drug use, 222
  gender, 218–221, 226
  gender of presentation, 218–219
  personalities in and out of drag, 221

Drag queen study (*continued*)
  politics of vulgarity, 226–228
  politics *vs.* entertainment, 219–221
  transgender, 218–219
Drug use, 222
  war on drugs, 58–59
Duneier, Mitchell, 49–60

E
East Harlem, sociological imagination, 43–44
Elderly Chicano men, borderlands research,
    195–196, 205
Emotional labor, 64–65
  theoretical framework, 64–65
Empathy, most difficult interview, 233–235
Entertainment work, 94–95, 218–228
Ethnography, *see also* Specific type
  art, compared, 37–38
  behavior compared to self-report, 54–56
  Black middle class, 17–18
  both inductive and deductive, 38
  challenges with insider knowledge, 17–18
  changed conditions, 58–59
  coaching combined, 28–40
  context, 57–59
  as craft, 37–38
  disagreements in moral terms, 50
  film making, compared, 56
  importance, 38–39
  in-depth, context-driven fieldwork, 59
  Latino neighborhoods, 27
  longitudinal, 180–181
  mass incarceration, policy implications,
    132–133
  mixed methods, 131–132
  need for, 38–39
  peer relationships, 38
  people's definition of situation, 54
  sociology, contrasted, 17–18
  tacit assumptions, 55
  theory
    as iterative process, 52–53
    necessity *vs.* contaminant, 52–53
    social world actualities, 53–54
  time period, 212
  transparency, 50–51
    positivist legacy, 51–52
Exclusionary boundary work, Black middle
    class, 172–173
Exploitation, most difficult interview, 59
Ex-prisoners, 50

F
Family context, women factory workers, 82

Fatherhood, 126–128
  absentee, 44
  "father-away" families, 94
  gender, 44–45
  low-income African American men, 44–45
    situated knowledge, 45
Fathering
  feminism, 115–116
  gender, 115–116
  sociological imagination, 115
Feeling rules, 64
Feminism
  backlash against feminism, 182–183
  demonization, 106
  fathering, 115–116
  truth telling, 108
Feminist criminology, 101
  career aspirations, 101–102
  covert aggression, 104–105
  "mean girls," 104–105
  methodology, 107–108
Feminist scholars, 116–117
  anti-racist feminism, 182–183
  marginalization, 104
Feminist sociology, 215–216
  Chicana professionals, 199–200
  feminist methods, 104
  grounded knowledge of feminist sociologists,
    94–95
Feminists of color, University of California,
    200–201
Fieldwork
  actually employed as worker, 211
  most difficult interview, 26, 231
    adolescents, 26
    boundaries, 71–72
    crack death, 137
    drag queen's mother, 229–230
    empathy, 233–235
    exploitation, 59
    gender, 39–40
    honesty, 79–80
    hostility, 79–80
    job seekers, 216
    life threatened, 118
    marriage proposal, 86
    Mexican immigrant woman, 203–204
    racism, 96
    researcher self-centeredness, 159–160
    setting, 233–234
    sexual violence, 109
    sex workers, 188–189
  researcher's age, 209–210
  worker *vs.* interviewer, 211–212

Filipino women, serial migration, 89
Film making, ethnography, compared, 56
Follow-up study, 87
Freakonomics, sociological alternative, 60

G
Gangs, 29, 120–124, 126, 138
    Latino youth, patterns of surveillance, 114
Gay sociologists
    graduate students, 225
    high-risk activism, 224–225
Gender
    borderlands feminist projects, 198–199
    crack epidemic, 125
    criminal justice, 101–110, 102–103
        intellectual inspirations, 105
        vs. feminist criminology, 103
    drag queen study, 218–221, 226
    fatherhood, 44–45
    fathering, 115–116
    intellectual inspirations, 23–24
    lines of difference, 79
    low-income African American men, 47
    most difficult interview, 39–40
    non-traditional jobs, 206–208
    in organizations, 232–233
    Philippines, 90–91
    race, relationship, 67
    sex, naturalization of gender, 90–91
    urban ethnography, 19
Gendered institutions, 204–209
    dynamic character of gendering, 209
Gender emancipation, women migrant workers,
    95–96
Global diasporic movements, 73
Globalization, 85–86
Globalized workers, 88–89
Grounded knowledge, feminist sociologists,
    94–95
Grounded theoretical approach, 28
Guilt, 71

H
Higher education, token women, 232–233
Honesty, most difficult interview, 79–80
Hostility, most difficult interview, 79–80
Housewives/homemakers, 86, 205, 232
Housing, random assignment, 175
Housing projects, African American girls, 80
Humanities, social sciences and
    degree of convergence, 46–47
    interdisciplinary efforts, 46–47
Human rights work, 72
Hurston, Zora Neale, 24

Hybridity, 179

I
Identity, 32–33
    Black middle class, 172
    multiple identities, 32–33
    public identity, 28–30
    racial identity characterized, 22
Immigration, 67–68, 125–126, *see also* Return
    migration
    impact on homeland, 75
Incarceration, *see* Mass incarceration
Indigenous ethnographers, 19–20
    African American youth, 112–113
        intersecting identities, 113–114
    Latino youth, 112–113
        intersecting identities, 113–114
Inequality, future, 215–216
Inner city
    Black urban poverty, 16
    change, 124–126
    punitive social control of youth, 111–113
Institutional change, 212–214
    Chicana/o faculty, 193–194
    Latina/o faculty, 193–194
Institutional home, urban sociologists, 117
Institutional racism, anti-racism work,
    212–214
Intellectual inspirations, 23–24
    gender, 23–24
Interdisciplinary approaches, 24–25, 179
Interracial friendships, military, 189–190
Intersecting identities, 32–33
Intersectionality, 2
    methodology, 206–208

J
Jenness, Valerie, 139–161
Job seekers, most difficult interview, 216
Journalism, 86

K
Kang, Miliann, 63–72
Kibria, Nazli, 81–87
Korean merchants, African American clients,
    relations, 63–68

L
Labor migration
    brain drain, 91–92
    contradictions, 93
    contradictory class mobility, 93
Labor organizer, 97
Lacy, Karyn, 165–175

Latina/o faculty, 191–193
    institutional change, 193–194
Latino neighborhoods, ethnography, 27
Latino youth, 111
    gangs, patterns of surveillance, 114
    indigenous ethnographers, 112–113
        intersecting identities, 113–114
    punitive social control, 111–113
Law, 60
Lesbian sociologists
    graduate students, 225
    high-risk activism, 224–225
    maiden aunts study, 230
    "the professors of lesbian love," 224–225
Lines of difference
    class, 79
    gender, 79
Low-income African American men
    fatherhood, 44–45
        situated knowledge, 45
    gender, 47
    meaning construction, 41–43
Low-income African American women, gender,
    47

M
Marginality, sociologists' own feelings, 92–93
Marginalization, feminist scholars, 104
Marginalized populations, resilience, 119
Marriage migration, 73
    Vietnamese women, 78
Masculinity
    "father-away" families, 94
    transnational fathers, 94
Mass incarceration, 18
    conditions in which girls are confined, 108–109
    cost, 106–107
    ethnography, policy implications, 132–133
    nation's shifting priorities, 106–107
Mass school shooting, 130–131
Meaning construction, low-income African
    American men, 41–43
Men in female jobs study, 206–208
Mentoring, 36–37, 45–46, 76, 114–115
    Black faculty, 36–37
        outside mentors, 37
    youth development program, 36
Methodology, 206–208
    Black middle class, 166–168
    feminist criminology, 107–108
    intersectionality, 206–208
    mixed methods, 179
        ethnography, 131–132
    race, 184–185

Mexican immigrant woman, most difficult
    interview, 203–204
Middle-class Blacks, *see* Black middle class
Middle East, sociological imagination, 34–35
Migrant Filipina workers, 88
    children left behind, 88, 92
    imagined global community, 89–90
    wide scale, 89
Migrant health professionals, race, 97
Military, interracial friendships, 189–190
Mixed methods, 179
    ethnography, 131–132
Mobility, 42–43
    class, 42–43
    race, 42–43
    social connections, 42–43
Model minority stereotype, Asian American
    women, 68–69
Moral worth, 49–50
Mothering standards, Asian American women,
    69–70
Multiple identities, 32–33
Music, 138
Muslim, sociological imagination, 34–35
Muslim religious identity, post-9/11 climate, 84

N
Nail salons, 63–68
Nakakabobo, brain drain, 91–92
Non-traditional jobs, gender, 206–208
Normative discourses
    Asian American women, 68–69
    middle-class Blacks, 68–69

O
Obama's presidency, sociological questions,
    25–26
"Opt-out" debate, Asian American women,
    69–70
Organized crime, 122
Out-migration, Black middle class, 16

P
Parrenas, Rhacel, 88–97
Pattillo, Mary, 15–27
Peer recognition, public identity, 28–30
Peer relationships, ethnography, 38
Penn Ethnography Conference, 31
Personal responsibility narrative, 42–43
Philippine emigration, 88–97
    hierarchy of destinations, 89
    institutionalization, 89
Philippines, gender, 90–91
Political consultant, 160–161

Politician, 230
Politics of vulgarity, drag queen study, 226–228
Post eras, 2
"Post-racial" America, 85
Pressure situations, 31–32
Privilege, 76
  academics' lives of privilege, 76
  students' lives of privilege, 76
Privileged status position, urban ethnography, 20–21
  representation, 20–21
  respect for subjects, 20–21
Prostitutes' rights movement, 157–158
Psychoanalytic training, 216
Public education system, California, 187
Public identity, 28–30
  peer recognition, 28–29, 29–30
  scholars, 28–29
Public sociology, 116
  research/teaching/social change relationship, 196–198

R
Race
  Bangladeshi Diaspora, 85
  gender, relationship, 67
  methodology, 184–185
  migrant health professionals, 97
  mobility, 42–43
  researcher status position, 128–130
Racial identity, characterized, 22
Racism
  Brazil, 178–179
  most difficult encounter, 96
Reciprocity, 48
Reflexivity, 58
Representation, 20–21
  of women, urban ethnography, 19
Research
  age doing fieldwork, 209–210
  crossing lines of difference, 78–79
  as foundation for policy, 84
  policy implications, 116
  research/teaching/social change relationship, 196–198
  sustaining research agenda, 186–187
  turning dissertation into book, 74
Researchers
  childhood of, in sociological imagination, 181–182
  knowledge, subjects as co-constructors, 64–66
  personal sharing, Bangladeshi Diaspora, 82–83

public identity, 28–29
  self-centeredness, most difficult interview, 159–160
  status position, Black middle class, 169–170
Research questions, origins, 28–29
Research subjects
  in co-construction of knowledge, 64–66
  respect for, 20–21
Resilience, marginalized populations, 119
Respectability, 49–50
Return migration
  Bangladesh
    constraints of context, 83–84
    policy implications, 84
    transnational status dynamics, 83
  Vietnam, 77
    interactional styles, 77–78
Rios, Victor, 111–119
Rupp, Leila, 217–230

S
Scholars, public identity, 28–29
School shooting, 130–131
  violence, 130–131
Segura, Denise, 191–205
Self-reflexivity, 58
Sellout, 21
Serial migration, Filipino women, 89
Sex, naturalization of gender, 90–91
Sexual assault, transgender inmates, 146–148
  face-to-face interviews, 153–156
Sexual harassment, 228
Sexual violence, most difficult interview, 109
Sex work, 94–95
Sex workers, most difficult interview, 188–189
Shark experts, 40
Shock, 226–228
Social change, 196–198, 212–214
Social connections, mobility, 42–43
Social isolation, 42–43
Socialization, sociological imagination, 34–36
Social movement theory, 218
Social sciences, humanities
  degree of convergence, 46–47
  interdisciplinary efforts, 46–47
Sociological imagination, 1
  adolescent shaping of, 34–36
  double consciousness, 34–35
  East Harlem, 43–44
  fathering, 115
  Middle East, 34–35
  Muslim, 34–35
  researchers' childhood, 181–182
  socialization, 34–36

Sociological questions, Obama's presidency,
    25–26
Sociologists
    public identity, 28–29
Sociology, *see also* Fieldwork; Public sociology
    America-centric perspectives, 85
    Black middle-class scholars, changing
        sociology, 18–20
    demographics, 1–2
    diverse, 1
    ethnography, contrasted, 17–18
    professionalization of, 2
Soetoro, S. Ann Dunham, 110
Statistics, transparency, 50–51
Status position, 32–33
Stigma, body forms, 161
Students' lives of privilege, 76
Sullivan, Mercer, 120–138

T
Tattoo artists, body labor, 66
Taylor, Verta, 217–230
Teenage pregnancy, male role, 126–128, 133
Textbook editing, 223–224
Thai, Hung Cam, 73–80
Theory, ethnography
    as iterative process, 52–53
    necessity *vs.* contaminant, 52–53
    social world actualities, 53–54
Thrift shopping, 110
Token women, higher education, 232–233
Transgender studies, 139–160
    assumptions, 142
    drag queen study, 218–219
    inmates, 144–160
        avoiding victimization, 156
        changing researcher, 158–159
        face-to-face interviews, 153–156
        origins, 144–146
        prison officers, 148–152
        sexual assault, 146–148
    origins, 140–142
Transnational families
    fathers, bondage of masculinity, 94
    mothers, doing gender, 94
    perspective of children, 88, 92
Transnationalism, impact on homeland, 75
Transnational marriage, Vietnamese women, 78
Transparency
    ethnography, 50–51
        positivist legacy, 51–52
    statistics, 50–51
Truth telling, feminism, 108

Twine, France Winddance, 176–190

U
University of California, feminists of color,
    200–201
Urban ethnography
    context, 57–59
    gender, 19
    privileged status position, 20–21
        representation, 20–21
        respect for subjects, 20–21
    representation of women, 19
Urban sociologists, institutional home, 117

V
Validity, 94–95
Vietnam, 73
    American students in, 75
    return migration, 77
        interactional styles, 77–78
Vietnamese Diaspora, researcher connections,
    73–76
Vietnamese women
    marriage migration, 78
    transnational marriage, 78
Violence, 120–124
Violence, school shooting, 130–131
Visual ethnography, 185–186
Visual sociology, 185–186

W
War on drugs, 58–59
Watts Old Timers' study, 195–196, 205
Welfare reform, 58
White mothers, Black children, 179–181
Whiteness
    need for study of, 183–184
    third wave whiteness, 183–184
White solipsism, 207
Williams, Christine, 206–216
Women factory workers, family context, 82
Women faculty, student expectations, 70–71
Women migrant workers, 88–97
    gender emancipation, 95–96
Women political leaders, 87
Worker self-esteem, 214–215
Worldviews, 41–43
Writing, 72

Y
Young, Alford A. Jr., 41–48
Youth development program, mentoring, 36
Youth violence, 120–124